THE O'LEARY SERIES

Microsoft® Word 2000

Brief Version

Timothy J. O'Leary
Arizona State University

Linda I. O'Leary

Irwin
McGraw-Hill

Boston   Burr Ridge, IL   Dubuque, IA   Madison, WI   New York
San Francisco   St. Louis   Bangkok   Bogotá   Caracas   Lisbon
London   Madrid   Mexico City   Milan   New Delhi   Seoul
Singapore   Sydney   Taipei   Toronto

McGraw-Hill Higher Education

A Division of **The McGraw-Hill** Companies

MICROSOFT® WORD 2000, BRIEF EDITION

This book is printed on acid-free paper.

1 2 3 4 5 6 7 8 9 0 BAN/BAN 9 0 9 8 7 6 5 4 3 2 1 0 9

ISBN 0-07-233738-9

Vice president/Editor-in-chief: *Michael W. Junior*
Sponsoring editor: *Trisha O'Shea*
Developmental editor: *Stephen Fahringer*
Senior marketing manager: *Jodi McPherson*
Senior project manager: *Beth Cigler*
Manager, new book production: *Melonie Salvati*
Freelance design coordinator: *Gino Cieslik*
Cover design: *Francis Owens*
Supplement coordinator: *Marc Mattson*
Compositor: *Rogondino & Associates*
Typeface: *11/13 Century Book*
Printer: *The Banta Book Group*

Library of Congress Catalog Card Number 99-60730

http://www.mhhe.com

THE O'LEARY SERIES

Microsoft® Word 2000

Brief Version

Timothy J. O'Leary
Arizona State University

Linda I. O'Leary

Irwin
McGraw-Hill

Boston   Burr Ridge, IL   Dubuque, IA   Madison, WI   New York
San Francisco   St. Louis   Bangkok   Bogotá   Caracas   Lisbon
London   Madrid   Mexico City   Milan   New Delhi   Seoul
Singapore   Sydney   Taipei   Toronto

At McGraw-Hill Higher Education, we publish instructional materials targeted at the higher education market. In an effort to expand the tools of higher learning, we publish texts, lab manuals, study guides, testing materials, software, and multimedia products.

At **Irwin/McGraw-Hill** (a division of McGraw-Hill Higher Education), we realize that technology has created and will continue to create new mediums for professors and students to use in managing resources and communicating information with one another. We strive to provide the most flexible and complete teaching and learning tools available as well as offer solutions to the changing world of teaching and learning.

Irwin/McGraw-Hill **is dedicated to providing the tools for today's instructors and students to successfully navigate the world of Information Technology.**

■ **Seminar series**—Irwin/McGraw-Hill's Technology Connection seminar series offered across the country every year demonstrates the latest technology products and encourages collaboration among teaching professionals.

■ **Osborne/McGraw-Hill**—This division of The McGraw-Hill Companies is known for its best-selling Internet titles *Harley Hahn's Internet & Web Yellow Pages* and the *Internet Complete Reference*. Osborne offers an additional resource for certification and has strategic publishing relationships with corporations such as Corel Corporation and America Online. For more information visit Osborne at **www.osborne.com**.

■ **Digital solutions**—Irwin/McGraw-Hill is committed to publishing digital solutions. Taking your course online doesn't have to be a solitary venture, nor does it have to be a difficult one. We offer several solutions that will allow you to enjoy all the benefits of having course material online. For more information visit **www.mhhe.com/solutions/index.mhtml**.

■ **Packaging options**—For more about our discount options, contact your local Irwin/McGraw-Hill Sales representative at 1-800-338-3987 or visit our Web site at **www.mhhe.com/it**.

Preface

Goals/Philosophy

The goal of **The O'Leary Series** is to give students a basic understanding of computing concepts and to build the skills necessary to ensure that information technology is an advantage in whatever path they choose in life. Because we believe that students learn better and retain more information when concepts are reinforced visually, we feature a unique visual orientation coupled with our trademark "learn by doing" approach.

Approach

The O'Leary Series is the true *step-by-step way to develop computer application skills*. The new Microsoft Office 2000 design emphasize the step-by-step instructions with full screen captures that illustrate the results of each step performed. Each Tutorial (chapter) follows the 'learn by doing' approach in combining conceptual coverage with detailed, software-specific instructions. A running case study that is featured in each tutorial highlights the real-world capabilities of each of the software applications and leads students step by step from problem to solution.

About the Book

The O'Leary Series offers 2 *levels* of instruction: Brief and Introductory. Each level builds upon the previous level.

- **Brief**—This level covers the basics of an application and contains two to three chapters.

- **Introductory**—This level includes the material in the Brief textbook plus two to three additional chapters. The Introductory text prepares students for the *Microsoft Office User Specialist Exam (MOUS Certification)*.

Each tutorial features:

- **Common Office 2000 Features**—This section provides a review of several basic procedures and Windows features. Students will also learn about many of the features that are common to all Microsoft Office 2000 applications.

- **Overview**—The Overview contains a "Before You Begin" section which presents both students and professors with all the information they need to know before starting the tutorials, including hardware and software settings. The Overview appears at the beginning of each lab manual and describes (1) what the program is,

(2) what the program can do, (3) generic terms the program uses, and (4) the Case Study to be presented.

- **Working Together sections**—These sections provide the same hands-on visual approach found in the tutorials to the integration and new collaboration features of Office 2000.

- **Glossary**—The Glossary appears at the end of each text and defines all key terms that appear in boldface type throughout the tutorials and in the end-of-tutorial Key Terms lists.

- **Index**—The Index appears at the end of each text and provides a quick reference to find specific concepts or terms in the text.

Brief Version

The Brief Version is divided into three tutorials, followed by Working Together, which shows the intregration of Word 2000 with the World Wide Web.

Tutorial 1: Adventure Travel has developed four new tours for the upcoming year and needs to promote them, partly through informative presentations held throughout the country. Your first job as advertising coordinator is to create a flyer advertising the four new tours and the presentations about them.

Tutorial 2: Your next project is to create a letter to be sent to past clients along with your flyer. The letter briefly describes Adventure Travel's four new tours and invites clients to attend an informational presentation.

Tutorial 3: Part of your responsibility, as advertising coordinator is to gather background information about the various tour locations. You will write a report providing information about Tanzania and Peru for two of the new tours.

Working Together: Adventure Travel Company has a World Wide Web site for the company. You think the flyer you developed to promote the new tours and presentations could be used on the Web site.

Each tutorial features:

- **Step-by-step instructions**—Each tutorial consists of step-by-step instructions along with accompanying screen captures. The screen captures represent how the student's screen should appear after completing a specific step.

- **Competencies**—Listed at the beginning of each tutorial, the Competencies describe what skills will be mastered upon completion of the tutorial.

- **Concept Overview**—Located at the start of each tutorial, the Concept Overviews provide a brief introduction to the concepts to be presented.

- **Concept boxes**–Tied into the Concept Overviews, the Concept boxes appear throughout the tutorial and provide clear, concise explanations of the concepts under discussion, which makes them a valuable study aid.

- **Marginal notes**–Appearing throughout the tutorial, marginal notes provide helpful hints, suggestions, troubleshooting advice, and alternative methods of completing tasks.

- **Case study**–The running case study carried throughout each tutorial and is based on real use of software in a business setting.

- **End-of-tutorial material**–At the end of each tutorial the following is provided:

  Concept Summary–This two-page spread presents a visual summary of the concepts presented in the tutorial and can be used as a study aid for students.

  Key Terms–This page-referenced list is a useful study aid for students.

  Matching/Multiple Choice/True False Questions

  Command Summary–The Command Summary includes keyboard and toolbar shortcuts.

  Screen Identifications–These exercises ask students to demonstrate their understanding of the applications by identifying screen features.

  Discussion Questions–These questions are designed to stimulate in-class discussion.

  Hands-On Practice Exercises–These detailed exercises of increasing difficulty ask students to create Office documents based on the skills learned in the tutorial.

  On Your Own–These problems of increasing difficulty ask students to employ more creativity and independence in creating Office documents based on new case scenarios.

Acknowledgments

The new edition of the Microsoft Office 2000 has been made possible only through the enthusiasm and dedication of a great team of people. Because the team spans the country, literally from coast to coast, we have utilized every means of working together including conference calls, FAX, e-mail, and document collaboration . . . we have truly tested the team approach and it works!

Leading the team from Irwin/McGraw-Hill are Kyle Lewis, Senior Sponsoring Editor, Trisha O'Shea, Sponsoring Editor, and Steve Fahringer, Developmental Editor. Their renewed commitment, direction, and support have infused the team with the excitement of a new project.

The production staff is headed by Beth Cigler, Senior Project Manager whose planning and attention to detail has made it possible for us to successfully meet a very challenging schedule. Members of the production team include. Gino Cieslik and Francis Owens, art and design, Pat Rogondino, layout, Susan Defosset and Joan Paterson, copy editing. While all have contributed immensely, I would particularly like to thank Pat and Susan . . . team members for many past editions whom I can always depend on to do a great job. My thanks also go to the project Marketing Manager, Jodi McPherson, for her enthusiastic promotion of this edition.

Finally, I am particularly grateful to a small but very dedicated group of people who help me develop the manuscript. My deepest appreciation is to my co-author, consultant, and lifelong partner, Tim, for his help and support while I have been working on this edition. Colleen Hayes who has been assisting me from the beginning, continues to be my right arm, taking on more responsibility with each edition. Susan Demar and Carol Dean have also helped on the last several editions and continue to provide excellent developmental and technical support. New to the project this year are Bill Barth, Kathy Duggan, and Steve Willis, who have provided technical expertise and youthful perspective.

Reviewers

We would also like to thank the reviewers for their insightful input and criticism. Their feedback has helped to make this edition even stronger.

Josephine A. Braneky, *New York City Technical College*
Robert Breshears, *Maryville University*

Gary Buterbaugh, *Indiana University of Pennsylvania*
Mitchell M. Charkiewicz, *Bay Path College*
Seth Hock, *Columbus State Community College*
Katherine S. Hoppe, *Wake Forest University*
Lisa Miller, *University of Central Oklahoma*
Anne Nelson, *High Point University*
Judy Tate, *Tarrant County Junior College*
Dottie Sunio, *Leeward Community College*
Charles Walker, *Harding University*
Mark E. Workman, *Blinn College*

Additionally, each semester I hear from students at Arizona State University who are enrolled in the Introduction to Computers course. They constantly provide great feedback from a student's perspective . . . I thank you all.

Features of This Text

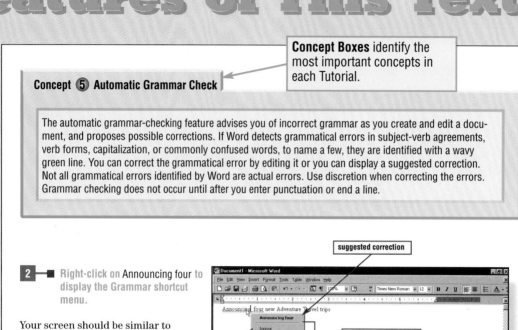

Concept Boxes identify the most important concepts in each Tutorial.

Concept ⑤ Automatic Grammar Check

The automatic grammar-checking feature advises you of incorrect grammar as you create and edit a document, and proposes possible corrections. If Word detects grammatical errors in subject-verb agreements, verb forms, capitalization, or commonly confused words, to name a few, they are identified with a wavy green line. You can correct the grammatical error by editing it or you can display a suggested correction. Not all grammatical errors identified by Word are actual errors. Use discretion when correcting the errors. Grammar checking does not occur until after you enter punctuation or end a line.

2 ■ Right-click on Announcing four to display the Grammar shortcut menu.

Your screen should be similar to Figure 1–10.

suggested correction

Announcing four new Adventure Travel trips

related menu options

Grammar shortcut menu

Figure 1–10

Tables provide quick summaries of toolbar buttons, key terms, and procedures for specific tasks.

Yellow **Additional Information** boxes appear throughout each tutorial and explain additional uses of the application or of a specific topic.

Additional Information

A dimmed option means it is currently unavailable.

A shortcut menu showing a suggested correction is displayed. The Grammar shortcut menu also includes several related menu options described below.

Option	Effect
Ignore	Instructs Word to ignore the grammatical error in this sentence.
Grammar	Opens the Grammar Checker and displays an explanation of the error.
About this Sentence	If the Office Assistant feature is on, this option is available. It also provides a detailed explanation of the error.

Because you cannot readily identify the reason for the error, you will open the Grammar Checker.

Other Features

Real World Case—Each O'Leary Lab Manual provides students with a fictitious running case study. This case study provides students with the real-world capabilities for each software application. Each tutorial builds upon the gained knowledge of the previous tutorial with a single case study running throughout each Lab Manual.

End-of-Chapter Material—Each Tutorial ends with a visual **Concept Summary**. This two-page spread presents a concept summary of the concepts presented in the tutorial and can be used as a study aid for

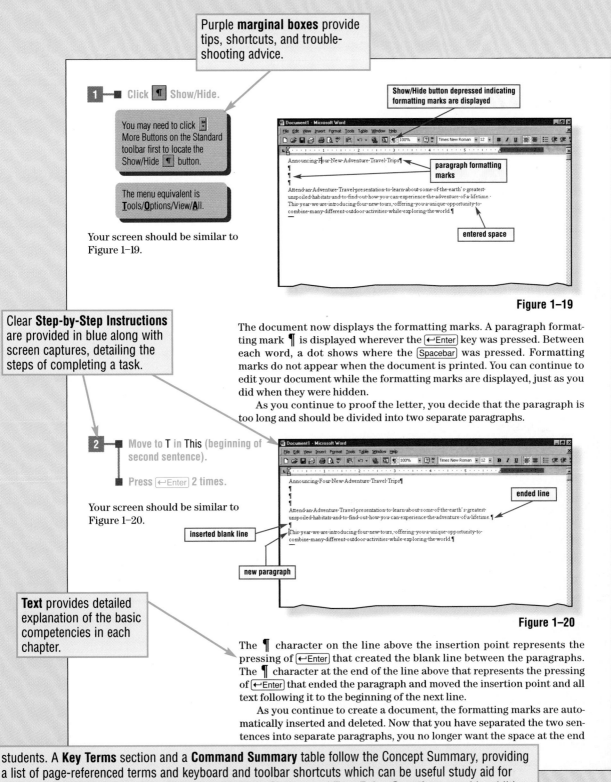

Purple **marginal boxes** provide tips, shortcuts, and trouble-shooting advice.

1 ➤ ■ Click ¶ Show/Hide.

You may need to click ⏷ More Buttons on the Standard toolbar first to locate the Show/Hide ¶ button.

The menu equivalent is **T**ools/**O**ptions/View/**A**ll.

Your screen should be similar to Figure 1–19.

Show/Hide button depressed indicating formatting marks are displayed

paragraph formatting marks

entered space

Figure 1–19

Clear **Step-by-Step Instructions** are provided in blue along with screen captures, detailing the steps of completing a task.

The document now displays the formatting marks. A paragraph formatting mark ¶ is displayed wherever the ⏎Enter key was pressed. Between each word, a dot shows where the ⎵Spacebar was pressed. Formatting marks do not appear when the document is printed. You can continue to edit your document while the formatting marks are displayed, just as you did when they were hidden.

As you continue to proof the letter, you decide that the paragraph is too long and should be divided into two separate paragraphs.

2 ■ Move to **T** in **This** (beginning of second sentence).

■ Press ⏎Enter 2 times.

Your screen should be similar to Figure 1–20.

inserted blank line

new paragraph

ended line

Figure 1–20

Text provides detailed explanation of the basic competencies in each chapter.

The ¶ character on the line above the insertion point represents the pressing of ⏎Enter that created the blank line between the paragraphs. The ¶ character at the end of the line above that represents the pressing of ⏎Enter that ended the paragraph and moved the insertion point and all text following it to the beginning of the next line.

As you continue to create a document, the formatting marks are automatically inserted and deleted. Now that you have separated the two sentences into separate paragraphs, you no longer want the space at the end

students. A **Key Terms** section and a **Command Summary** table follow the Concept Summary, providing a list of page-referenced terms and keyboard and toolbar shortcuts which can be useful study aid for students. **Screen Identification**, **Matching**, **Multiple Choice**, and **True False Questions** provide additional reinforcement to the Tutorial Material. **Discussion Questions**, **Hands-on Practice Exercises**, and **On Your Own Exercises** develop critical thinking skills and offer step-by-step practice. These exercises have a rating system from Easy to Difficult and test the student's ability to apply the knowledge they have gained in each tutorial. Each O'Leary Lab Manual provides at least two **On the Web** exercises where students are asked to use the Web to solve a particular problem.

Teaching Resources

The following is a list of supplemental material that can be used to help teach this course.

Active Testing and Learning Assessment Software (ATLAS)

Available for The O'Leary Series is our cutting edge "Real Time Assessment" ATLAS software. ATLAS is web enabled and allows students to perform timed tasks while working live in an application. ATLAS will track how a specific task is completed and the time it takes to complete that task and so measures both proficiency and efficiency. ATLAS will provide full customization and authoring capabilities for professors and can include content from any of our application series.

Instructor's Resource Kits

Instructor's Resource Kits provide professors with all of the ancillary material needed to teach a course. Irwin/McGraw-Hill is committed to providing instructors with the most effective instructional resources available. Many of these resources are available at our Information Technology Supersite, found at **www.mhhe.com/it**. Our Instructor's Resource Kits are available on CD-ROM and contain the following:

- **Diploma by Brownstone**—Diploma is the most flexible, powerful, and easy to use computerized testing system available in higher education. The Diploma system allows professors to create an exam as a printed version, as a LAN-based Online version, or as an Internet version. Diploma also includes grade book features, which automate the entire testing process.

- **Instructor's Manual**—The Instructor's Manual includes solutions to all lessons and end of the unit material, teaching tips and strategies, and additional exercises.

- **Student Data Files**—Students must have student data files in order to complete practice and test sessions. The instructor and students using this text in classes are granted the right to post student data files on any network or stand-alone computer, or to distribute the files on individual diskettes. The student data files may be downloaded from our IT Supersite at **www.mhhe.com/it**

- **Series Web site**—Available at **www.mhhe.com/cit/oleary**.

Digital Solutions

- **Pageout Lite**–This software is designed for you if you're just beginning to explore Web site options. Pageout Lite will help you to easily post your own material online. You may choose one of three templates, type in your material, and PageOut Lite will instantly convert it to HTML.

- **Pageout**–Pageout is our Course Web Site Development Center. Pageout offers a syllabus page, Web site address, Online Learning Center content, online exercises and quizzes, gradebook, discussion board, an area for students to build their own Web pages, plus all features of Pageout Lite. For more information please visit the Pageout Web site at **www.mhla.net/pageout**.

- **OLC/Series Web Sites**–Online Learning Centers (OLCs)/series sites are accessible through our Supersite at **www.mhhe.com/it**. Our Online Learning Centers/series sites provide pedagogical features and supplements for our titles online. Students can point and click their way to key terms, learning objectives, chapter overviews, PowerPoint slides, exercises, and Web links.

- **The McGraw-Hill Learning Architecture (MHLA)**–MHLA is a complete course delivery system. MHLA gives professors ownership in the way digital content is presented to the class through online quizzing, student collaboration, course administration, and content management. For a walk-through of MHLA, visit the MHLA Web Site at **www.mhla.net**.

Packaging Options

For more about our discount options, contact your local Irwin/McGraw-Hill sales representative at 1-800-338-3987 or visit our Web site at **www.mhhe.com/it**.

Contents

Introducing Common Office 2000 Features

This section will review several basic procedures and Windows features. In addition, you will learn about many of the features that are common to all Microsoft Office 2000 applications. Although Word 2000 will be used to demonstrate how the features work, only common features will be addressed. The features that are specific to each application will be introduced individually in each tutorial.

Turning on the Computer

If necessary, follow the procedure below to turn on your computer.

1

- **Turn on the power switch.** The power switch is commonly located on the back or right side of your computer. It may also be a button that you push on the front of your computer.

- **If necessary, turn your monitor on and adjust the contrast and brightness.** Generally, the button to turn on the monitor is located on the front of the monitor. Use the dials (generally located in the panel on the front of the monitor) to adjust the monitor.

- **If you are on a network, you may be asked to enter your User Name and Password. Type the required information in the boxes. When you are done, press** [←Enter].

Do not have any disks in the drives when you start the computer.

Press [Tab ⇄] to move to the next box.

The Windows program is loaded into the main memory of your computer and the Windows desktop is displayed.

Your screen should be similar to Figure 1.

Figure 1

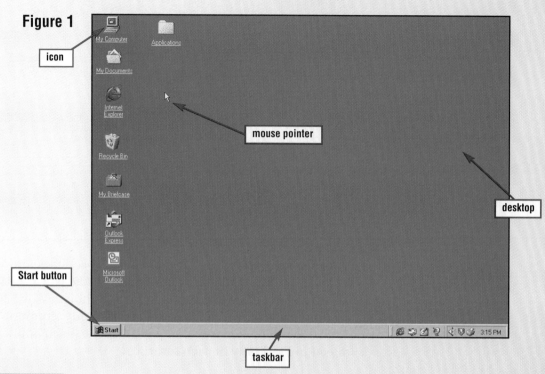

The **desktop** is the opening screen for Windows and is the place where you begin your work using the computer. Figure 1 shows the Windows 98 desktop. If you are using Windows 95, your screen will look slightly different. Small pictures, called icons, represent the objects on the desktop. Your desktop will probably display many different **icons** than those shown here. At the bottom of the desktop screen is the **taskbar**. It contains buttons that are used to access programs and features. The **Start button** on the left end of the taskbar is used to start a program, open a document, get help, find information, and change system settings.

> If a Welcome box is displayed, click ⊠ (in the upper right corner of the box) to close it.

> If you are already familiar with using a mouse, skip to Loading an Office Application.

Using a Mouse

The arrow-shaped symbol on your screen is the **mouse pointer**. It is used to interact with objects on the screen and is controlled by the hardware device called a **mouse** that is attached to your computer.

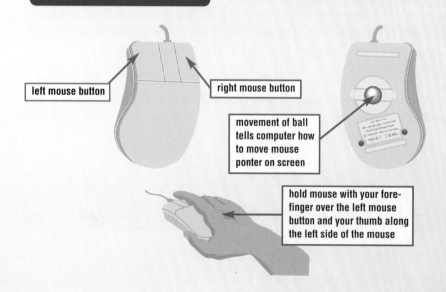

The mouse pointer changes shape on the screen depending on what it is pointing to. Some of the most common shapes are shown in the table below.

Pointer Shape	Meaning
⌖	Normal select
☝	Link select
⧗	Busy
⊘	Area is not available

If your system has a stick, ball or touch pad, the buttons are located adjacent to the device.

On top of the mouse are two or three buttons that are used to choose items on the screen. The mouse actions and descriptions are shown in the table below.

Action	Description
Point	Move the mouse so the mouse pointer is positioned on the item you want to use.
Click	Press and release a mouse button. The left mouse button is the primary button that is used for most tasks.
Double-click	Quickly press and release the left mouse button twice.
Drag	Move the mouse while holding down a mouse button.

Throughout the labs, "click" means to use the left mouse button. If the right mouse button is to be used, the directions will tell you to right-click on the item.

1 ■ Move the mouse in all directions (up, down, left, and right) and note the movement of the mouse pointer.

■ Point to the 🖳 My Computer icon.

Your screen should be similar to Figure 2.

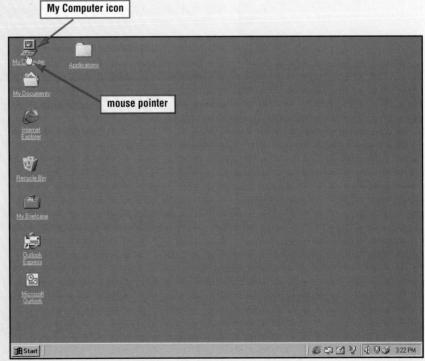

Figure 2

Depending on the version of Windows you are using and the setup, the mouse pointer may be ⇧ and you will need to click on the icon to select it.

The pointer on the screen moved in the direction you moved the mouse and currently appears as a 🖑. The icon appears highlighted, indicating it is the selected item and ready to be used. A **ScreenTip** box containing a brief description of the item you are pointing to may be displayed.

Loading an Office Application

There are several ways to start an Office application. One is to use the Start/New Office Document command and select the type of document you want to create. Another is to use Start/Documents and select the document name from the list of recently used documents. This starts the associated application and opens the selected document at the same time. The two most common ways to start an Office 2000 application are by choosing the application name from the Start menu or by clicking a desktop shortcut for the program if it is available.

Point to a Start menu option to select it; click it to choose it.

1 ■ Click **Start** to display the Start menu.

■ Select **Programs**

■ Choose **[W] Microsoft Word** .

or

If you are using Windows 98, depending on your setup, you may only need to single-click the shortcut.

■ Double-click the **Word 2000** shortcut.

After a few moments, the Word application window is displayed, and your screen should be similar to Figure 3.

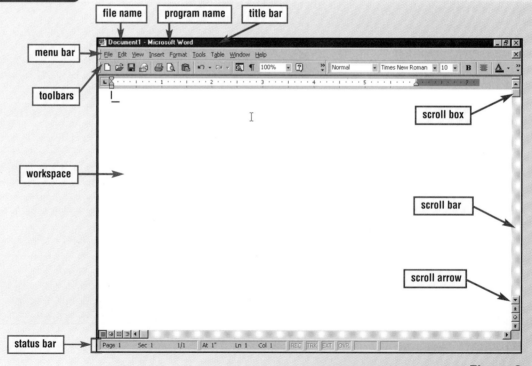

Figure 3

Basic Windows Features

As you can see, many of the features in the Word window are the same as in other Windows applications. Among those features is a title bar, a menu bar, toolbars, a document window, scroll bars, and mouse compatibility. You can move and size Office application windows, select commands, use Help, and switch between files and programs, just as you can in Windows. The common user interface makes learning and using new applications much easier.

TITLE BAR

The Word window title bar displays the file name Document1, the default name of the file displayed in the window, followed by the program name, Microsoft Word. The left end of the title bar contains the Word application window ▦ Control-menu icon, and the right end displays the ▬ Minimize, ▣ Restore, and ✕ Close buttons. They perform the same functions and operate in the same way as in Windows 95 and Windows 98.

1 ▬■ If necessary, click ▢ in the title bar to maximize the application window.

MENU BAR

The **menu bar** below the title bar displays the Word program menu, which consists of nine menus. The right end displays the document window ✕ Close button. As you use the Office applications, you will see that the menu bar contains many of the same menus, such as File, Edit, and Help. You will also see several menus that are specific to each application. You will learn about using the menus in the next section.

TOOLBARS

The **toolbar** located below the menu bar contains buttons that are mouse shortcuts for many of the menu items. Commonly, the Office applications will display two toolbars when the application is first opened: Standard and Formatting. They may appear together on one row, or on separate rows. You will learn about using the toolbars shortly.

WORKSPACE

The **workspace** is the large center area of the Word application window where documents are displayed in open windows. Currently, there is one open document window, which is maximized and occupies the entire area. Multiple documents can be open and displayed in the work area at the same time.

STATUS BAR

The **status bar** at the bottom of the window displays location information and the status of different settings as they are used. Different information is displayed in the status bar for different applications.

SCROLL BARS

A **scroll bar** is used with a mouse to bring additional lines of information into view in a window. It consists of **scroll arrows** and a **scroll box**.

Clicking the arrows moves the information in the direction of the arrows, allowing new information to be displayed in the space. You can also move to a general location within the area by dragging the scroll box up or down the scroll bar. The location of the scroll box on the scroll bar indicates your relative position within the area of available information. Scroll bars can run vertically along the right side or horizontally along the bottom of a window. The vertical scroll bar is used to move vertically, and the horizontal scroll bar moves horizontally in the space.

Using Office 2000 Features

MENUS

A **menu** is one of many methods you can use to tell a program what you want it to do. When opened, a menu displays a list of commands. Most menus appear in a menu bar. Other menus pop up when you right-click (click the right mouse button) on an item. This type of menu is called a **shortcut menu**.

1 ▬▬■ **Click File to open the File menu.**

Your screen should be similar to Figure 4.

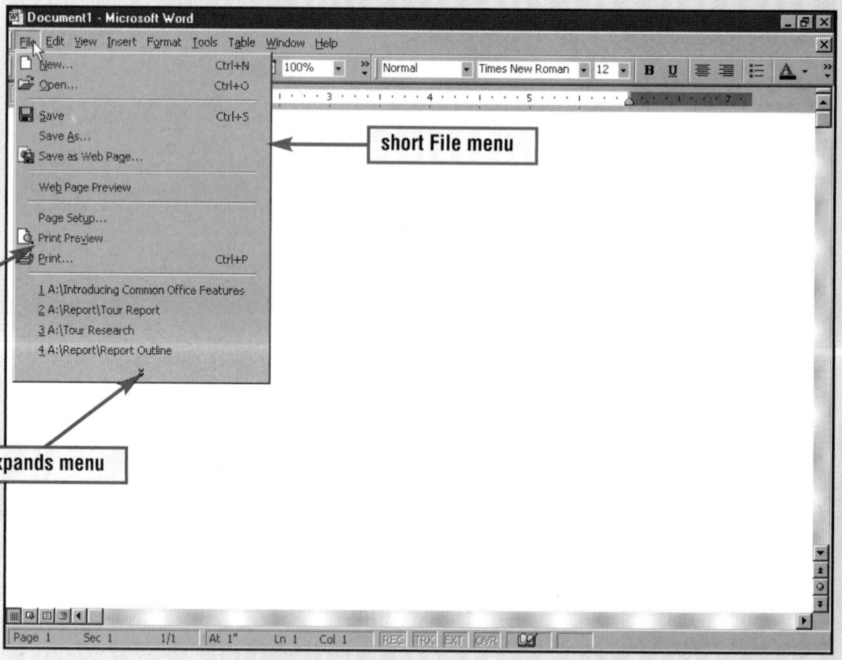

menu command

short File menu

expands menu

Figure 4

When a menu is first opened, it displays a short version of commands. The short menu displays basic commands when the application is first used. As you use the application, those commands you use frequently are listed on the short menu and others are hidden. Because the short menu is personalized automatically to the user's needs, different commands may be listed on your File menu than appear in Figure 4 above.

An expanded version will display automatically after the menu is open for a few seconds (see Figure 5). If you do not want to wait for the expanded version to appear, you can click ❤ at the bottom of the menu and the menu list expands to display all commands.

> You can double-click the menu name to show the expanded menu immediately.

Your screen should be similar to Figure 5.

Figure 5

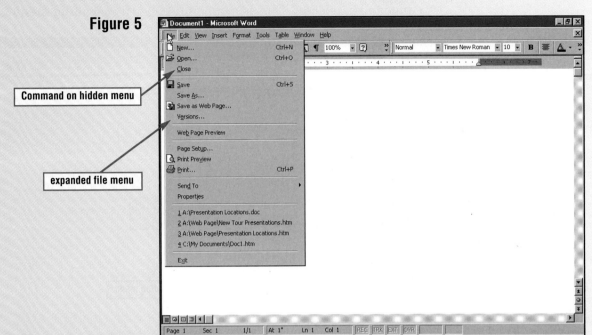

Command on hidden menu

expanded file menu

The commands that are in the hidden menu appear on a light gray background. Once one menu is expanded, others are expanded automatically until you choose a command or perform another action.

2 ■ Point to each menu in the menu bar to see the expanded menu for each.

■ Point to the File menu again.

Many commands have images next to them so you can quickly associate the command with the image. The same image appears on the toolbar button for that feature.

Menus may include the following features (not all menus include all features):

Feature	Meaning
Ellipsis (...)	Indicates a dialog box will be displayed.
▶	Indicates a cascading menu will be displayed.
Dimmed	Indicates the command is not available for selection until certain other conditions are met.
Shortcut key	A key or key combination that can be used to execute a command without using the menu.
Checkmark ✔	Indicates a toggle type of command. Selecting it turns the feature on or off. A checkmark indicates the feature is on.

Once a menu is open, you can *select* a command from the menu by pointing to it. A colored highlight bar, called the **selection cursor**, appears over the selected command. If the selected command line displays a right-facing arrow, a submenu of commands automatically appears when the command is selected. This is commonly called a **cascading menu**.

3 ■ Point to the Send To command to display the cascading menu.

Your screen should be similar to Figure 6.

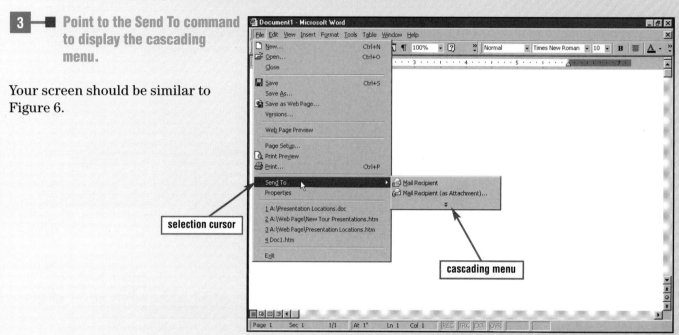

Figure 6

Then to *choose* a command, you click on it. When the command is chosen, the associated action is performed. You will use a command in the Help menu to access the Microsoft Office Assistant and Help feature.

Note: If your Office Assistant feature is already on, as shown in Figure 7, skip step 4.

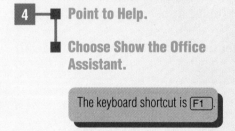
You can also type the underlined command letter to choose a command. If the command is already selected, you can press ⏎Enter to choose it.

4 ■ Point to Help.

■ Choose Show the Office Assistant.

The keyboard shortcut is F1.

Your screen should be similar to Figure 7.

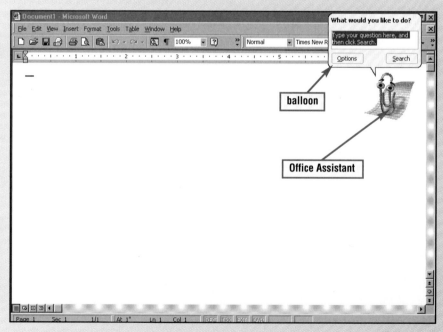

Figure 7

The command to display the Assistant has been executed, and the Office Assistant character is displayed.

Note: If the Assistant does not appear, this feature has been disabled. If this is the case, Choose **H**elp/Microsoft Word **H**elp or press (F1) and skip to the section Using Help.

Using the Office Assistant

When the Office Assistant is on, it automatically suggests help topics as you work. It anticipates what you are going to do and then makes suggestions on how to perform a task. In addition, you can activate the Assistant at any time to get help on features in the Office application you are using. When active, the Office Assistant balloon appears and displays a prompt and a text box in which you can type the topic you want help on.

1 — ■ **If the balloon is not displayed as in Figure 7 above, click the Office Assistant character to activate it.**

You will ask the Office Assistant to provide information on the different ways you can get help while using the program.

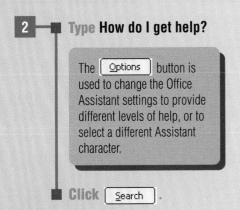

2 — ■ Type **How do I get help?**

The [Options] button is used to change the Office Assistant settings to provide different levels of help, or to select a different Assistant character.

■ Click [Search].

Your screen should be similar to Figure 8.

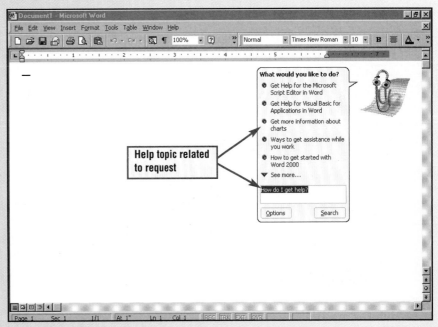

Figure 8

The balloon displays a list of related topics from which you can select.

3 — ■ Select Ways to get assistance while you work.

Your screen should be similar to Figure 9.

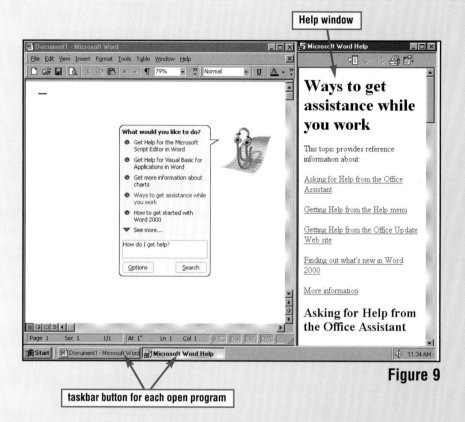

Figure 9

The Help program has been opened and displays the selected topic. Because Help is a separate program within Word, it appears in its own window. The taskbar displays a button for both open windows. Now that Help is open, you no longer need to see the Assistant.

4 — ■ Right-click the Assistant to display the shortcut menu.

■ Click Hide.

■ Click 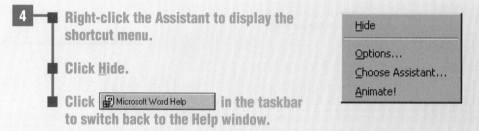 in the taskbar to switch back to the Help window.

Using Help

- -

In the Help window, the toolbar buttons help you use different Help features and navigate within Help. The ⬅▤ Show button displays the Help Tabs frame.

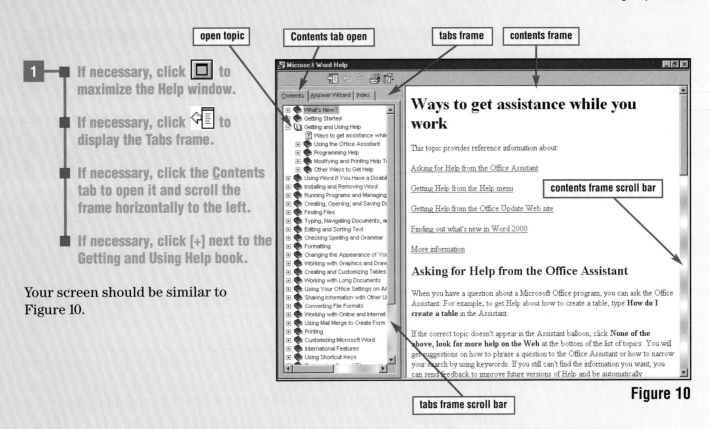

1 If necessary, click ▢ to maximize the Help window.

If necessary, click ◁▤ to display the Tabs frame.

If necessary, click the Contents tab to open it and scroll the frame horizontally to the left.

If necessary, click [+] next to the Getting and Using Help book.

Your screen should be similar to Figure 10.

Figure 10

The Help window is divided into two vertical frames. **Frames** divide a window into separate, scrollable areas that can display different information. The left frame in the Help window is the Tabs frame. The three folder-like tabs—Contents, Index, and Search—in the left frame are used to access the three different means of getting Help information. The open tab appears in front of the other tabs and displays the available options for the feature. The right frame is the content frame. It displays the content for the located information.

The Contents tab displays a table of contents listing of topics in Help. Clicking on an item preceded with a 📖 opens a "chapter," which expands to display additional chapters or specific Help topics. Chapters are preceded with a 📂 icon and topics with a ？ icon.

The content frame displays the selected Help topic. It contains more information than can be displayed at one time.

2 Using the scroll bar, scroll the right frame to the bottom of the Help topic.

Scroll back to the top of the Help topic.

USING A HYPERLINK

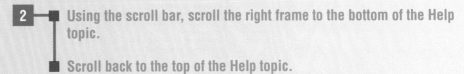
The mouse pointer appears as 🖑 when pointing to a hyperlink.

Another way to move in Help is to click a hyperlink. A **hyperlink** is a connection to a location in the current document or the World Wide Web. It commonly appears as colored or underlined text. Clicking the hyperlink moves to the location associated with the hyperlink.

1 ■ **Click the** Asking for Help from the Office Assistant **hyperlink.**

Your screen should be similar to Figure 11.

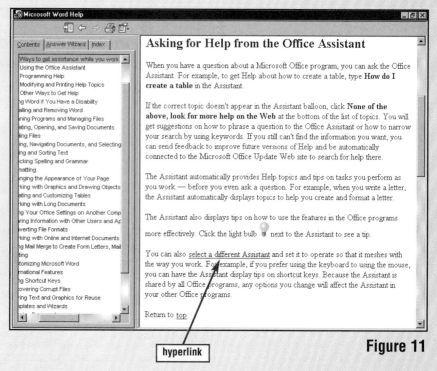

hyperlink

Figure 11

Help quickly jumps to the selected topic and displays the topic heading at the top of the frame.

currently displayed help topic

2 ■ **Read the information displayed on this topic.**

■ **Click the** select a different Assistant **hyperlink.**

Your screen should be similar to Figure 12.

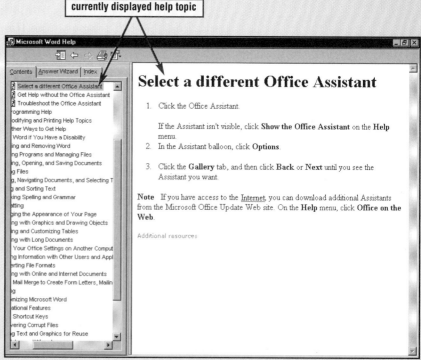

Figure 12

The Help topic about selecting a different Assistant is displayed. Notice the Contents list now highlights this topic, indicating it is the currently selected topic. Other hyperlinks may display a definition of a term.

3 ━■ Click the Internet hyperlink.

Your screen should be similar to Figure 13.

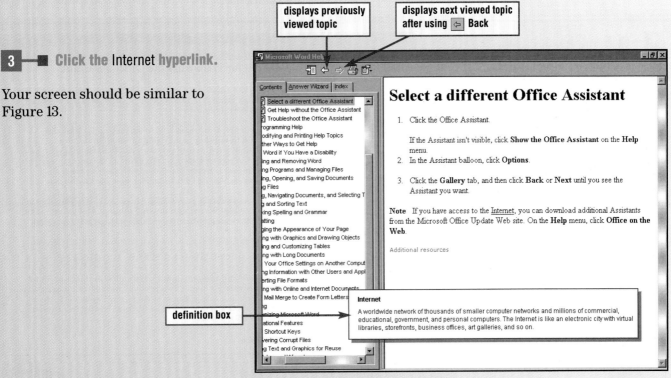

Figure 13

A box containing a definition of the Internet is displayed.

4 ━■ Click on the definition box to clear it.

To quickly return to the previous topic,

5 ━■ Click ⇦ Back.

The previous topic is displayed again.

The ⇨ Forward button appears after using ⇦ Back and can be used to move to the next viewed topic.

USING THE INDEX TAB

To search for Help information by entering a word or phrase for a topic, you can use the Index tab.

1 ■— ■ Open the <u>I</u>ndex tab.

Your screen should be similar to Figure 14.

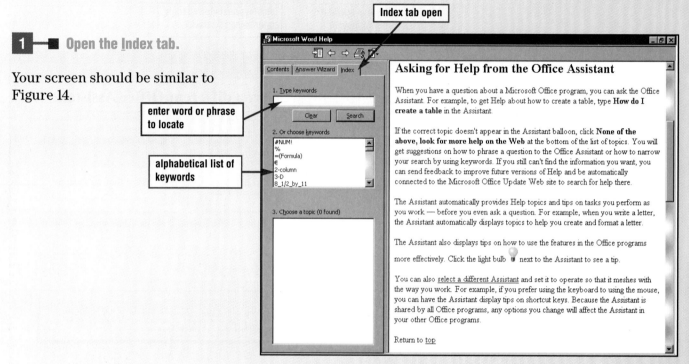

Figure 14

The Index tab consists of a text box where you can type a word or phrase that best describes the topic you want to locate. Below it is a list box displaying a complete list of Help keywords in alphabetical order. You want to find information about using the Index tab.

2 ■— ■ Type **index** in the text box.

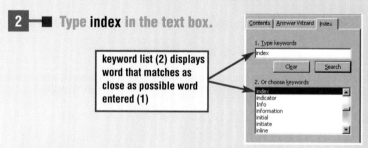

The keyword list jumps to the word "index." To locate all Help topics containing this word,

3 ━■ Click [Search] .

Your screen should be similar to Figure 15.

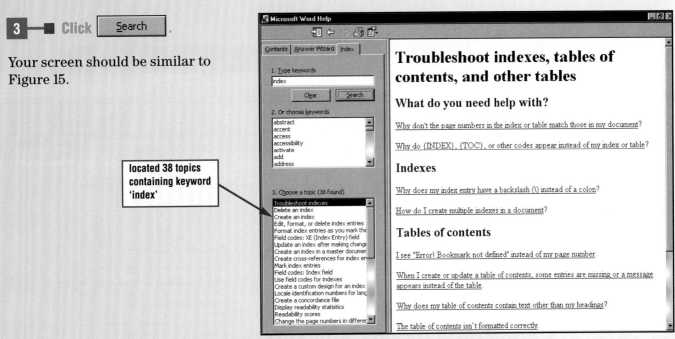

located 38 topics containing keyword 'index'

Figure 15

The topic list has located 38 Help topics containing this word and displays the information on the first topic in the content frame. However, many of the located topics are not about the Help Index feature. To narrow the search more, you can add another word to the keyword text box.

4 ━■ Type **help** in the keyword text box following the word index.

■ Click [Search] .

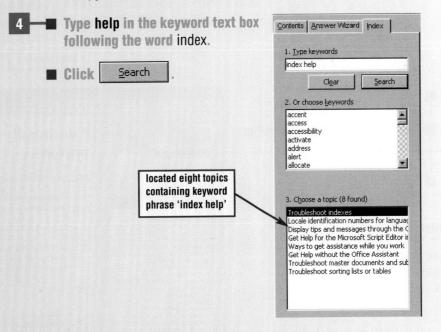

located eight topics containing keyword phrase 'index help'

Now only eight topics were located that contain both keywords.

5 ━■ Click the Get Help without the Office Assistant.

■ Read the information on this topic.

Your screen should be similar to Figure 16.

Figure 16

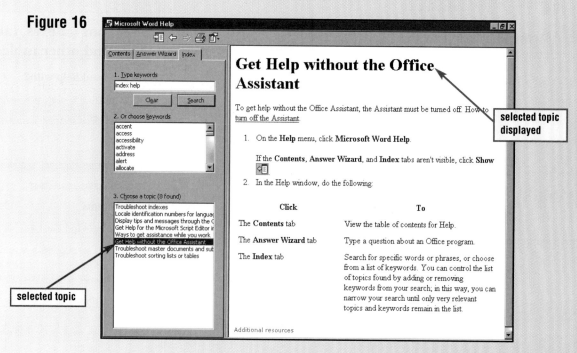

selected topic displayed

selected topic

USING THE ANSWER WIZARD

Another way to locate Help topics is to use the Answer Wizard tab. This feature works just like the Office Assistant to locate topics. You will use this method to locate Help information on toolbars.

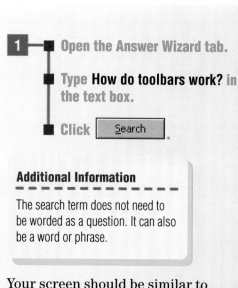

1 ■ Open the Answer Wizard tab.

■ Type **How do toolbars work?** in the text box.

■ Click ⬚ Search ⬚.

Additional Information

The search term does not need to be worded as a question. It can also be a word or phrase.

Your screen should be similar to Figure 17.

enter question

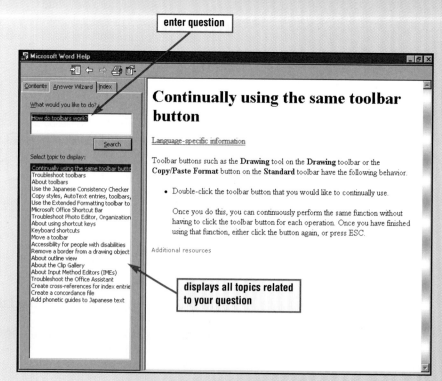

displays all topics related to your question

Figure 17

The topic list box displays all topics that the Answer Wizard considers may be related to the question you entered.

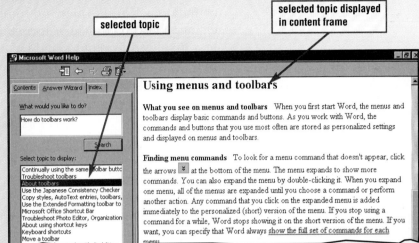

Figure 18

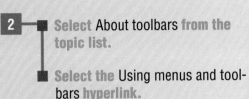

2 ■ Select About toolbars from the topic list.

■ Select the Using menus and toolbars hyperlink.

Your screen should be similar to Figure 18.

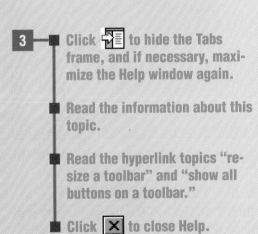

3 ■ Click 🖥 to hide the Tabs frame, and if necessary, maximize the Help window again.

■ Read the information about this topic.

■ Read the hyperlink topics "resize a toolbar" and "show all buttons on a toolbar."

■ Click ✖ to close Help.

Your screen should be similar to Figure 19.

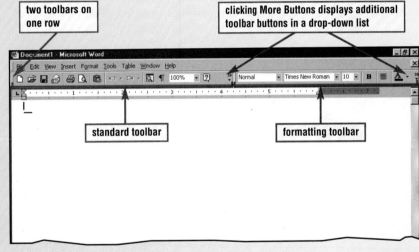

Figure 19

The Help window is closed, and the Word window is displayed again.

Using Toolbars

While using Office 2000, you will see that many toolbars open automatically as different tasks are performed. Toolbars initially display the basic buttons. Like menus they are personalized automatically, displaying those buttons you use frequently and hiding others. The More Buttons ≫ button located at the end of a toolbar displays a drop-down button list of those buttons that are not displayed. When you use a button from this list, it then is moved to the toolbar, and a button that has not been used recently is moved to the More Buttons list.

Initially, Word displays two toolbars, Standard and Formatting, on one row below the menu bar (See Figure 19). The Standard toolbar contains buttons that are used to complete the most frequently used menu commands. The Formatting toolbar contains buttons that are used to change the appearance or format of the document. However, your screen may display different toolbars in different locations. If you right-click on a toolbar, the toolbar shortcut menu is displayed. Using this menu, you can specify which toolbars are displayed. To see which toolbars are open,

1 ─■ **Right-click on any toolbar.**

> The menu equivalent is View/Toolbars.

Your screen should be similar to Figure 20.

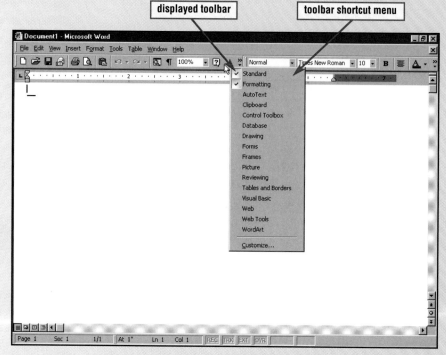

Figure 20

The toolbar shortcut menu displays a list of toolbar names. Those that are currently displayed are checked. Clicking on a toolbar from the list will display it onscreen. Clicking on a checked toolbar will hide the toolbar.

2 ─■ **If necessary, clear the checkmark from all toolbars other than the Standard and Formatting toolbars.**

There should now only be two open toolbars. When a toolbar is opened, it may appear docked or floating. A **docked** toolbar is fixed to an edge of the window and displays the move handle ▯. Dragging this bar up or down allows you to move the toolbar. If multiple toolbars share the same row, dragging the bar left or right adjusts the size of the toolbar. A docked toolbar can occupy a row by itself, or several can be on a row together. A **floating** toolbar appears in a separate window that can be moved by dragging the title bar.

3 ▪— Drag the move handle of the Standard toolbar into the workspace.

Your screen should be similar to Figure 21.

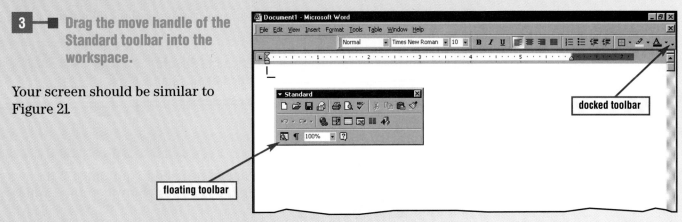

Figure 21

The Standard toolbar is now floating and can be moved to any location in the window. If you move it to the edge of the window, it will attach to that location and become a docked toolbar. A floating toolbar can also be sized by dragging the edge of toolbar.

4 ▪— Move the floating toolbar to the left end of the row below the menu bar.

▪ If necessary, move the Formatting toolbar to the right end of the same row as the Standard toolbar.

Your screen should be similar to Figure 22.

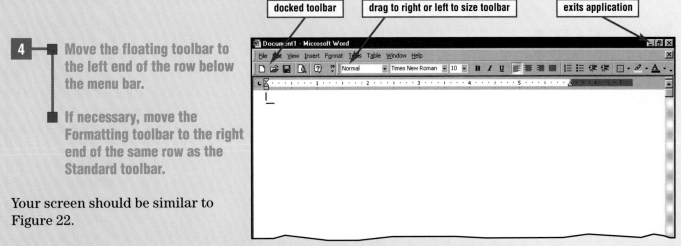

Figure 22

The two toolbars now occupy a single row. The size of each toolbar can be adjusted to show more or fewer buttons by dragging the move handle.

The mouse pointer appears as ✛ when you point to the ▯ of any toolbar.

5 ▪— Drag the ▯ of the Formatting toolbar to the right or left as needed until each bar occupies approximately half the row space.

Double-clicking the bar when multiple toolbars share the same row minimizes or maximizes the toolbar size.

To quickly identify the toolbar buttons, you can display the button name by pointing to the button.

6 ▬ Point to any button on the Standard toolbar to see the ScreenTip displaying the button name.

Exiting an Office Application

The Exit command on the File menu can be used to quit most Windows programs. In addition, you can click the ☒ Close button in the application window title bar.

1 ▬ Click ☒ Close.

The application window is closed, and the desktop is visible again.

Key Terms

cascading menu xxviii	ScreenTip xxiv
desktop xxii	scroll arrows xxv
docked xxxviii	scroll bar xxv
floating xxxviii	scroll box xxv
frame xxi	selection cursor xxvii
hyperlink xxxi	shortcut menu xxvi
icon xxii	Start button xxii
menu xxvi	status bar xxv
menu bar xxv	taskbar xxii
mouse xxii	toolbar xxv
mouse pointer xxii	workspace xxv

Command Summary

Command	Shortcut Keys	Button	Action
Start/Programs			Opens program menu
File/Exit	Alt + F4	☒	Exits Word program
View/Toolbars			Hides or displays toolbars
Help/Microsoft Word Help	F1		Opens help window
Help/Show the Office Assistant.			Displays Help's Office Assistant.

Overview

What Is Word Processing?

Word 2000 is a word processing software application whose purpose is to help you create any type of written communication. A word processor can be used to manipulate text data to produce a letter, a report, a memo, an e-mail message or any other type of correspondence. Text data is any letter, number, or symbol that you can type on a keyboard. The grouping of the text data to form words, sentences, paragraphs, and pages of text results in the creation of a document. Through a word processor you can create, modify, store, retrieve, and print part or all of a document.

Word processors are one of the most widely used applications software programs. Putting your thoughts in writing, from the simplest note to the most complex book, is a time-consuming process. Even more time-consuming is the task of editing and retyping the document to make it better. Word processors make errors nearly nonexistent—not because they are not made, but because they are easy to correct. Word processors let you throw away the correction fluid, scissors, paste, and erasers. Now, with a few keystrokes, you can easily correct errors, move paragraphs, and reprint your document.

Announcing
New Adventure Travel Tours

This year we are introducing four new tours offering you a unique opportunity to combine many different outdoor activities while exploring the world.

Hike the Inca trail to Machu Picchu
Camping Safari in Tanzania
Climb Mount Kilimanjaro
Explore the Costa Rican Rainforests

Attend an Adventure Travel presentation to learn about some of the earth's greatest unspoiled habitats and find out how you can experience the adventure of a lifetime.

Presentation dates and times are January 5 at 7 PM, February 3 at 7:30 PM and March 8 at 7 PM. All presentations are held at convenient hotel locations. The hotels are located in downtown Los Angeles, Santa Clara and at the airport.

Call 1-800-777-0004 for presentation locations, a full color brochure, and itinerary information, costs, and trip dates.

Visit our
Web site at
AdventureTravelTours.com

January 10, 2001

Dear Adventure Traveler,

Imagine hiking and paddling your way through the rain forests of Costa Rica, camping under the stars in Africa, or following in the footsteps of the ancient Inca as you backpack along the Inca trail to Machu Picchu. Turn these dreams of adventure into memories you will cherish forever by joining us on one of our four new adventure tours.

To learn more about these exciting new adventures, we are offering several presentations. These presentations will focus on the features and cultures of the area. We will also show you pictures of places and activities you will participate in. Also presented is a detailed agenda and package costs. Plan on attending one of the following presentations:

Date	Time	Location	Room
January 5	7:00 PM	Town Center Hotel	Room 284B
February 3	7:30 PM	Airport Manor	Conference Room A
March 8	7:00 PM	Country Inn	Mountainside Room

In appreciation for your past patronage, we are pleased to offer you a 10% discount off the price of any of the new tour packages. You must book the trip at least 60 days prior to the departure date. Please turn in this letter to qualify for the discount.

Our vacation tours are professionally planned and designed solely for your enjoyment. Nearly everything is included in the price of your tour while giving you the best possible value for your dollar. All trips include:

- **Professional tour manager and local guides**
- **All accommodations and meals**
- **All entrance fees, excursions, transfers and tips**

We hope you will join us this year on another special Adventure Travel journey. Your memories of fascinating places and challenging physical adventures should linger for a long, long time. For reservations, please see your travel agent, or contact us directly at 1-800-777-0004. You can also visit us at our new Web site at www.AdventureTravelTours.com.

Best regards,

Student Name

A flyer and letter created using Word 2000

Word 2000 Features

Word 2000 excels in its ability to change or edit a document. Editing involves correcting spelling, grammar, and sentence structure errors. In addition, you can easily revise or update existing text by inserting or deleting text. For example, a document that lists prices can easily be updated to reflect new prices. A document that details procedures can be revised by deleting old procedures and inserting new ones. This is especially helpful when a document is used repeatedly. Rather than recreating the whole document, you change only the parts that need to be revised.

Revision also includes the rearrangement of selected areas of text. For example, while writing a report, you may decide to change the location of a single word or several paragraphs or pages of text. You can do it easily by cutting or removing selected text from one location, then pasting or placing the selected text in another location. The selection can also be copied from one document to another.

Another time-saver is word wrap. As you enter text, you do not need to decide where to end each line, as you do on a typewriter. When a line is full, the program automatically wraps the text down to the next line.

To help you produce a perfect document, Word 2000 includes many additional support features. The AutoCorrect feature checks the spelling and grammar in a document as text is entered. Many common errors are corrected automatically for you. Others are identified and a correction suggested. While you enter text, the AutoComplete feature may suggest entire phrases that can be quickly inserted based on the first few characters you type. The words and phrases are included in a list of AutoText entries provided with Word 2000, or they may be ones you have included yourself. A thesaurus can be used to display alternative words that have a meaning similar or opposite to a word you entered. A Find and Replace feature can be used to quickly locate specified text and replace it with other text throughout a document.

A variety of Wizards are included in Word 2000 that provide step-by-step assistance while you produce many common types of documents such as business letters, faxes, resumes, or reports. Templates also can be used to produce many of these documents without the step-by-step guidance provided by the wizard.

You can also easily control the appearance or format of the document. Formatting includes such operations as changing the line spacing and margin widths, adding page numbers, and displaying page headers and footers. You can also quickly change how your text is aligned with the left or right margin. For example, text can be centered between the margins, or justified—evenly aligned on both the left and right margins. Perhaps the most noticeable formatting feature is the ability to apply different fonts (type styles and sizes) and text appearance changes such as bold, italics, and color to all or selected portions of the document. Additionally, you can add color shading behind individual pieces of text or entire paragraphs and pages to add emphasis. Automatic formatting can be turned on to automatically format text as you type by detecting when to apply selected formats to text as it is entered. In addition, Word 2000 includes a variety of tools that automate the process of many common tasks, such as creating tables, form letters, and columns.

Group collaboration on projects is common in industry today. Word 2000 includes many features to help streamline how documents are developed and changed by group members. A discussion feature allows multiple people to insert remarks in the same document without having to route the document to each person or reconcile multiple reviewers' comments. A feature called versioning allows you to save multiple versions of the same document so that you can see exactly who did what on a document and when. You can easily consolidate all changes and comments from different reviewers in one simple step and accept or reject changes as needed.

To further enhance your documents, you can insert many different types of graphic elements. You can select from over 150 border styles that can be applied to areas of text such as headings, or around graphics or entire pages. The drawing tools supplied with Word 2000 can be used to create your own drawings. Or you can select from over 100 adjustable AutoShapes and modify them to your needs. All drawings can be further enhanced with 3-D effects, shadows, colors, and textures. Additionally, you can produce fancy text effects using the WordArt tool. More complex pictures can be inserted in documents by scanning your own, using supplied or purchased clip art, or downloading images from the World Wide Web.

Word 2000 is closely integrated with the World Wide Web. It detects when you are typing a Web address and converts it to a hyperlink automatically for you. You can also create your own hyperlinks to locations within documents, or to other documents, including those at external locations such as a Web site or file server. Its many Web-editing features help you quickly create a Web page. Among these is a Web Page Wizard that guides you step-by-step through the process of creating a Web page. Themes can be used to quickly apply unified design elements and color schemes to your Web pages. Frames can be created to make your Web site easier for users to navigate. Pictures, graphic elements, animated graphics, sound, and movies can all be used to increase the impact of your Web pages.

You can also create and send e-mail messages directly from within Word, using all its features to create and edit the message. You can also send an entire document directly by e-mail. The document becomes the message. This makes collaboration easy, because you can edit the document directly without having to open or save an attachment.

Case Study for Word 2000 Tutorials

As a recent college graduate, you have accepted a job as advertising coordinator for Adventure Travel, a specialty travel company that organizes active adventure vacations. The company is headquartered in Los Angeles and has locations in other major cities throughout the country. You will coordinate many kinds of promotional materials: the advertising program for all locations. Your duties include the creation of brochures, flyers, form letters, news releases, advertisements, and a monthly newsletter. You will also create Web pages for the company Web site.

Before You Begin

To the Student

The following assumptions have been made:

■ Microsoft Word 2000 has been properly installed on your computer system.

■ The data disk contains the data files needed to complete the series of Word 2000 Tutorials and practice exercises. These files are supplied by your instructor.

■ You are already familiar with how to use Windows and a mouse.

To the Instructor

By default, Office 2000 installs the most commonly used components and leaves others, such as the Thesaurus and HTML editor, to be installed when first accessed. It is assumed that these additional features have been installed prior to students using the tutorials.

Please be aware that the following settings are assumed to be in effect for the Word 2000 program. These assumptions are necessary so that the screens and directions in the manual are accurate.

■ Language is set to English [US]. (Use Tools/Language/Set Language).

■ The ScreenTips feature is active. (Use Tools/Options/View.)

■ The Office Assistant feature is not on. (Click on the Assistant, click Option, and clear the Use the Office Assistant option.)

■ The Normal view is on. Zoom is 100 percent. (Use View/Normal; View/Zoom/100%.)

■ The Wrap to Window setting is off. (Use Tools/Options/View.)

■ All default settings for the Normal document template are in effect.

■ In addition, all figures in the manual reflect the use of a standard VGA display monitor set at 800 by 600. If another monitor setting is used, there may be more or fewer lines of text displayed in the windows than in the figures. This setting can be changed using Windows setup.

Microsoft Office 2000 Shortcut Bar

The Microsoft Office Shortcut Bar (shown below) may be displayed automatically on the Windows desktop. Commonly, it appears in the right side of the desktop; however, it may appear in other locations, depending upon your setup. The Shortcut Bar on your screen may display different buttons. This is because the Shortcut Bar can be customized to display other toolbar buttons.

The Office Shortcut Bar makes it easy to open existing documents or to create new documents using one of the Microsoft Office applications. It can also be used to send e-mail, add a task to a to-do list, schedule appointments using Schedule+, or access Office Help.

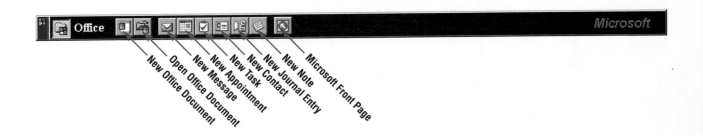

Instructional Conventions

Hands-on instructions you are to perform appear as a sequence of numbered blue steps. Within each step, a series of pink bullets identifies the specific actions that must be performed. Step numbering begins new within each main topic heading throughout the tutorial.

Command sequences you are to issue appear following the word "Choose." Each menu command selection is separated by a /. If the menu command can be selected by typing a letter of the command, the letter will appear underlined. Items that need to be selected will follow the word "Select" and appear in black text. You can select items with the mouse or directional keys.

EXAMPLE

The menu equivalent is **F**ile/**O**pen and the keyboard shortcut is Ctrl + O.

1 Choose **F**ile/**O**pen.

   Select Trip Flyer.

Commands that can be initiated using a button and the mouse appear following the word "Click." The icon (and the icon name if the icon does not include text) is displayed following Click. The menu equivalent and keyboard shortcut appear in a margin note when the action is first introduced.

EXAMPLE

Black text identifies items you need to select or move to. Information you are asked to type appears in black and bold.

EXAMPLE

Creating and Editing a Document

Competencies

After completing this tutorial, you will know how to:

1. Develop a document as well as enter and edit text.
2. Insert and delete text and blank lines.
3. Use AutoCorrect, AutoText, and AutoComplete.
4. Use automatic spelling and grammar checking.
5. Save, close, and open files.
6. Select text.
7. Undo and redo changes.
8. Change fonts and type sizes.
9. Bold and color text.
10. Change alignment.
11. Insert, size, and move graphics.
12. Preview and print a document.

Case Study

As a recent college graduate, you have accepted a job as advertising coordinator for Adventure Travel, a specialty travel company that organizes active adventure vacations. The company is headquartered in Los Angeles and has locations in other major cities throughout the country. You are responsible for coordination of the advertising program for all locations. This includes the creation of many kinds of promotional materials: brochures, flyers, form

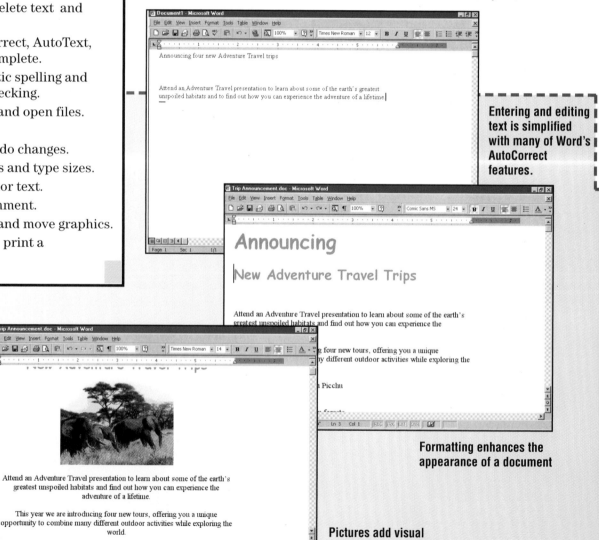

Entering and editing text is simplified with many of Word's AutoCorrect features.

Formatting enhances the appearance of a document

Pictures add visual interest to a document

letters, news releases, advertisements, and a monthly newsletter. You are also responsible for creating Web pages for the company Web site.

Adventure Travel is very excited about four new tours planned for the upcoming year. They want to promote them through informative presentations held throughout the country. Your first job as advertising coordinator will be to create a flyer advertising the four new tours and the presentations about them. The flyer will be modified according to the location of the presentation.

The software tool you will use to create the flyer is the word processing application Word 2000. It helps you create documents such as letters, reports, and research papers. In this tutorial, you will learn how to enter, edit, and print a document while you create the flyer (shown here) to be distributed in a mailing to Adventure Travel clients.

Announcing
New Adventure Travel Tours

This year we are introducing four new tours, offering you a unique opportunity to combine many different outdoor activities while exploring the world.

Hike the Inca trail to Machu Picchu
Camp on safari in Tanzania
Climb Mt. Kilimanjaro
Explore the Costa Rican rain forests

Attend an Adventure Travel presentation to learn about some of the earth's greatest unspoiled habitats and find out how you can experience the adventure of a lifetime.

Presentation dates and times are January 5 at 7 PM, February 3 at 7:30 PM, and March 8 at 7 PM. All presentations are held at convenient hotel locations located in downtown Los Angeles, Santa Clara and at the airport.

Call 1-800-777-0004 for presentation locations, a full color brochure, and itinerary information, costs, and trip dates.

Concept Overview

The following concepts will be introduced in this tutorial:

1 **Template**   A template is a document file that includes predefined settings that are used as a pattern to create many common types of documents.

2 **Document Development**   The development of a document follows several steps: plan, enter, edit, format, and preview and print.

3 **AutoCorrect**   The AutoCorrect feature makes some basic assumptions about the text you are typing and, based on these assumptions, automatically identifies and/or corrects the entry as you type.

4 **Automatic Spelling Check**   The automatic spelling-checking feature advises you of misspelled words as you create and edit a document, and proposes possible corrections.

5 **Automatic Grammar Check**   The automatic grammar-checking feature advises you of incorrect grammar as you create and edit a document, and proposes possible corrections.

6 **AutoText and AutoComplete**   The AutoText feature includes entries, such as commonly used phrases, that can be quickly inserted into a document. If the AutoComplete feature is on, a ScreenTip appears as you type the first four characters of an AutoText entry that suggests the remainder of the AutoText entry you may want to use.

7 **Word Wrap**   The word wrap feature automatically decides where to end a line and wrap text to the next line based on the margin settings.

8 **Font**   A font, also commonly referred to as a typeface, is a set of characters with a specific design.

9 **Character Effects**   Different character effects can be applied to selections to add emphasis or interest to a document.

10 **Alignment**   Alignment is how text is positioned on a line between the margins or indents. There are four types of paragraph alignment: left, center, right, and justified.

11 **Graphics**   A graphic is a non-text element or object, such as a drawing or picture, that can be added to a document.

Exploring the Word Window

See Introducing Common Office 2000 Features for information on how to start the application and for a discussion of features common to all Office 2000 applications.

Adventure Travel has recently upgraded their computer systems at all locations across the country. As part of the upgrade, they have installed the latest version of the Microsoft Office suite of applications, Office 2000. You will use the word processing application included in the Office suite, Word 2000, to create a flyer promoting the new tours and presentations. You are very excited to see how this new and powerful application can help you create professional letters and reports as well as eye-catching flyers and newsletters.

1 Start the Word application.

■ If necessary, maximize the Word application window.

Your screen should be similar to Figure 1–1

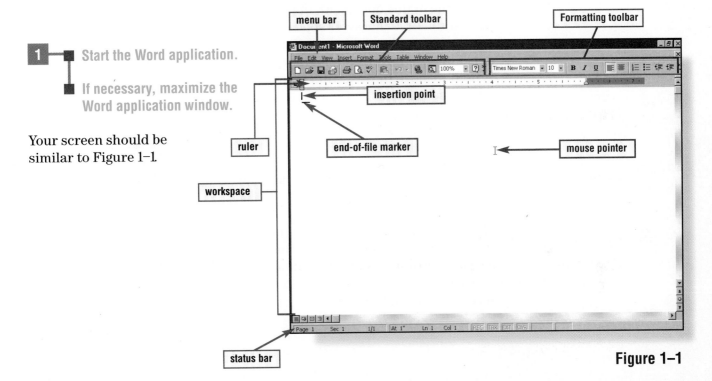

Figure 1–1

The menu bar below the title bar displays the Word program menu. It consists of nine menus that provide access to the commands and features you will use to create and modify a document.

The toolbars, normally located below the menu bar, contain buttons that are mouse shortcuts for many of the menu items. The **Standard toolbar** contains buttons for the most frequently used menu commands. The **Formatting toolbar** contains buttons that are used to change the appearance or format of the document. Word includes 16 different toolbars, many of which appear automatically as you use different features. Your screen may display other toolbars if they were on when the program was last exited.

Because Word remembers settings that were on when the program was last exited, your screen may look slightly different.

The **ruler** is displayed below the toolbars. The ruler shows the line length in inches and is used to set margins, tab stops, and indents.

> **2** ■ If the ruler is not displayed, choose View/Ruler.
>
> ■ If your screen also displays a vertical ruler, choose View/Normal.

You will learn about the different Word views shortly.

The workspace currently displays a blank document window, which is maximized and occupies the entire space. The **insertion point**, also called the **cursor**, is the blinking vertical bar that marks your location in the document. The solid horizontal line is the **end-of-file marker**. Because there is nothing in this document, the insertion point and end-of-file marker appear at the first character space on the first line. The mouse pointer may appear as an I-beam ⌶ (see Figure 1-1) or a left- or right-facing arrow, depending on its location in the window. When it appears as an I-beam, it is used to move the insertion point, and when it appears as an arrow, it is used to select items.

> **3** ■ Move the mouse pointer to the menu bar to see it appear as ⬉.
>
> ■ Move the mouse pointer into the left edge of the document window to see it appear as ◿.

The indicators on the status bar (shown below) show both the location of the text that is displayed in the document window as well as the location of the insertion point in a document. The numbers following the indicators specify the exact location in the document. The indicators are described in the table below.

Indicator	Meaning
Page	Indicates the page of text displayed onscreen.
Sec	Indicates the section of text displayed onscreen. A large document can be broken into sections.
1/1	Indicates the number of pages from the beginning of the document to the displayed page, and the total pages in the document.
At	Indicates the vertical position of the insertion point from the top edge of the page.
Ln	Indicates the vertical position of the insertion point from the top margin of the page.
Col	Indicates the horizontal position of the insertion point from the left margin of the page.

Starting a New Document

When you first start Word, a new blank Word document is opened. It is like a blank piece of paper that already has many predefined settings. These settings, called **default** settings, are generally the most commonly used settings and are stored as a document template.

Concept ① Templates

A **template** is a document file that includes predefined settings that can be used as a pattern to create many common types of documents. Every Word document is based on a document template. The default document settings are stored in the Normal document template. Whenever you create a new document using this template, the same default settings are used. The Normal document template is referred to as a **global template** because it contains settings that are available to all documents.

Normal Document Template

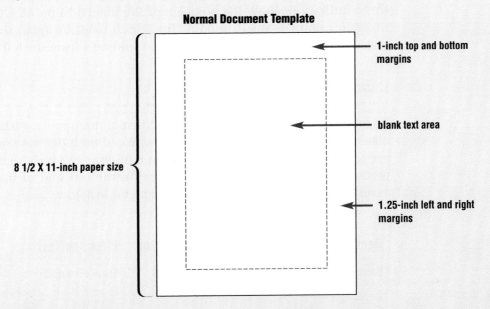

1-inch top and bottom margins

blank text area

8 1/2 X 11-inch paper size

1.25-inch left and right margins

Word also includes many other templates that are designed to help you create professional-looking documents. They include templates that create different styles of memos, letters, and reports. Unlike global templates, the settings included in these specialized templates are available only to documents based on that template. You can also design and save your own document templates.

Contemporary Memo

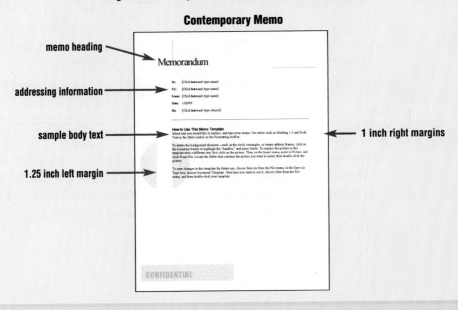

memo heading

addressing information

sample body text

1.25 inch left margin

1 inch right margins

When you first start Word, it displays a new blank document based on the Normal template. The Normal document template settings include 1-inch top and bottom margins, and 1.25-inch left and right margins. Other default settings include a standard paper-size setting of 8.5 by 11 inches, tab settings at every half inch, and single line spacing.

To verify several of the default settings, you can look at the information displayed in the status bar (shown on page WD12). As you can see from the first three indicators in the status bar, page 1 of section 1 of a document consisting of only 1 page (1/1) is displayed on your screen. The next three indicators show the position of the insertion point. Currently, the insertion point is positioned at the 1-inch location from the top of the page, on line 1 from the top margin and column 1 from the left margin.

Changing Views

To more easily verify several of the Normal document settings, you can also switch to another document view. Word includes several views that are used for different purposes. You can change views using the View menu commands or the view buttons on the left end of the horizontal scroll bar. The views are described in the table below.

Document View	Command	Button	Effect on Text
Normal view	**V**iew/**N**ormal		Shows text formatting and simple layout of the page. This is the best view to use when typing, editing, and formatting text.
Web Layout view	**V**iew/**W**eb Layout		Shows the document as it will appear when viewed in a Web browser.
Print Layout view	**V**iew/**P**rint Layout		Shows how the text and objects will appear on the printed page. This is the view to use when adjusting margins, working in columns, drawing objects, and placing graphics.
Outline view	**V**iew/**O**utline		Shows the structure of the document. This is the view to use to move, copy, and reorganize text in a document.

The view you see when first starting Word is the view that was in use when the program was last exited. Figure 1–2 shows the document window in Normal view. You can tell which view is in use by looking at the view buttons. The button for the view that is in use appears recessed as if it were depressed.

1 Point to each view button to display the ScreenTip.

If necessary, click ▤ to switch to Normal view.

If your ruler does not show the right margin boundary as in Figure 1–2, choose View/Zoom/100%/✕.

You will learn about zooming the window in Tutorial 2.

Your screen should be similar to Figure 1–2.

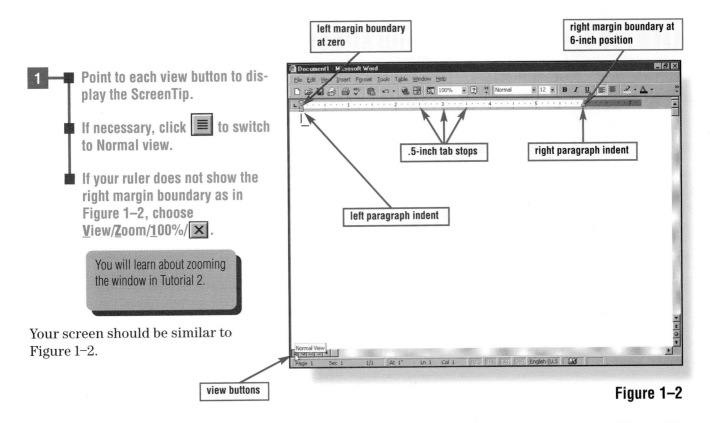

left margin boundary at zero

right margin boundary at 6-inch position

.5-inch tab stops

right paragraph indent

left paragraph indent

view buttons

Figure 1–2

Normal view is the all-purpose view for typing, editing, and formatting text. Normal view shows text formatting but simplifies the layout of the page so that you can type and edit quickly.

To verify several more Normal document settings, you can look at the information displayed in the ruler. The margin boundaries on both ends of the ruler show the location of the left and right margins. The symbol ⧖ at the zero position on the ruler marks the location of the left paragraph indent, and the symbol ⌂ on the right end of the ruler line at the 6-inch position marks the right paragraph indent. The default paragraph indent locations are the same as the margin settings. The ruler shows that the distance between the left and right margins is 6 inches. Knowing that the default page size is 8.5 inches wide, this leaves 2.5 inches for margins: 1.25 inches for equal-sized left and right margins. The ruler also displays dimmed tab marks below each half-inch position along the ruler, indicating a default tab setting of every half inch.

Although Normal view displays the default settings, they are easier to see when you are in Print Layout view.

2 Click ▣ Print Layout view.

■ If your screen does not display the top and sides of the page as in Figure 1–3, choose **V**iew/**Z**oom/**P**age Width/ OK .

Your screen should be similar to Figure 1–3.

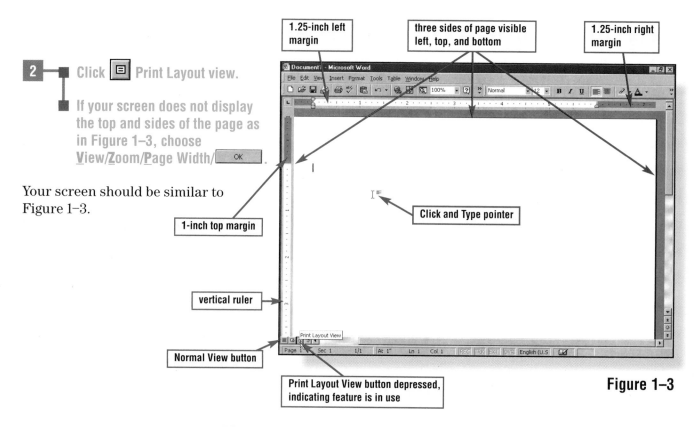

1.25-inch left margin

three sides of page visible left, top, and bottom

1.25-inch right margin

Click and Type pointer

1-inch top margin

vertical ruler

Normal View button

Print Layout View button depressed, indicating feature is in use

Figure 1–3

This view displays the current page of your document as it will appear when printed. The top edge of the paper is visible below the horizontal ruler, and the left and right edges are visible along the sides of the window. The top margin is 1 inch from the top of the page, and the left margin setting is 1.25 inches from the left edge of the page.

This view also displays a vertical ruler that shows the vertical position of text. Also notice in this view that the mouse pointer appears as Ɪ▤. This is the Click and Type pointer, which indicates the Click and Type feature is on. This feature allows you to quickly insert text into a blank area of a document while applying certain design features automatically. You will learn more about this feature in later tutorials.

3 Switch back to Normal view.

Developing a Document

Your first project with Adventure Travel is to create a flyer about this year's new tours.

Concept ② Document Development

The development of a document follows several steps: plan, enter, edit, format, and preview and print.

Plan The first step in the development of a document is to understand the purpose of the document and to plan what your document should say.

Enter After planning the document, you can begin entering the content of the document by typing the text using the word processor.

Edit Making changes to your document is called **editing**. While typing, you are bound to make typing and spelling errors that need to be corrected. This is one type of editing. Another is to revise the content of what you have entered to make it clearer, or to add or delete information.

Format Enhancing the appearance of the document to make it more readable or attractive is called **formatting**. This step is usually performed when the document is near completion. It includes many features such as boldfaced text, italics, and bulleted lists.

Preview and Print The last step is to preview and print the document. Previewing displays the document onscreen as it will appear when printed, allowing you to check the document's overall appearance and make any final changes before printing.

You will find that you will generally follow these steps in the order listed above for your first draft of a document. However, you will probably retrace steps such as editing and formatting as the final document is developed.

Planning the Document

During the planning phase, you spoke with your manager regarding the purpose of the flyer and the content in general. The primary purpose of the flyer is to promote the new tours. A secondary purpose is to advertise the company in general. To do this you plan to include specific information about the new tours in the flyer as well as general information about Adventure Travel. The content also needs to include information about the upcoming new tour presentations. Finally, you want to include information about the Adventure Travel Web site.

Entering Text

Now that you understand the purpose of the flyer and have a general idea of the content, you are ready to enter the text.

To enter text in a new document, simply begin typing the text. On the first line of the flyer you will enter "Announcing Four New Adventure Travel Trips." As you enter the text, it will include several intentional errors. Type the entries exactly as they appear.

1 ■ **Type** anouncing

Your screen should be similar to Figure 1–4.

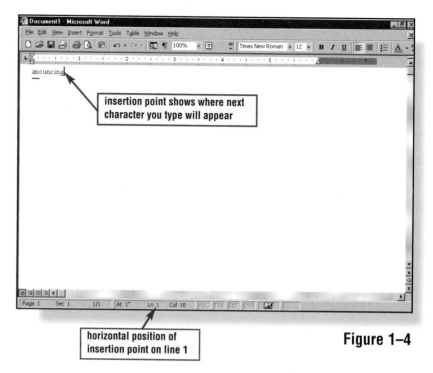

Figure 1–4

Notice that as you type, the character appears to the left of the insertion point. The location of the insertion point shows where the next character will appear as you type. Also, the status bar reflects the new horizontal position of the insertion point on the line. It shows the insertion point is currently positioned on column 10 of line 1.

Using AutoCorrect

To end this word, you need to enter a space. As soon as you complete a word, the program checks the word for accuracy. This is part of the automatic correcting feature of Word.

Concept ③ AutoCorrect

The **AutoCorrect** feature makes some basic assumptions about the text you are typing and, based on these assumptions, automatically identifies and/or corrects the entry. The AutoCorrect feature automatically inserts proper capitalization at the beginning of sentences and in the names of days of the week. It will also change to lowercase letters any words that were incorrectly capitalized due to the accidental use of the [Caps Lock] key. In addition, it also corrects many common spelling errors automatically.

The program automatically corrects by looking for certain types of errors. For example, if two capital letters appear at the beginning of a word, Word changes the second capital letter to a lowercase letter. If a lowercase letter appears at the beginning of a sentence, Word capitalizes the first letter of the first word. If the name of a day begins with a lowercase letter, Word capitalizes the first letter.

In some cases, you may want to exclude an abbreviation or capitalized item from automatic correction. You can do this by adding the word to an exception list. Alternatively, you can add words to the list of words you want to be automatically corrected. For example, if you commonly misspell a word, you can add the word to the list and it will be automatically corrected as you type.

1 ■ Press Spacebar twice.

Your screen should be similar to
Figure 1–5.

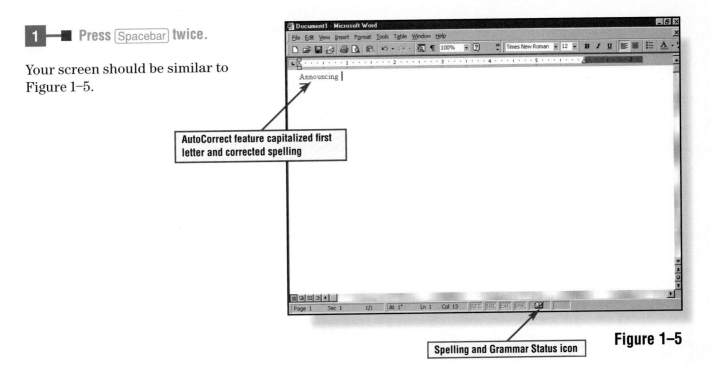

AutoCorrect feature capitalized first
letter and corrected spelling

Spelling and Grammar Status icon

Figure 1–5

Word automatically capitalized the first letter of the word and corrected
the spelling error.

Automatically Checking Spelling

Next you will continue entering the flyer heading. As you do, observe the
Spelling and Grammar Status icon [icon] in the status bar. It will display an
animated pencil icon while you are typing, indicating Word is checking for
errors as you type. Currently it displays a red checkmark, indicating the
program does not detect any errors.

1 ■ Type **four new Adventure Travell**

■ Press Spacebar.

Your screen should be similar to
Figure 1–6.

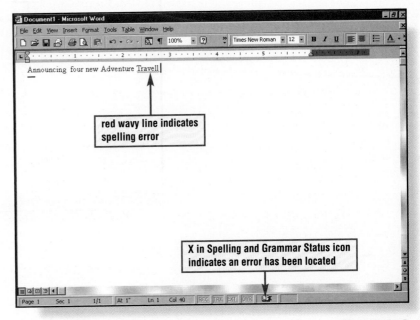

red wavy line indicates
spelling error

X in Spelling and Grammar Status icon
indicates an error has been located

Figure 1–6

This time Word has identified the word as misspelled by underlining it with a wavy red line. It is not automatically corrected because the misspelled word is not on the list of commonly misspelled words. Also notice the Spelling and Grammar Status icon changes to ▨ when a document contains errors.

Concept ④ Automatic Spelling Check

The automatic spelling-checking feature advises you of misspelled words as you create and edit a document, and proposes possible corrections. The Spelling Checker compares each word you type to a **main dictionary** of words supplied with the program. Although this dictionary includes most common words, it may not include proper names, technical terms, and so on. If the word does not appear in the main dictionary, it checks the **custom dictionary**, a dictionary that you can create to hold words you commonly use but that are not included in the main dictionary. If the word does not appear in either dictionary, the program identifies it as misspelled by displaying a red wavy line below the word. You can then correct the misspelled word by editing it. Alternatively, you can display a list of suggested spelling corrections for that word and select the correct spelling from the list to replace the misspelled word in the document.

The quickest way to correct a misspelled word is to select the correct spelling from a list of suggested spelling corrections displayed on the Spelling shortcut menu.

2 ■ Right-click on Travell to display the Spelling shortcut menu.

Your screen should be similar to Figure 1–7.

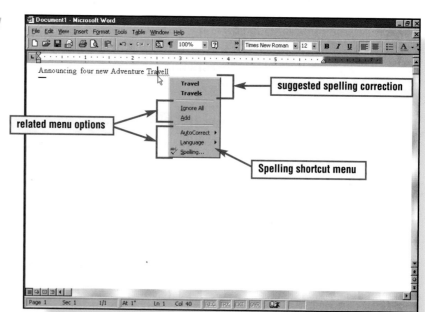

Figure 1–7

A shortcut menu of suggested correct spellings is displayed. In this case, two correct spellings are suggested. The menu also includes several related menu options described below.

Option	Effect
Ignore All	Instructs Word to ignore the misspelling of this word throughout the rest of this session.
Add	Adds the word to the custom dictionary list. When a word is added to the custom dictionary, Word will always accept that spelling as correct.
AutoCorrect	Adds the word to the AutoCorrect list so Word can correct misspellings of it automatically as you type.
Language	Sets the language format, such as French, English or German, to apply to the word.
Spelling	Starts the spell-checking program to check the entire document. You will learn about this feature in Tutorial 2.

Notice that the suggested replacements reflect the same capitalization as used in the document. Sometimes there are no suggested replacements, because Word cannot locate any words in its dictionary that are similar in spelling; or the suggestions are not correct. If this happens, you need to edit the word manually. In this case, the first suggestion is correct. To select it,

3 ──■ Choose Travel.

Your screen should be similar to Figure 1–8.

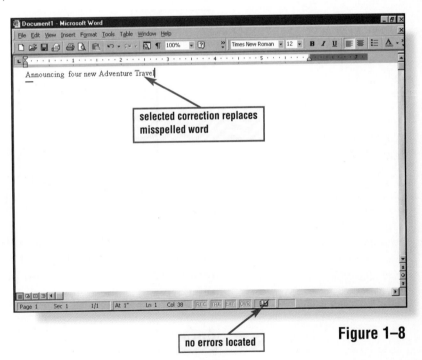

selected correction replaces misspelled word

no errors located

Figure 1–8

The spelling correction you selected replaces the misspelled word in the document.

The Spelling and Grammar status icon again displays a red checkmark ⊞ indicating that as far a Word is able to detect, the document is clear of errors.

Ending a Line and Inserting Blank Lines

Now you are ready to complete the first line of the announcement. To end a line and begin another line, you simply press ⏎Enter. The insertion point moves to the beginning of the next line. If you press ⏎Enter at the beginning of a line, a blank line is inserted into the document. If the insertion point is in the middle of a line of text and you press ⏎Enter, all the text to the right of the insertion point moves to the beginning of the next line.

1 ■ Press Spacebar.

■ Type **trips**

■ Press ⏎Enter **4 times.**

Your screen should be similar to Figure 1–9.

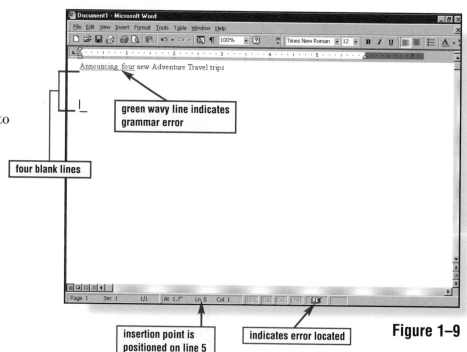

Figure 1–9

Pressing the first ⏎Enter ended the first line of text and inserted a blank line. The next three inserted three more blank lines. The status bar now shows that the insertion point is positioned on line 5, column 1 of the page.

Automatic Grammar Checking

Also notice that now there is a green wavy line under "Announcing four". This means Word has located a grammatical error.

Concept ⑤ Automatic Grammar Check

The automatic grammar-checking feature advises you of incorrect grammar as you create and edit a document, and proposes possible corrections. If Word detects grammatical errors in subject-verb agreements, verb forms, capitalization, or commonly confused words, to name a few, they are identified with a wavy green line. You can correct the grammatical error by editing it or you can display a suggested correction. Not all grammatical errors identified by Word are actual errors. Use discretion when correcting the errors. Grammar checking does not occur until after you enter punctuation or end a line.

2 ■ Right-click on Announcing four to display the Grammar shortcut menu.

Your screen should be similar to Figure 1–10.

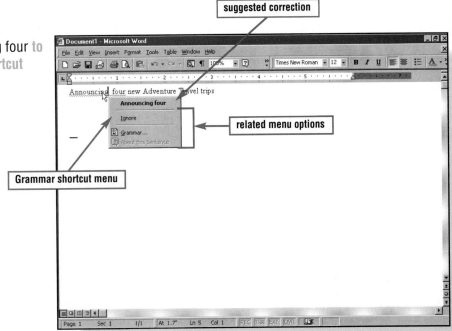

Figure 1–10

A shortcut menu showing a suggested correction is displayed. The Grammar shortcut menu also includes several related menu options described below.

Option	Effect
Ignore	Instructs Word to ignore the grammatical error in this sentence.
Grammar	Opens the Grammar Checker and displays an explanation of the error.
About this Sentence	If the Office Assistant feature is on, this option is available. It also provides a detailed explanation of the error.

Additional Information

A dimmed option means it is currently unavailable.

Because you cannot readily identify the reason for the error, you will open the Grammar Checker.

3 ■ Choose Grammar.

Your screen should be similar to Figure 1–11.

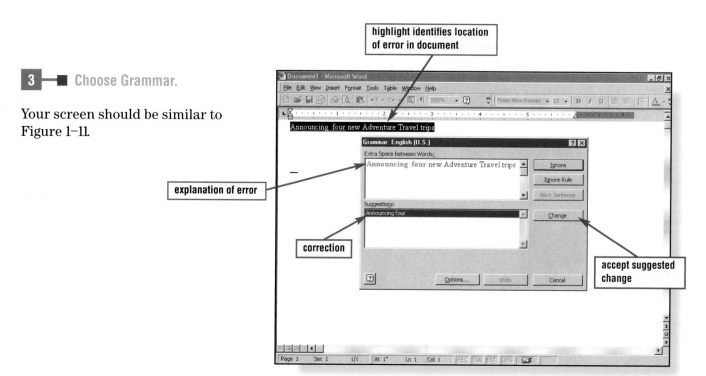

Figure 1–11

The Grammar dialog box is open. It tells you that the grammatical error is an extra space between words, in this case between the words "Announcing" and "four." The suggested correction is correct. To make the suggested change,

4 ■ Click  .

Your screen should be similar to Figure 1–12.

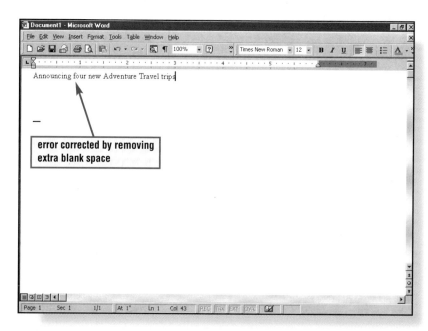

Figure 1–12

The error is corrected, the wavy green line is removed, and the Spelling and Grammar Status icon returns to 📖 .

Using AutoText and AutoComplete

Now you are ready to type the text for the first paragraph of the flyer. Do not worry about making typing errors as you enter the text; you will learn how to correct them next.

1 Press ↓ 4 times.

   Type **Atte**

Your screen should be similar to Figure 1–13.

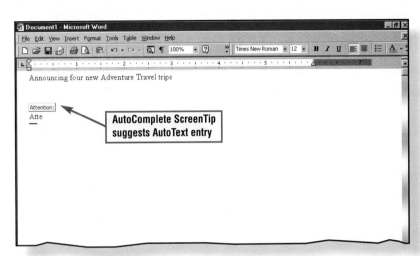

Figure 1–13

> If a ScreenTip is not displayed, you may need to turn on this feature using **I**nsert/**A**utoTe**x**t/AutoTe**x**t and activate the **S**how AutoComplete tip for AutoText and dates option.

A ScreenTip displaying the word "Attention:" appears. This is Word's AutoText and AutoComplete feature.

Concept **6** AutoText and AutoComplete

The **AutoText** feature includes entries, such as commonly used phrases, that can be quickly inserted into a document. The AutoText entries can be selected and inserted into the document using the Insert/AutoText command. Word's standard AutoText entries include salutations and closing phrases, and you can also add your own entries to the AutoText list. These can consist of text or graphics you may want to use again. Common uses are for a company name, mailing address, and a distribution list for memos.

Additionally, if the **AutoComplete** feature is on, a Screen Tip appears as you type the first four characters of an AutoText entry that suggests the remainder of the AutoText entry you may want to use. You can choose to accept the suggestion to insert it into the document, or continue typing to ignore it.

The AutoComplete ScreenTip suggests that you may be typing the word "Attention." When the suggestion appears, you can press ←Enter or F3 to accept it, and the AutoText suggestion is entered automatically for you. If you keep typing, the AutoText suggestion will disappear. In this case, you do not want to enter the suggested word and will continue typing the word "Attend."

2 ■ Type **nd**

■ Press ⟨Spacebar⟩.

The AutoComplete ScreenTip has cleared, and the text as you typed it is displayed.

Using Word Wrap

Now you will continue entering more of the paragraph. As you type, when the text gets close to the right margin, do not press ⟨←Enter⟩ to move to the next line. Word will automatically wrap words to the next line as needed.

Concept ⑦ Word Wrap

The **word wrap** feature automatically decides where to end a line and wrap text to the next line based on the margin settings. This saves time when entering text, as you do not need to press ⟨←Enter⟩ at the end of a full line to begin a new line. The only time you need to press ⟨←Enter⟩ is to end a paragraph, to insert blank lines, or to create a short line such as the salutation. In addition, if you change the margins or insert or delete text on a line, the program automatically readjusts the text on the line to fit within the new margin settings. Word wrap is common to all word processors.

---

1 ■ Type: **an Adventure Travel presentation to learn about some of the earth's greatest unspoiled habitats and to find out how you can experience the adventure of a lifetime.**

> Do not worry about typing errors, you will learn more about correcting them shortly.

Your screen should be similar to Figure 1–14.

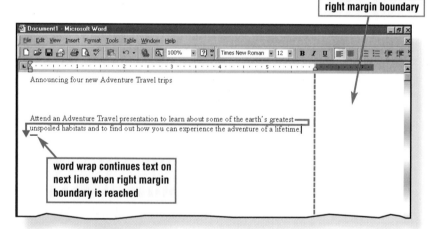

Figure 1–14

The program has wrapped the text that would overlap the right margin to the beginning of the next line. You will continue the paragraph by entering a second sentence.

2 ■ Press Spacebar.

■ Type **This year we are introducing four new tours, offering you a unique opportunity to combine many different outdoor activities while exploring the world.**

Your screen should be similar to Figure 1–15.

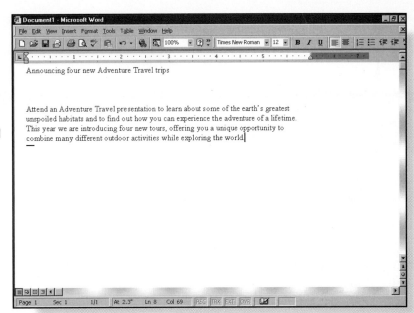

Figure 1–15

Additional Information

Generally, when using a word processor, separate sentences with a single space rather than a double space, which was common when using typewriters.

Once text is entered into a document, it is important to know how to move around within the text to correct errors or make changes. As soon as you learn about moving through a document, you will correct any errors you have made.

Moving Around the Document Window

Either the mouse or the keyboard can be used to move through the text in the document window. Depending on what you are doing, the mouse is not always the quickest means of moving. For example, if your hands are already on the keyboard as you are entering text, it may be quicker to use the keyboard rather than take your hands off to use the mouse. Therefore, you will learn how to move through the document using both methods.

You will learn about selecting text using this feature shortly.

You use the mouse to move the insertion point to a specific location in a document. When you can use the mouse to move the insertion point, it is shaped as an I-beam. However, when the mouse pointer is positioned in the unmarked area to the left of a line (the left margin), it changes to an arrow. This area is called the **selection bar** (see Figure 1–16). When the mouse is in this area, it can be used to highlight (select) text.

To move the insertion point, position the I-beam at the location in the text where you want it to be, then click the left mouse button.

1 ■ Click on the p of presentation (first sentence).

■ Move the mouse pointer out of the way so you can see the insertion point better.

> Make sure the pointer is an I-beam before clicking to move the insertion point. If text appears highlighted, click anywhere in the document where the mouse pointer is an I-beam to clear the highlighting.

Your screen should be similar to Figure 1–16.

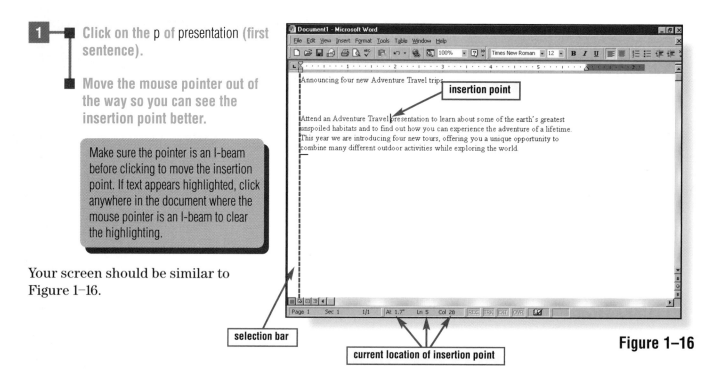

Figure 1–16

> Throughout these tutorials, you will be instructed to move to a specific letter in the text. This means to move the insertion point to the *left* side of the character so the character to the right is selected.

> If you are using the arrows on the numeric keypad, be sure the Num Lock key is off.

The insertion point should now be positioned on one side or the other of the p, with the status bar showing the new location of the insertion point. If it is positioned to the left of the p, this means that the I-beam was positioned more to the left side of the character when you pressed the mouse button. The letter to the right of the insertion point is the selected character, in this case the p. If it is positioned to the right of the p, this means the I-beam was positioned more to the right side of the character when you clicked the mouse button. The letter to the right of the insertion point is the selected character, in this case the r.

The insertion point can also be moved around the window using the arrow keys located on the numeric keypad or the directional keypad. The directional keys and key combinations are described in the table below.

Key	Movement
→	One character to right
←	One character to left
↑	One line up
↓	One line down
Ctrl + →	One word to right
Ctrl + ←	One word to left
Home	Left end of line
End	Right end of line

Holding down a directional key or key combination moves quickly in the direction indicated, saving multiple presses of the key. Many of the Word insertion point movement keys can be held down to execute multiple moves. You will use many of these keys to quickly move through the text.

2

Press ← 7 times.

Press Ctrl + → 4 times.

Hold down → until the insertion point is positioned on the e in earth's. If you move too far to the right along the line of text, use ← to move back to the correct position.

Press ↓ 2 times.

Your screen should be similar to Figure 1–17.

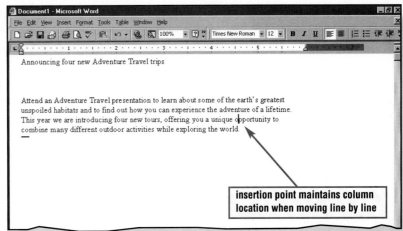

Figure 1–17

The insertion point first moved seven character spaces to the left, then four words to the right, then quickly character by character to the right, and finally down two lines to the p in "opportunity." It moved to that position because it was located in a line containing text at that position. The insertion point will attempt to maintain its position in a line of text as you move up or down through the document.

Editing Text

While entering text and creating a document, you will find that you will want to edit or make changes and corrections to the document. You have decided to make several changes to the text you just entered. The changes you want to make are shown below.

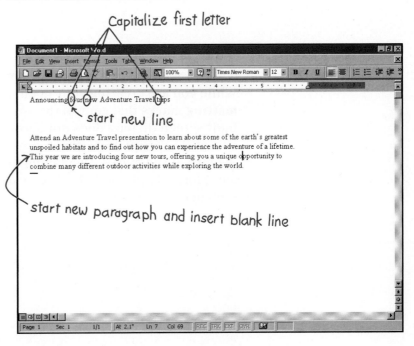

Using Backspace and Delete

Two of the most basic editing keys are the [Backspace] key and the [Delete] key. The [Backspace] key removes a character or space to the left of the insertion point. It is particularly useful when you are moving from right to left (backward) along a line of text. The [Delete] key removes the character or space to the right of the insertion point and is most useful when moving from right to left along a line. You will use these keys to capitalize the first letter of each word in the flyer title.

1 ■ Move to the t in trips.

■ Press [Delete].

■ Type **T**

■ Press [Ctrl] + [←] 4 times.

■ Capitalize the first letter of new.

■ Press [←] 5 times.

■ Press [Backspace].

■ Type **F**

Your screen should be similar to Figure 1–18.

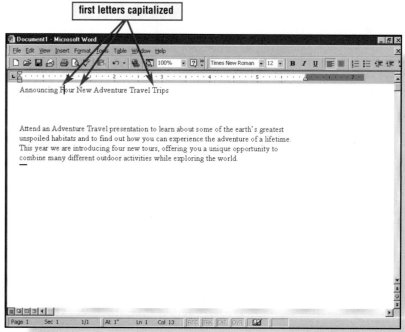

Figure 1–18

Displaying Formatting Marks

While you are creating your document, Word automatically inserts **formatting marks** that control the appearance of your document. Word's default screen display does not show the formatting marks, because they clutter the screen. Sometimes, however, it is helpful to view the underlying formatting marks. Displaying these marks makes it easy to see if you have, for example, added an extra space between words or at the end of a sentence.

1 ■ Click ¶ Show/Hide.

You may need to click ⟩⟩ More Buttons on the Standard toolbar first to locate the Show/Hide ¶ button.

The menu equivalent is **T**ools/**O**ptions/View/**A**ll.

Your screen should be similar to Figure 1–19.

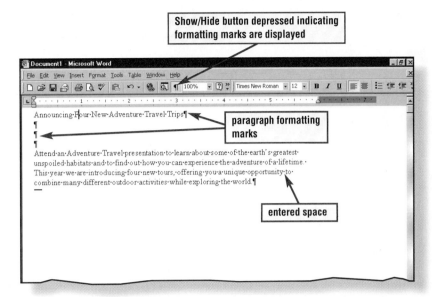

Show/Hide button depressed indicating formatting marks are displayed

paragraph formatting marks

entered space

Figure 1–19

The document now displays the formatting marks. A paragraph formatting mark ¶ is displayed wherever the ⟨←Enter⟩ key was pressed. Between each word, a dot shows where the ⟨Spacebar⟩ was pressed. Formatting marks do not appear when the document is printed. You can continue to edit your document while the formatting marks are displayed, just as you did when they were hidden.

As you continue to proof the letter, you decide that the paragraph is too long and should be divided into two separate paragraphs.

2 ■ Move to T in This (beginning of second sentence).

■ Press ⟨←Enter⟩ 2 times.

Your screen should be similar to Figure 1–20.

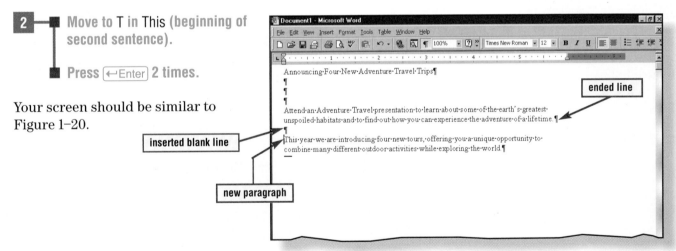

ended line

inserted blank line

new paragraph

Figure 1–20

The ¶ character on the line above the insertion point represents the pressing of ⟨←Enter⟩ that created the blank line between the paragraphs. The ¶ character at the end of the line above that represents the pressing of ⟨←Enter⟩ that ended the paragraph and moved the insertion point and all text following it to the beginning of the next line.

As you continue to create a document, the formatting marks are automatically inserted and deleted. Now that you have separated the two sentences into separate paragraphs, you no longer want the space at the end of the first sentence. You also want to separate the title into two lines. To make these changes,

3 ■ Press ← 2 times.

■ Press Backspace

■ Move to the F in Four

■ Press ←Enter 2 times.

■ Delete the blank space following the word Announcing.

Your screen should be similar to Figure 1–21.

Figure 1–21

The formatting marks are added and deleted as appropriate as you edit the document. In many editing situations, it is necessary to display the formatting marks; however, this is not needed for simple text deletions. For normal entry of text, you will probably not want the marks displayed. To hide the formatting marks again,

Show/Hide button not depressed, indicating formatting marks are not displayed

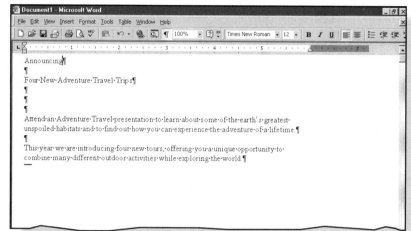

4 ■ Click ¶ Show/Hide.

Your screen should be similar to Figure 1–22.

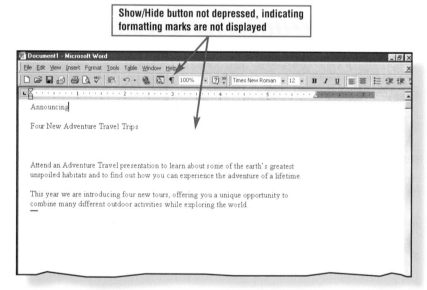

Figure 1–22

The screen returns to normal display. Now that you know how to turn this feature on and off, you can use it whenever you want when entering and editing text.

5 ■ Now that you know how to move around and edit text, move to any errors you may have made while entering the text and correct them.

When complete, your edited document should like Figure 1–22 above.

Saving a New Document and Closing a File

You have a meeting you need to attend shortly, so you want to save your work to a file and close the file. As you enter and edit text to create a new document, the changes you make are immediately displayed onscreen and are stored in your computer's memory. However, they are not permanently stored until you save your work to a file on your disk.

As a backup against the accidental loss of work due to power failure or other mishap, Word includes an AutoRecovery feature. When this feature is on, as you work you may see a pulsing disk icon briefly appear in the status bar. This indicates the program is saving your work to a temporary recovery file. The time interval between automatic saving can be set to any period you specify; the default is every 10 minutes. When you start up again, the recovery file is automatically opened containing all changes you made up to the last time it was saved by AutoRecover. You then need to save the recovery file. If you do not save it, it is deleted when closed. While AutoRecover is a great feature for recovering lost work, it should not be used in place of regularly saving your work.

You will save your work as a file on your data disk.

1 ■ Place your data disk in drive A (or the appropriate drive for your system).

■ Choose File/Save.

> The keyboard shortcut is
> Ctrl + S.

Your screen should be similar to Figure 1–23.

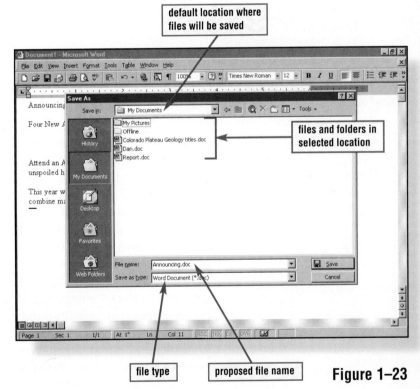

default location where files will be saved

files and folders in selected location

file type

proposed file name

Figure 1–23

This Save As dialog box is used to specify the location to save the file and the file name. The Save In drop-down list box displays the default folder as the location where the file will be saved, and the File Name text box displays the proposed file name. The file list box displays the names of any Word documents in the default location. Only Word-type documents are listed, because Word Document is the specified file type in the Save As Type list box. First you need to change the location where the file will be saved to the drive containing your data disk.

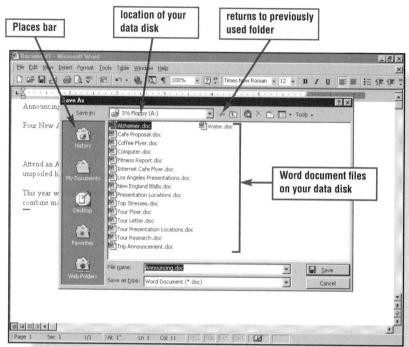

2   Open the Save In drop-down list box.

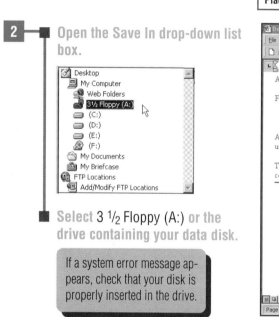

■ Select 3 ½ Floppy (A:) or the drive containing your data disk.

> If a system error message appears, check that your disk is properly inserted in the drive.

Your screen should be similar to Figure 1–24.

Figure 1–24

Now the large list box displays the names of all Word files on your data disk. You can also select the location to save your file from the Places bar along the left side of the dialog box. The icons bring up a list of recently accessed files and folders, the contents of the My Documents and Favorites folder, the Windows desktop, and the remote WebFolders list. Selecting a folder from one of these lists changes to that location. You can also click the ⬅ button in the toolbar to return to folders that were previously opened during the current session.

Next you need to enter a file name. The File Name list box displays the default file name, consisting of the first few words from the document. The file name can be edited using the same features you used to edit text in the document. You will change the file name to Announcement.

Additional Information: Windows documents can have up to 256 characters in the file name. Names can contain letters or numbers; special symbols, with the exception of the underscore, cannot be used. Word files are identified by the file extension .doc, which is automatically added to the file name when the file is saved.

3 ■ Click in the File Name text box.

■ Change the file name to **Announcement**.

■ Click 🔲 Save .

The document is saved on disk. Finally, you want to close the document while you attend your meeting.

4 ■ Click ☒ in the menu bar.

Because you did not make any changes to the document since saving it, the document window is closed immediately. If you had made additional changes, Word would ask if you wanted to save the file before closing it. This prevents the accidental closing of a file that has not been saved first. Now the Word window displays an empty workspace, and the status bar indicators are blank because there are no open documents.

Opening a File

You asked your assistant to enter the remaining information in the flyer for you while you attend the meeting. Upon your return, you find a disk and a note from your assistant on your desk. The note explains that he had a little trouble entering the information and tells you that he saved the revised file as Trip Announcement. You want to open the file and continue working on the flyer.

1 ■ Click 📂 Open.

Your screen should be similar to Figure 1–25.

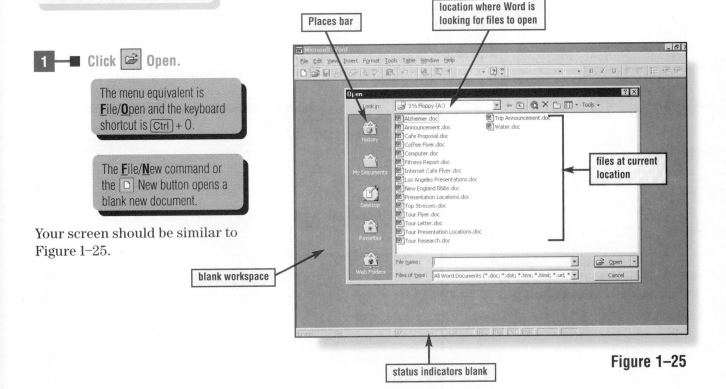

Figure 1–25

In the Open dialog box, you specify the location and name of the file you want to open. The Look In drop-down list box displays the drive you specified when saving as the location where the program will look for files. The location should be the drive containing your data disk. The large list box displays the names of all Word files on your data disk. As in the Save As dialog box, the Places bar can be used to quickly access recently used files. When selecting a file to open, it may be helpful to see a preview of the file first. To do this you can change the dialog box view.

2 ■ If the Look In location is not correct, select the appropriate location from the Look In drop-down list box.

■ Select Trip Announcement.doc.

■ Open the 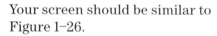 Views drop-down list.

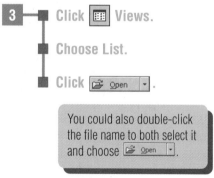

■ Choose Pre**v**iew.

Your screen should be similar to Figure 1–26.

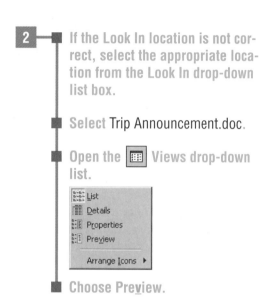

Figure 1–26

A preview of the selected file is displayed in the right side of the dialog box. To return the view to the list of file names and open this file,

3 ■ Click 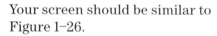 Views.

■ Choose List.

■ Click Open.

> You could also double-click the file name to both select it and choose Open.

Your screen should be similar to Figure 1–27.

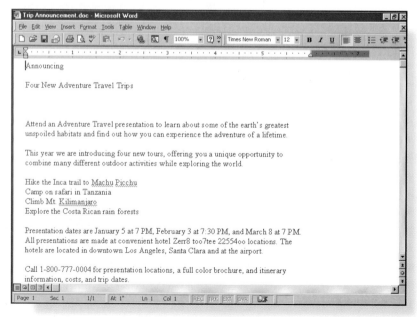

Figure 1–27

The file is loaded and displayed in the document window. This file contains the text of the rest of the first draft of the flyer.

Ignoring Spelling Errors

After entering the text of a document, you should proofread it for accuracy and completeness and modify or edit the document as needed. You first notice that the spelling checker has identified the names of several locations as misspelled when they are in fact spelled correctly. This is because they are not in the dictionary and consequently they are identified. You will instruct Word to accept the spelling of these words and for all other words that it encounters having the same spelling throughout the remainder of the current Word session.

1 ■ Right-click on Machu.

■ Choose Ignore All.

■ In the same manner, tell Word to ignore the spelling of the other identified words.

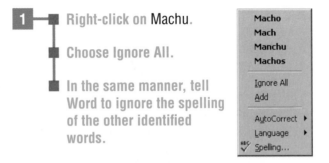

The red underlines are cleared from each word. If you type any of these words again during this Word session, they will not be identified as misspelled.

Inserting Text

As you continue to check the document, you see that the first sentence of the paragraph below the list of trips is incorrect. It should read: "Presentation dates *and times* are. . . ." The sentence is missing the words "and times." In addition, you want to change the word "made" to "held" in the following sentence. These words can easily be entered into the sentence without retyping using either Insert or Overtype mode.

In **Insert mode** new characters are inserted into the existing text by moving the existing text to the right to make space for the new characters. You will insert the words "and times" after the word "dates" in the first sentence.

1   ■ Move to a in are (in the paragraph below the list of tours).

■ Type **and times**

■ Press ⌷Spacebar⌷.

Your screen should be similar to Figure 1–28.

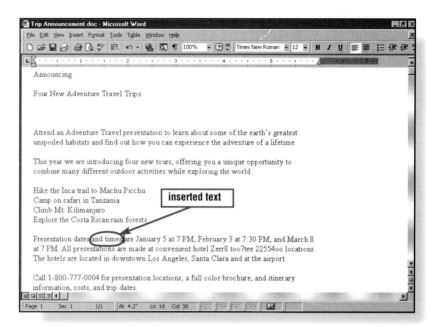

Figure 1–28

In the second sentence, you want to change the word "made" to "held." You could delete this word and type in the new word, or you can use the Overtype mode to enter text in a document. When you use **Overtype mode**, new text replaces existing text as you type. To switch to this mode and change the word,

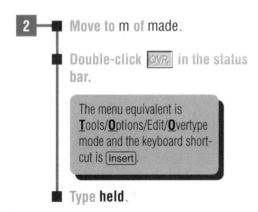

2   ■ Move to m of made.

■ Double-click OVR in the status bar.

> The menu equivalent is **T**ools/**O**ptions/Edit/**O**vertype mode and the keyboard shortcut is ⌷Insert⌷.

■ Type **held**.

Your screen should be similar to Figure 1–29.

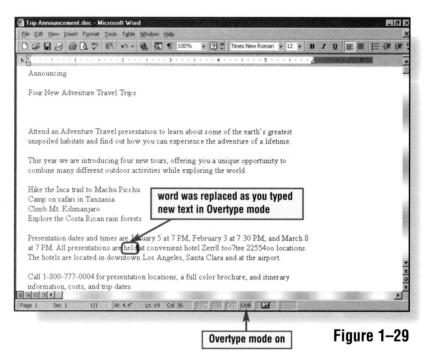

Overtype mode on

Figure 1–29

As each character was typed, the selected character (or space) was replaced with the character being typed. Also notice the OVR status indicator button letters are now bold, indicating the Overtype mode is on. To turn it off again,

3   ■ Double-click OVR.

Deleting a Word

Looking back at the title, you decide to delete the word "Four" from the second line. The ⌈Ctrl⌉ + ⌈Delete⌉ key combination deletes the word to the right of the insertion point to the beginning of the next group of characters. In order to delete an entire word, you must position the insertion point at the beginning of the word.

1 ■ Move to F in Four (second title line).

 ■ Press ⌈Ctrl⌉ + ⌈Delete⌉.

Your screen should be similar to Figure 1–30.

entire word "Four" was deleted

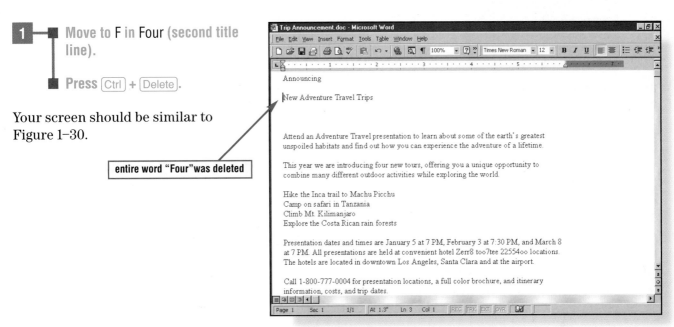

Figure 1–30

Selecting and Deleting Text

As you continue proofreading the flyer, you see the second line of the paragraph below the list of trips contains several sections of junk characters. To remove these characters, you could use ⌈Delete⌉ and ⌈Backspace⌉ to delete each character individually, or ⌈Ctrl⌉ + ⌈Delete⌉ or ⌈Ctrl⌉ + ⌈Backspace⌉ to delete each word. This is very slow, however. Several characters, words, or lines of text can be deleted at once by first **selecting** the text and then pressing ⌈Delete⌉. Text is selected by highlighting it. To select text, first move the insertion point to the beginning or end of the text to be selected, then drag the mouse. You can select as little as a single letter or as much as the entire document.

The first area of characters to be removed follows the word "hotel" in the second line of the paragraph below the list of trips. To position the insertion point on the first character of the text to be selected,

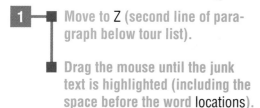

1 ▪ Move to Z (second line of paragraph below tour list).

▪ Drag the mouse until the junk text is highlighted (including the space before the word locations).

> When you start dragging over a word, the entire word including the space after it is automatically selected.

Your screen should be similar to Figure 1-31.

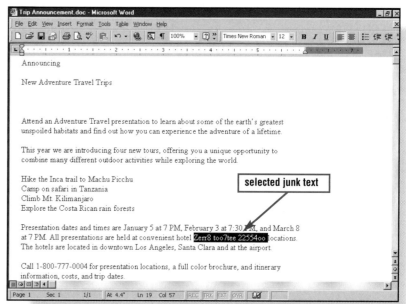

Figure 1–31

The junk text is selected. Text that is selected can then be modified using many different Word features. In this case, you want to remove the selected text.

2 ▪ Press Delete

You also decide to delete the entire last sentence of the paragraph. You can also quickly select a standard block of text. A standard block consists of a sentence, paragraph, page, tabular column, rectangular portion of text, or the entire document. The following table summarizes the techniques used to select standard blocks.

To Select	Procedure
Word	Double-click in the word.
Sentence	Press Ctrl and click within the sentence.
Line	Click in the selection bar next to the line.
Multiple lines	Drag in the selection bar next to the lines.
Paragraph	Triple-click on the paragraph or double-click in the selection bar next to the paragraph.
Multiple paragraphs	Drag in the selection bar next to the paragraphs.
Document	Triple-click in the selection bar or press Ctrl and click in the selection bar.

To select and delete the sentence,

3 ■ Press Ctrl and click anywhere in third sentence of the third paragraph.

Your screen should be similar to Figure 1–32.

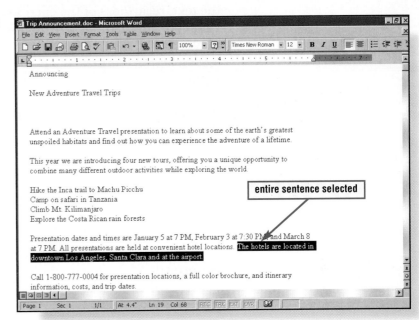

entire sentence selected

Figure 1–32

4 ■ Press Delete.

Undoing Editing Changes

After removing the sentence, you decide it may be necessary after all. To quickly restore this sentence, you can use  Undo to reverse your last action or command.

1 ■ Click ↺ ▾ Undo.

The menu equivalent is Edit/Undo or Ctrl + Z.

Your screen should be similar to Figure 1–33.

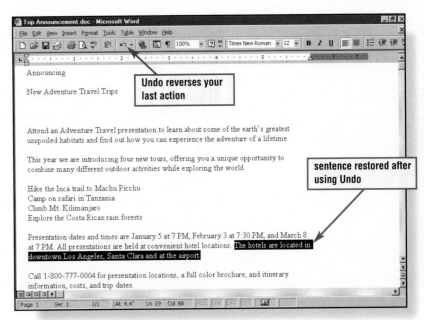

Undo reverses your last action

sentence restored after using Undo

Figure 1–33

Undo returns your last deletion and restores it to its original location in the text, regardless of the current insertion point location. Notice that the Undo button includes a drop-down list button. Clicking this button displays a list of the most recent actions that can be reversed. When you select an action from the drop-down list, you also undo all actions above it in the list.

 Open the Undo button drop-down list.

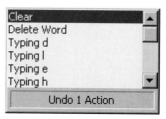

The drop-down list displays the actions you have performed, with the most recent action at the top of the list. To undo the last two actions you performed,

3 ■ Select Delete Word.

The junk characters and the word "Four" are restored. Immediately after you Undo an action, the Redo button is available so you can restore the action you just undid. To restore your corrections,

4 ■ Click [⌒ ▾] Redo 2 times.

Repeatedly using the [↶ ▾] Undo or [↷ ▾] Redo buttons performs the actions in the list one by one.

> The menu equivalent is **E**dit/**R**edo or Ctrl + Y.

> You may need to click [»] More Buttons on the Standard toolbar to locate the [⌒ ▾] button.

Formatting the Document

Because this document is a flyer, you want it to be easy to read and interesting to look at. Applying different formatting to characters can greatly enhance the appearance of the document.

Changing Fonts and Type Sizes

One way to enhance the appearance of a document is to use different fonts and font sizes.

Concept ⑧ Font

A **font**, also commonly referred to as a **typeface**, is a set of characters with a specific design. The designs have names such as Times New Roman and Courier. Using fonts as a design element can add interest to your document and give readers visual cues to help them find information quickly.

There are two basic types of fonts, serif and sans serif. **Serif fonts** have a flair at the base of each letter that visually leads the reader to the next letter. Two common serif fonts are Roman and Times New Roman. Serif fonts generally are used in paragraphs. **Sans serif fonts** do not have a flair at the base of each letter. Arial and Helvetica are two common sans serif fonts. Because sans serif fonts have a clean look, they are often used for headings in documents. It is good practice to use only two types of fonts in a document, one for text and one for headings. Too many styles can make your document look cluttered and unprofessional.

Each font has one or more sizes. Size is the height and width of the character and is commonly measured in points, abbreviated "pt". One point equals about 1/72 inch, and text in most documents is 10. pt or 12 pt.

Several common fonts in different sizes are shown in the following table.

Font Name	Font Type	Font Size	Font Style (Bold)
Arial	Sans serif	This is 10 pt. / This is 16 pt.	Bold 10 pt. / Bold 16 pt.
Courier New	Serif	This is 10 pt. / This is 16 pt.	Bold 10 pt. / Bold 16 pt.
Times New Roman	Serif	This is 10 pt. / This is 16 pt.	Bold 10 pt. / Bold 16 pt.

To change the font before typing the text, use the command and then type. All text will appear in the specified setting until another font setting is selected. To change a font setting for existing text, select the text you want to change first and then use the command. If you want to apply font formatting to a word, simply move the insertion point to the word and the formatting is automatically applied to the entire word.

First you want to increase the font size of all the text in the flyer to make it easier to read.

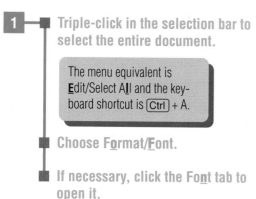

1 ■ Triple-click in the selection bar to select the entire document.

> The menu equivalent is **E**dit/Select A**l**l and the keyboard shortcut is Ctrl + A.

■ Choose Fo**r**mat/**F**ont.

■ If necessary, click the Fo**n**t tab to open it.

Your screen should be similar to Figure 1–34.

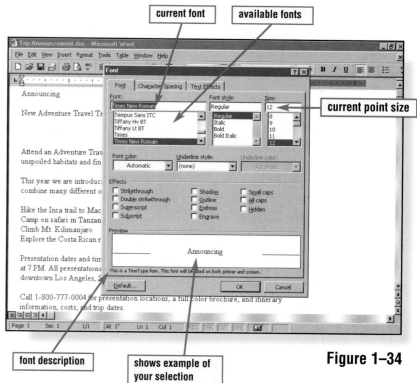

Figure 1–34

The Font list box displays the fonts supported by your active printer in alphabetical order. The current font settings are selected and reflect the Normal template default of Times New Roman with a size of 12 points. The Preview box displays an example of the currently selected font setting.

Notice the description of the font below the Preview box. It states that the selected font is a TrueType font. TrueType fonts are fonts that are automatically installed when you install Windows. They appear onscreen exactly as they will appear when printed. Some fonts are printer fonts, which are available only on your printer and may look different onscreen than when printed. Courier is an example of a printer font.

You will increase the font to a type size of 14 points. As you make the selections, the Preview box displays how your selections will appear.

2 ▪ Scroll the Size list box and select 14.

▪ Click [OK] .

Your screen should be similar to Figure 1-35.

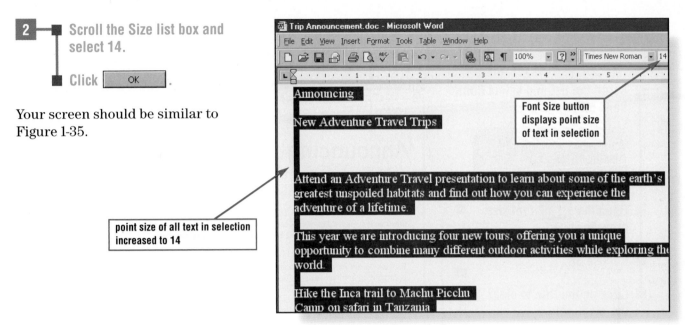

point size of all text in selection increased to 14

Font Size button displays point size of text in selection

Figure 1–35

The point size of all text in the document has increased to 14 points, making the text much easier to read. The Font Size button in the Formatting toolbar displays the new point size setting for the text at the location of the insertion point.

Next you will change the font and size of the two title lines. A quicker way to change the font and size is to use the toolbar buttons.

3 ▪ Move to the word Announcing.

▪ Open the [Times New Roman] Font drop-down list.

Your screen should be similar to Figure 1-36.

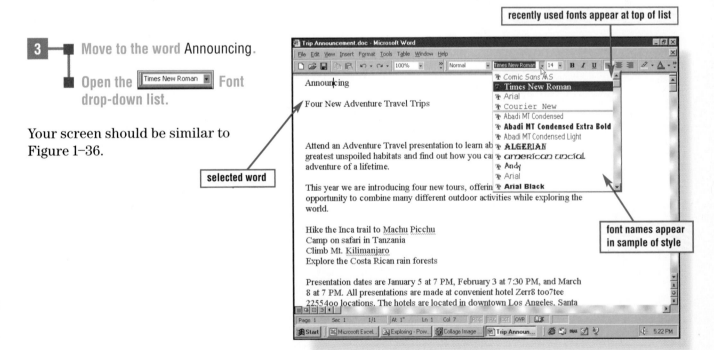

recently used fonts appear at top of list

selected word

font names appear in sample of style

Figure 1–36

The name of each font is displayed using a sample of the font. The names of any fonts that have been used during the current session appear at the top of the list.

4 Scroll the list and select Comic Sans MS.

> Choose a similar font if your machine does not have this font.

Open the `12` font size drop-down list.

Choose 36.

Click on the title to clear the highlight.

Your screen should be similar to Figure 1-37.

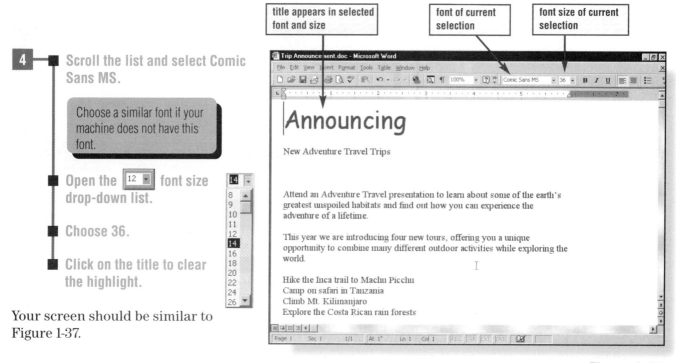

Figure 1–37

The selected font and size have been applied to the selection, making the title line much more interesting and eye-catching. The font and font size buttons reflect the settings in use at the location of the insertion point.

5 Finally, select the second title line and change the font to Comic Sans MS with a point size of 24.

Changing Character Effects

In addition to changing font and font size, you can apply different character effects to enhance the appearance of text.

Concept 9 Character Effects

Different character effects can be applied to selections to add emphasis or interest to a document. The table below describes some of the effects and their uses.

Format	Example	Use
Bold, italic	**Bold** *Italic*	Adds emphasis
Underline	<u>Underline</u>	Adds emphasis
Strikethrough	~~Strikethrough~~	Indicates words to be deleted
Double strikethrough	~~Double Strikethrough~~	Indicates words to be deleted
Superscript	"To be or not to be."[1]	Used in footnotes and formulas
Subscript	H_2O	Used in formulas
Shadow	Shadow	Adds distinction to titles and headings
Outline	Outline	Adds distinction to titles and headings
Small caps	SMALL CAPS	Adds emphasis when case is not important
All caps	ALL CAPS	Adds emphasis when case is not important
Hidden	Displays, but does not print	Notes or comments you do not want printed
Color	**Color** Color Color	Adds interest

You will add color and bold effects to selected areas of the flyer.

1

Select both title lines.

Open the 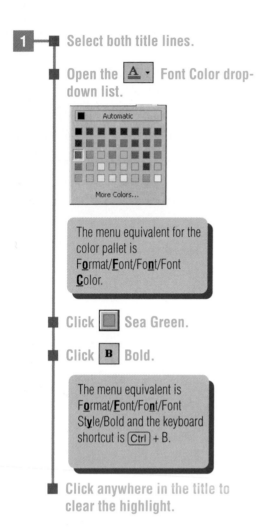 Font Color drop-down list.

The menu equivalent for the color pallet is Format/**F**ont/Font/Font **C**olor.

Click ▨ Sea Green.

Click **B** Bold.

The menu equivalent is Format/**F**ont/Font/Font St**y**le/Bold and the keyboard shortcut is ⎡Ctrl⎤ + B.

Click anywhere in the title to clear the highlight.

Your screen should be similar to Figure 1–38.

applies bold effect

button shows last selected color

Figure 1–38

The selected color and bold effect have been applied to all text in the selection. The Font button appears in the last selected color. You can now quickly apply the same color simply by clicking on the button.

2 — ■ Select the list of four trips.

■ Change the font to Comic Sans MS and color to sea green.

■ Clear the selection.

Your screen should be similar to Figure 1–39.

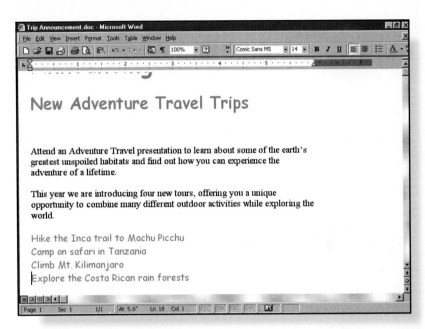

Figure 1–39

Setting Paragraph Alignment

The final formatting change you want to make is to change the paragraph alignment.

Concept ⑩ Alignment

Alignment is how text is positioned on a line between the margins or indents. There are four types of paragraph alignment: left, center, right, and justified.

Alignment		Effect on Text
Left		Aligns text against the left margin of the page, leaving the right margin ragged. This is the most commonly used paragraph alignment type and therefore the default setting in all word processing software packages.
Center		Centers each line of text between the left and right margins. Center alignment is used mostly for headings or centering graphics on a page.
Right		Aligns text against the right margin, leaving the left margin ragged. Use right alignment when you want text to line up on the outside of a page, such as a chapter title or a header.
Justified		Aligns text against the right and left margins and evenly spaces out the words. Newspapers commonly use justified alignment so the columns of text are even.

The alignment settings affect entire paragraphs. Word considers any text that ends with a paragraph mark to be a paragraph.

The commands to change paragraph alignment are under the Format/Paragraph menu. However, it is much faster to use the shortcuts shown below.

Alignment	Command	Keyboard Shortcut	Button
Left	F**o**rmat/**P**aragraph/**I**ndents and Spacing/Ali**g**nment/Left	Ctrl + L	
Center	F**o**rmat/**P**aragraph/**I**ndents and Spacing/Ali**g**nment/Center	Ctrl + E	
Right	F**o**rmat/**P**aragraph/**I**ndents and Spacing/Ali**g**nment/Right	Ctrl + R	
Justified	F**o**rmat/**P**aragraph/**I**ndents and Spacing/Ali**g**nment/Justified	Ctrl + J	

You want to change the alignment of all paragraphs in the flyer from the default of left-aligned to centered.

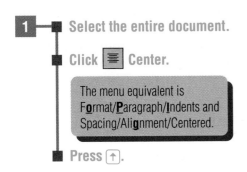

1 ■ Select the entire document.

■ Click ☰ Center.

> The menu equivalent is F**o**rmat/**P**aragraph/**I**ndents and Spacing/Ali**g**nment/Centered.

■ Press [↑].

Your screen should be similar to Figure 1–40.

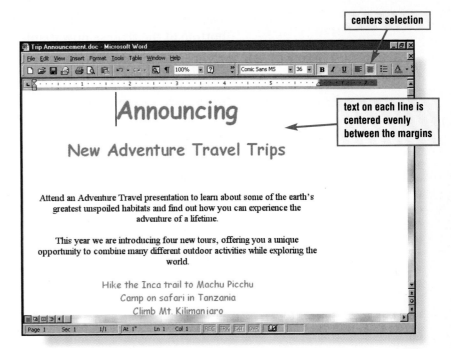

Figure 1–40

Each line of text is centered evenly between the left and right page margins.

Scrolling a Document

Now that the point sizes are larger, the workspace is no longer large enough to display the entire document. To bring additional text into view in the window, you can scroll the document using either the scroll bars or the keyboard. Again, both methods are useful, depending on what you are doing.

1 ■ Click the ▼ in the vertical scroll bar to scroll the document until the bottom line is displayed in the window.

Your screen should be similar to Figure 1–41.

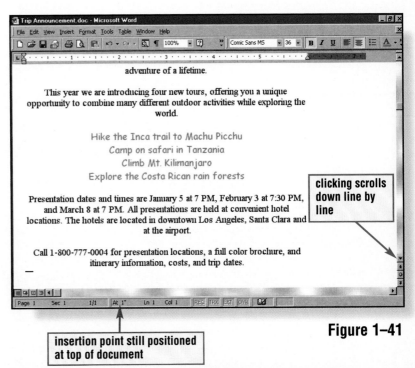

Figure 1–41

The text at the beginning of the flyer has scrolled off the window, and the bottom of the flyer is now displayed. Notice that the insertion point is no longer visible in the window; the insertion point location information in the status bar shows that the insertion point is still positioned at the top of the document. To actually move the insertion point, you must click in a location in the window.

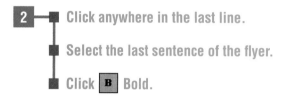

2 ■ Click anywhere in the last line.

■ Select the last sentence of the flyer.

■ Click **B** Bold.

You can also scroll the document using the keyboard. While scrolling using the keyboard, the insertion point also moves. To return to the top of the letter,

3 ■ Hold down ↑ for several seconds until the insertion point is on the word Announcing.

The document scrolled up and the insertion point is moved at the same time.

Inserting and Sizing Graphics

Finally, you want to add a picture from one of the past trips to the flyer to add interest. A picture is one of several different graphic objects that can be added to a Word document.

Concept 11 Graphics

A **graphic** is a non-text element or object, such as a drawing or picture, that can be added to a document. An **object** is an item that can be sized, moved, and manipulated. A graphic can be a simple drawing object consisting of shapes such as lines and boxes that can be created using features on the Drawing toolbar. A **drawing object** is part of your Word document. A **picture** is an illustration such as a scanned photograph. Pictures are graphics that were created from another program and and are inserted in your Word document as embedded objects. An **embedded object** becomes part of the Word document and can be opened and edited using the **source program**, the program in which it was created.

Examples of drawing objects

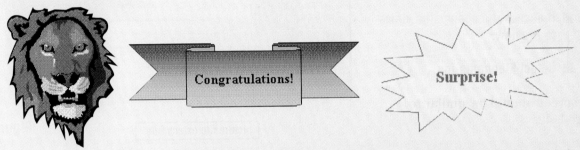

Picture files can be obtained from a variety of sources. Many simple drawings called **clip art** are available in the ClipArt gallery that comes with Office 2000. You can also create graphic files using a scanner to convert any printed document, including photographs, to an electronic format. Most images that are scanned and inserted into documents are stored as Windows bitmap files (.bmp). All types of graphics, including clip art, photographs, and other types of images, can be found on the Internet. These files are commonly stored as .jpg or .pcx files. Keep in mind that any images you locate on the Internet may be copyrighted and should only be used with permission. You can also purchase CD's containing graphics for your use.

A graphic object can be manipulated in many ways. You can change its size, add captions, borders, or shading, or move it to another location. A graphic object can be moved anywhere on the page, including in the margins or on top of or below other objects, including text. The only places you cannot place a graphic object are into a footnote, endnote, or caption.

Add graphics to your documents to help the reader understand concepts, to add interest, and to make your document stand out from others.

Additional Information

You can also scan a picture and insert it directly into a Word document without saving it as a file first.

You have a photograph taken during a recent safari tour that you scanned and saved as Elephant.jpg. You will add the picture to the flyer below the two title lines.

1 Move to the middle blank line below the second title line.

Choose Insert/Picture.

Select From File.

Change the Look In location to the drive containing your data disk.

If necessary, change the view to Preview.

Select Elephants.jpg.

Your screen should be similar to Figure 1–42.

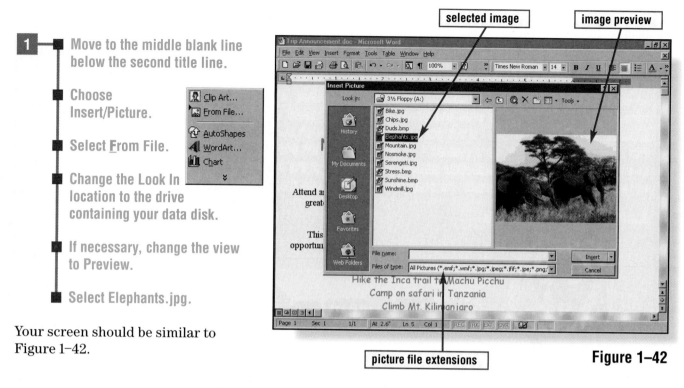

selected image

image preview

picture file extensions

Figure 1–42

The Insert Picture dialog box is similar to the Open and Save files dialog boxes. The only types of files listed, however, are files with picture file extensions.

2 Click Insert.

Your screen should be similar to Figure 1–43.

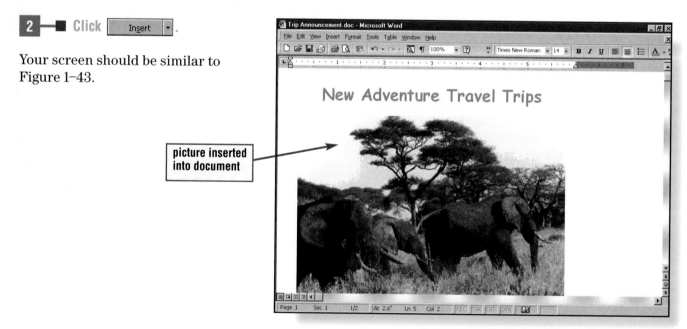

picture inserted into document

Figure 1–43

The picture is inserted in the document at the insertion point. It is centered because the paragraph formatting in which it was placed is centered. Usually, when a graphic is inserted, its size will need to be adjusted. In this case you want to reduce its size. To do this you must first select the object.

3 ■ Click on the picture.

Your screen should be similar to Figure 1–44.

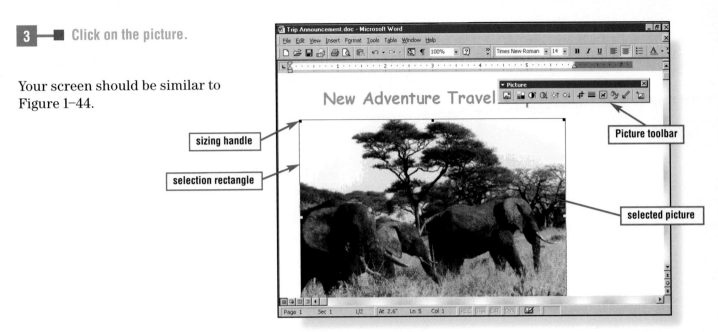

Figure 1–44

The picture is surrounded by a **selection rectangle** and eight boxes, called **sizing handles**, indicating it is a selected object and can now be sized and moved anywhere in the document. The handles are used to size the object, much as you would size a window. A graphic object is moved by dragging it to the new location.

The Picture toolbar is also automatically displayed. Its buttons (identified below) are used to modify the selected picture object. Your Picture toolbar may be floating or docked along an edge of the window, depending on where it was when last used.

If the Picture toolbar is not displayed, right-click on any toolbar to open the Shortcut menu and select Picture, or use View/Toolbars/Picture.

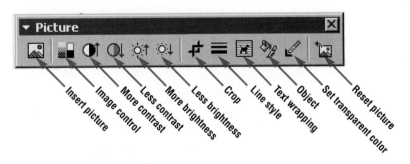

You want to reduce the image to approximately 3 inches wide by 2.25 inches high.

4 ■ Point to the lower right corner handle.

> The mouse pointer changes to ↖ just as it does when resizing a window.

> Dragging a corner handle maintains the original proportions of the picture.

■ Drag the mouse to reduce the size of the picture to approximately 3 by 2.25 inches (use the rulers as a guide and refer to Figure 1–45).

■ Click outside the picture to clear the selection.

Your screen should be similar to Figure 1–45.

picture size reduced

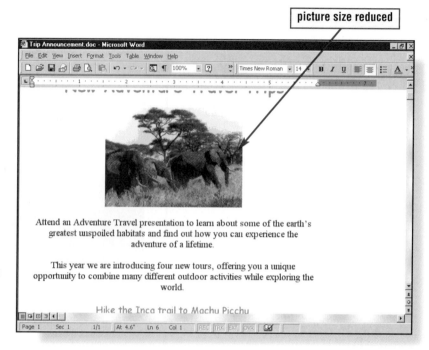

Figure 1–45

Saving an Existing Document

Now you are ready to save the changes you have made to the file on your data disk using the Save or Save As commands on the File menu. The Save command or the 🖫 Save button will save the active file using the same file name by replacing the contents of the existing file on disk with the document as it appears on your screen. The Save As command allows you to save the current file using a new file name. This leaves the original file unchanged. Because you may want to redo this tutorial and use the file again, you will save your edited version using a new file name.

1 ■ Choose File/Save As.

The file name of the file you opened, Trip Announcement, is displayed in the File Name text box of the Save As dialog box. To save the document as Trip Announcement1, you can type the new file name entirely, or you can edit the existing name. In this case, it is easier to edit the file name by adding the number to the end of the name.

> If you do not clear the highlight, the selected file name will be cleared and replaced with the new text as it is typed.

2 ■ Click at the end of the file name.

■ Type 1

The new file name, Trip Announcment1, is displayed in the window title bar. The original document file is unchanged on your data disk.

Previewing and Printing a Document

Although you still plan to make several formatting changes to the document, you want to give a copy of the flyer to the manager to get feedback regarding the content and layout. To save time and unnecessary printing and paper waste, it is always a good idea to preview onscreen how your document will appear when printed. The Print Preview feature displays each page of your document in a reduced size so you can see the layout. You can also make last-minute editing and formatting changes while previewing and then print directly from the Preview screen. To preview this document,

1 ■ Click [🔍] Print Preview.

> The menu equivalent is File/Print Preview.

Your screen should be similar to Figure 1–46.

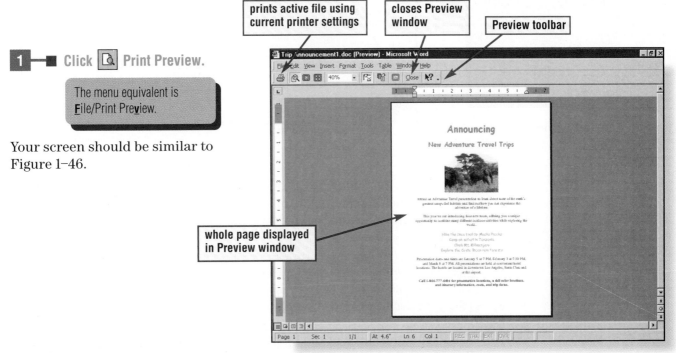

prints active file using current printer settings

closes Preview window

Preview toolbar

whole page displayed in Preview window

Figure 1–46

The Print Preview window displays a reduced view of how the current page will appear when printed. This view allows you to check your page layout before printing. The flyer looks good and does not appear to need any further modifications immediately.

The Preview window also includes its own toolbar. You can print the letter directly from the Preview window using the [🖨️] Print button; however, you do not want to send the document directly to the printer just yet. First you need to add your name to the flyer and check the print settings. To close the Print Preview window,

2 ■ Click [Close] .

■ Add "[your name] at" before the phone number in the last sentence of the flyer.

To check the print settings, you need to use the Print command in the File menu.

3 If necessary, make sure your printer is on and ready to print.

Choose <u>F</u>ile/<u>P</u>rint.

> Please consult your instructor for printing procedures that may differ from the following directions.

> The keyboard shortcut for the Print command is [Ctrl] + P. Clicking 🖨 Print on the Standard toolbar will send the document directly to the printer.

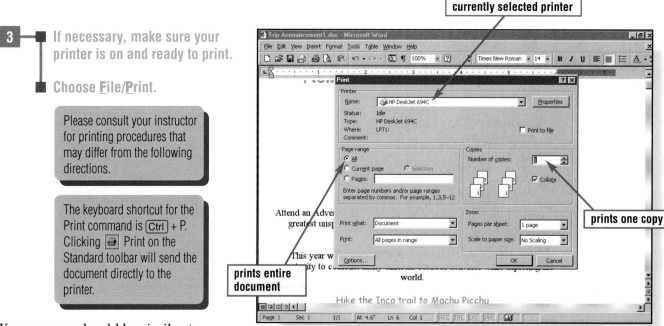

currently selected printer

prints one copy

prints entire document

Your screen should be similar to Figure 1–47.

Figure 1–47

From the Print dialog box, you need to specify the printer you will be using and the document settings. The printer that is currently selected is displayed in the Name drop-down list box in the Printer section of the dialog box.

4 If you need to change the selected printer to another printer, open the Name drop-down list box and select the appropriate printer (your instructor will tell you which printer to select).

The Page Range area of the Print dialog box lets you specify how much of the document you want printed. The range options are described in the following table:

Option	Action
All	Prints the entire document.
Current page	Prints selected page or the page the insertion point is on.
Pages	Prints pages you specify by typing page numbers in the text box.
Selection	Prints selected text only.

The default range setting, All, is the correct setting. In the Copies section, the default setting of one copy of the document is acceptable. To begin printing using the settings in the Print dialog box,

5 Click  .

Your printer should be printing out the document. The printed copy of the flyer should be similar to the document shown in the Case Study at the beginning of the tutorial.

Exiting Word

- -

The Exit command in the File menu is used to quit the Word program. Alternatively, you can click the ☒ Close button in the application window title bar. If you attempt to close the application without first saving your document, Word displays a warning asking if you want to save your work. If you do not save your work and you exit the application, all your changes are lost.

The keyboard shortcut for the Exit command is Alt + F4.

1 ■  Click ☒ Close.

The Windows desktop is visible again.

- -

Concept Summary

Tutorial 1: Creating and Editing a Document

Document development follows several steps: plan, enter, edit, format, and preview and print.

A **template** is a document file that includes predefined settings that are used as a pattern to create many common types of documents.

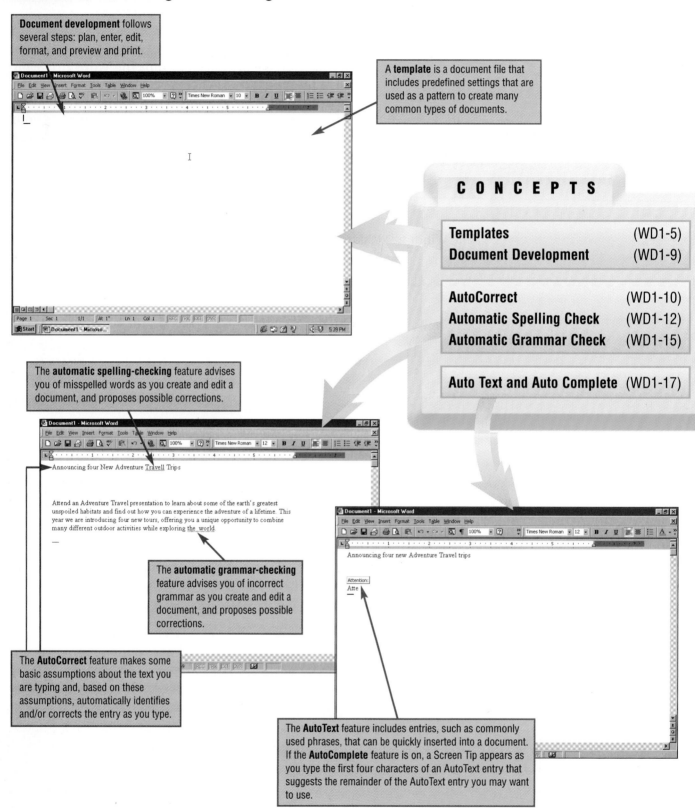

C O N C E P T S

Templates	(WD1-5)
Document Development	(WD1-9)

AutoCorrect	(WD1-10)
Automatic Spelling Check	(WD1-12)
Automatic Grammar Check	(WD1-15)

Auto Text and Auto Complete	(WD1-17)

The **automatic spelling-checking** feature advises you of misspelled words as you create and edit a document, and proposes possible corrections.

The **automatic grammar-checking** feature advises you of incorrect grammar as you create and edit a document, and proposes possible corrections.

The **AutoCorrect** feature makes some basic assumptions about the text you are typing and, based on these assumptions, automatically identifies and/or corrects the entry as you type.

The **AutoText** feature includes entries, such as commonly used phrases, that can be quickly inserted into a document. If the **AutoComplete** feature is on, a Screen Tip appears as you type the first four characters of an AutoText entry that suggests the remainder of the AutoText entry you may want to use.

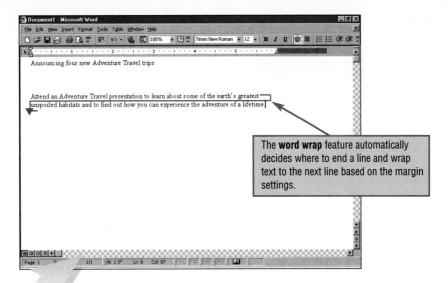

Announcing four new Adventure Travel trips

Attend an Adventure Travel presentation to learn about some of the earth's greatest unspoiled habitats and to find out how you can experience the adventure of a lifetime.

The **word wrap** feature automatically decides where to end a line and wrap text to the next line based on the margin settings.

Word Wrap	(WD1-18)
Font	(WD1-35)
Character Effects	(WD1-39)
Alignment	(WD1-42)
Graphics	(WD1-45)

A **font**, also commonly referred to as a typeface, is a set of characters with a specific design.

Different **character effects** can be applied to selections to add emphasis or interest to a document.

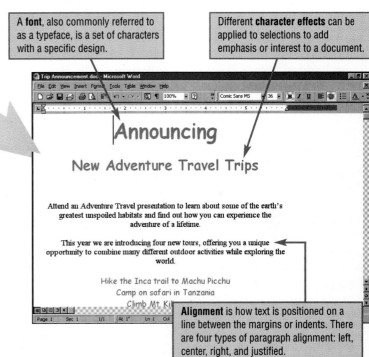

Announcing

New Adventure Travel Trips

Attend an Adventure Travel presentation to learn about some of the earth's greatest unspoiled habitats and find out how you can experience the adventure of a lifetime.

This year we are introducing four new tours, offering you a unique opportunity to combine many different outdoor activities while exploring the world.

Hike the Inca trail to Machu Picchu
Camp on safari in Tanzania
Climb Mt. Ki...

Alignment is how text is positioned on a line between the margins or indents. There are four types of paragraph alignment: left, center, right, and justified.

A **graphic** is a non-text element or object, such as a drawing or picture, that can be added to a document.

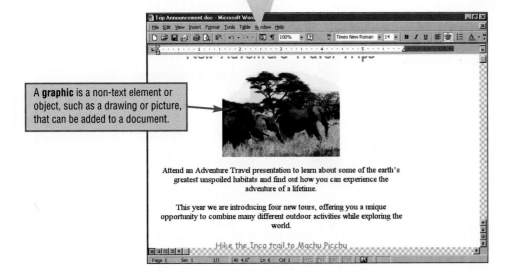

New Adventure Travel Trips

Attend an Adventure Travel presentation to learn about some of the earth's greatest unspoiled habitats and find out how you can experience the adventure of a lifetime.

This year we are introducing four new tours, offering you a unique opportunity to combine many different outdoor activities while exploring the world.

Hike the Inca trail to Machu Picchu

Tutorial Review

Key Terms

alignment WD1-42
AutoComplete WD1-17
AutoCorrect WD1-10
AutoText WD1-17
clip art WD1-45
cursor WD1-45
custom dictionary WD1-12
default WD1-4
drawing object WD1-45
edit WD1-9
embedded object WD1-45
end-of-file marker WD1-4
font WD1-35

format WD1-9
formatting mark WD1-22
Formatting toolbar WD1-3
global template WD1-5
graphic WD1-45
Insert mode WD1-29
insertion point WD1-4
main dictionary WD1-12
object WD1-45
Overtype mode WD1-30
picture WD1-45
points WD1-35
ruler WD1-4

sans serif font WD1-35
select WD1-31
selection bar WD1-19
selection rectangle WD1-47
serif font WD1-35
sizing handles WD1-47
source program WD1-45
status bar WD1-4
Standard toolbar WD1-3
template WD1-5
typeface WD1-35
word wrap WD1-18

Command Summary

Command	Shortcut Key	Button	Action
File/New	Ctrl + N		Opens new file
File/Open	Ctrl + O		Opens selected file
File/Close	Ctrl + F4		Closes file
File/Save	Ctrl + S		Saves file using same file name
File/Save As			Saves file using a new file name
File/Print Preview			Displays document as it will appear when printed
File/Print	Ctrl + P		Prints file using selected print settings
File/Exit	Alt + F4		Exits Word program
Edit/Undo	Ctrl + Z		Restores last editing change
Edit/Redo	Ctrl + Y		Restores last Undo or repeats last command or action
Edit/Select All	Ctrl + A		Selects all text in a document

Command	Shortcut Key	Button	Action
View/**N**ormal		☰	Displays document in Normal view
View/**P**rint Layout		▣	Displays document in Print Layout view
View/**T**oolbars			Displays or hides selected toolbar
View/**R**uler			Displays horizontal ruler bar
View/**Z**oom/**P**ageWidth			Fits display of document within right and left margins
Insert/**A**utoText/AutoTe**x**t/ **S**how AutoComplete tip for AutoText and dates			Turns on AutoComplete feature
Insert/**P**icture/**F**rom File			Inserts picture
F**o**rmat/**F**ont/**F**ont/Fo**n**t		Times New Roman	Changes typeface
F**o**rmat/**F**ont/Fo**n**t/**S**ize		12	Changes font size
F**o**rmat/**F**ont/Fo**n**t/Font St**y**le/Bold	Ctrl + B	**B**	Makes selected text bold
F**o**rmat/**F**ont/Fo**n**t/Font **C**olor		A	Changes text to selected color
F**o**rmat/**P**aragraph/**I**ndents and Spacing/ Ali**g**nment/Left	Ctrl + L	☰	Aligns text to left margin
F**o**rmat/**P**aragraph/**I**ndents and Spacing/ Ali**g**nment/Centered	Ctrl + E	☰	Centers text between left and right margins
F**o**rmat/**P**aragraph/**I**ndents and Spacing/ Ali**g**nment/Right	Ctrl + R	☰	Aligns text to right margin
F**o**rmat/**P**aragraph/**I**ndents and Spacing/ Ali**g**nment/Justified	Ctrl + J	☰	Aligns text equally between left and right margins
Tools/**O**ptions/View/**A**ll		¶	Displays or hides formatting marks
Tools/**O**ptions/Edit/**O**vertype mode	Insert	OVR	Switches between Insert and overtype modes

Screen Identification

1. In the following Word screen, letters identify important elements. Enter the correct term for each screen element in the space provided.

a. _____   f. _____   k. _____

b. _____   g. _____   l. _____

c. _____   h. _____   m. _____

d. _____   i. _____   n. _____

e. _____   j. _____   o. _____

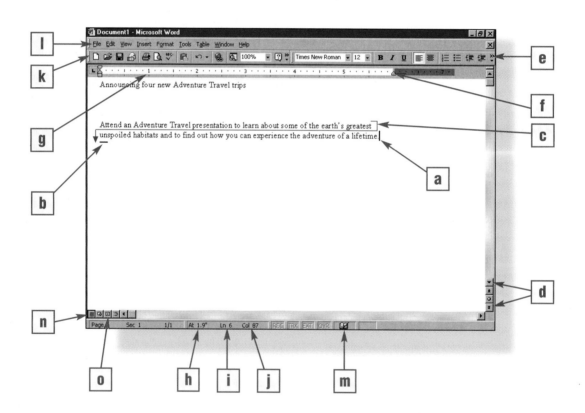

2. The following screen identifies several errors and changes that need to be made to a document. From the list below, match the letter to the procedure that will make the change.

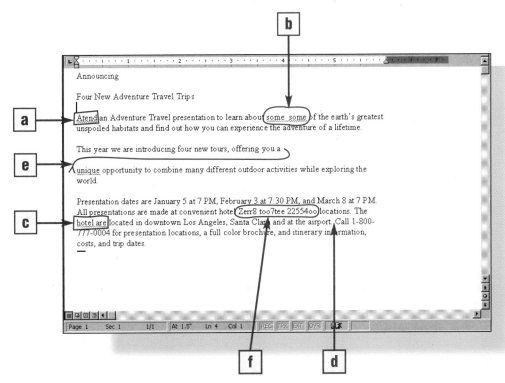

1. fix spelling ——————

2. remove second "some" ——————

3. fix grammar ——————

4. begin new paragraph ——————

5. combine with previous paragraph ——————

6. delete junk text ——————

a. Display the Grammar shortcut menu and make necessary correction.

b. Display the Spelling shortcut menu and select the correct spelling.

c. Move to the letter C and press ←Enter twice.

d. Select text and press Delete.

e. Display the Spelling shortcut menu and select Delete Repeated Word.

f. Move to the letter u and press Backspace three times.

Matching

Match the letter to the correct item in the numbered list.

1. [icon] _____   a. new text writes over existing text
2. template _____   b. type styles that can be applied to text
3. font _____   c. moves to the top of the document
4. OVR _____   d. constant adjustment of text to fill in extra space in a line without exceeding the margin setting
5. alignment _____   e. images that enhance a document
6. [Ctrl] + [Home] _____   f. displays the Print Preview window
7. graphics _____   g. predesigned document that is used as a pattern to create many common types of documents
8. [icon] _____   h. inserted into a document, can be opened and edited using the source program
9. word wrap _____   i. controls paragraph positioning between the margins
10. embedded object _____   j. saves a document using the same file name

Multiple Choice

Circle the correct response to the questions below.

1. Document development follows these steps:
   a. plan, edit, enter, format, preview and print
   b. enter, edit, format, preview and print
   c. plan, enter, edit, format, preview and print
   d. design, enter, edit, format, preview and print

2. The Word feature that makes some basic assumptions about the text entered and automatically makes changes based on those assumptions is _____.
   a. AutoChange
   b. AutoCorrect
   c. AutoText
   d. AutoFormat

3. Words that are not contained in the main dictionary can be added to the _____dictionary.
   a. custom
   b. additional
   c. add to
   d. user defined

4. The feature that allows you to preview a document before it is printed is _____.
   a. print review
   b. page review
   c. page preview
   d. print preview

5. When text is evenly aligned on both margins it is _____.
   a. center aligned
   b. justified
   c. left aligned
   d. right aligned

6. Words that may be spelled incorrectly in a document are indicated by a _____.
   a. green wavy line
   b. red wavy line
   c. blue wavy line
   d. underline

7. Font sizes are measured in _____.
   a. inches
   b. points
   c. bits
   d. pieces

8. A _____ is a document file that includes predefined settings that can be used as a pattern to create many common types of documents.
   a. template
   b. predesign
   c. design document
   d. format document

9. The _____ feature automatically decides where to end a line and where the next line of text begins based on the margin settings.
   a. line wrap
   b. word wrap
   c. wrap around
   d. end wrap

10. A non-text element or object, such as a drawing or picture, that can be added to a document is called a _____.
    a. picture
    b. drawing
    c. graphic
    d. image

True/False

Circle the correct answer to the following questions.

1. A wavy red line indicates a potential grammar error. True False

2. A template is a predesigned document. True False

3. The first three steps in developing a document are: plan, enter, and edit. True False

4. Text can be entered in a document in either the Insert or Overtype mode. True False

5. The D key erases the character to the right of the insertion point. True False

6. The automatic word wrap feature checks for typing errors. True False

7. The Word document file name extension is .wrd. True False

8. Font sizes are measured in inches. True False

9. Word inserts hidden marks into a document to control the display of text. True False

10. The AutoCorrect feature automatically identifies and corrects certain types of errors. True False

Discussion Questions

1. Discuss several uses you may have for a word processor. Then explain the steps you would follow to create a document.

2. Discuss how the AutoCorrect and Spelling and Grammar Checker features help you as you type. What types of corrections does the AutoCorrect feature make?

3. Discuss how word wrap works. What happens when text is added? What happens when text is removed?

4. Discuss three ways you can select text. Discuss when it would be appropriate to use the different methods.

5. Describe how the Undo and Redo features work. What are some advantages of these features?

6. Discuss how graphics can be used in a document. What should you consider when adding graphics to a document? Can the use of a graphic change the reader's response to a document?

Hands-On Practice Exercises

Step by Step

Rating System ☆ Easy
☆ ☆ Moderate
☆ ☆ ☆ Difficult

1. You work for a health organization that produces a newsletter for patients. The upcoming issue is focusing the effects of stress and how to handle stress. You have located information about the top stresses and want to include this information in a short article.

a. Enter the following information in a new Word document.

Top Stresses

The National Study of Daily Experiences has found over 50 different types of stress. However, 60 percent of all stresses people experience are from the top stresses listed below.

Arguments or tense moments

Disagreement on how something gets done at work

Concern over physical health of others

Work overload and demands

Worry about others' problems

Financial issues

Disciplining children

Family disagreements

Late or miss an appointment

Value differences

Home overload and demands

Household, car repairs

Tension over chores

b. Correct any spelling or grammar errors.

c. Remove any blank spaces at the end of short lines.

d. Change the title font to Broadway (or a font of your choice), 16 pt.

e. Center the title.

f. Center and bold the list of stresses.

g. Add italics and bold to the text "60 percent."

h. Insert the Stress clip art image on your data disk below the title. Size it appropriately and center it below the title.

i. Add your name and the current date several lines below the list.

j. Preview, then print the document.

k. Save the document as Top Stresses on your data disk.

2. You are about to open a bed and breakfast inn in the Pocono Mountains. You are going to advertise the B&B in a local travel guide.

a. Open a blank Word document and type the following information to create the first draft of the ad.

Pocono Mountain Retreat

124 Mountain Laurel Trail

Pocono Manor, PA 18349

Phone: 1-717-839-5555

Host: [Your Name]

Number of rooms: 4

Number of private baths: 1

Maximum number sharing baths: 4

Double rate for shared bath: $85.00

Double rate for private bath: $95.00

Single rate for shared bath: $65.00

Single rate for private bath: $75.00

Open: All year

Breakfast: Continental

Children: Welcome, over 12

Located in the heart of the Poconos is this rustic country inn where you can choose to indulge yourself in the quiet beauty of the immediate surroundings or take advantage of the numerous activities at nearby resorts, lakes, and parks.

In the winter, shuttle buses will transport you to the Jack Frost and Big Boulder ski resorts. We have trails for cross-country skiing right on the property. In the summer you can be whisked away to beautiful Lake Wallenpaupack for swimming and boating. The fall foliage is beyond compare, and you can hike our nature trails and take in the breathtaking scenery at any time of year.

In the evenings, you can relax in front of a cozy fire or take advantage of the Pocono nightlife. The choice is yours!

Be sure to call well in advance for reservations during the winter and summer months.

b. Correct any spelling and grammar errors that are identified.

c. Bold and center the first three lines. Change the font to a font of your choice, 16 pt. Add color of your choice to the three lines.

d. Bold the phone number and host lines.

e. Insert the text "Pets: No" above "Children: Welcome, over 12."

f. Center the list of features.

g. Change the font size of the four paragraphs to 11 pt and change the alignment to justified.

h. Insert the clip art image Sunshine above the phone number. Size it appropriately and center it.

i. Save the document as B&B Ad on your data disk.

j. Preview and print the document.

3. Universal Industries has banned smoking in all buildings. Mr. Biggs, the CEO, has sent a memo informing employees of this policy.

a. Open a blank Word document and create the memo with the following text. Press [Tab] after you type colons (:) in the To, From, and Date lines. This will make the information following the colons line up evenly.

To: [Your Name]

From: Mr. Biggs

Date: [Current date]

Effective next Monday, smoking will be banned in all buildings. Ashtrays will be placed outside each door, and smoking material must be extinguished before you enter.

Thank you for your cooperation in this matter.

JBB/xxx

To: [Your Name]
From: Mr. Biggs
Date: January 10, 2001
RE: No Smoking Policy

Effective next Monday, smoking will be banned in all buildings. Ashtrays will be placed outside each door, and smoking material must be extinguished before you enter.

Thank you for your cooperation in this matter.

JBB/xxx

b. Correct any spelling and grammar errors that are identified.

c. Change the font to 14 pt.

d. Change the alignment to justified.

e. Insert a blank line under the Date line and insert the AutoText reference line "RE:".

f. Press T and type "No Smoking Policy".

g. On the line above the first paragraph, insert the picture Nosmoke from your data disk. Size and position it appropriately.

h. Save the document as No Smoking Memo on your data disk.

i. Preview and print the document.

4. You are part owner of Debbie's Duds, a new clothing boutique located in Little Silver, a small town in New Jersey. In preparation for an upcoming sale, you want to create a flyer that you can give customers and also post in the windows of other local businesses.

a. Open a new document and change the font size to 14 point. Enter the following text:

Does Your Wardrobe Need Work?

Debbie's Duds Announces

Their Huge Labor Day Sale

If you're going out on the town this fall but don't have a thing to wear, make sure you visit Debbie's Duds. We're a new boutique on Telegraph Avenue that can turn your fashion disaster into a style triumph, all without breaking the bank. Our huge Labor Day sale features low, low prices on sport coats, khakis and cable knits. Sale runs Friday through Monday.

Debbie's Duds

2314 Telegraph Avenue

Phone: 555-1010

DOES YOUR WARDROBE NEED WORK?

DEBBIE'S DUDS ANNOUNCES
THEIR HUGE LABOR DAY SALE

If you're going out on the town this fall but don't have a thing to wear, make sure you visit **Debbie's Duds.** We're a new boutique on Telegraph Avenue that can turn your fashion disaster into a style triumph, all without breaking the bank.

Our huge Labor Day sale features low, low prices on sport coats, khakis and cable knits. Sale runs Friday through Monday.

Debbie's Duds
2314 Telegraph Avenue
Phone: 555-1010

Student Name
Current Date

b. Correct any spelling and grammar errors that are identified.

c. Save the document as Debbie on your data disk.

d. Insert a blank line at the top of the document and insert the graphic named Duds from your data disk.

e. Resize the graphic to be 1.5 by 2 inches.

f. Center the graphic on the page, keeping it at the top of the page.

g. Center the first three lines, change the font color to blue, font type to Copperplate Gothic or a font of your choice, and size to 22 pt.

h. Insert a blank line between the first and second lines.

i. Bold the store name "Debbie's Duds" at the end of the first sentence.

j. Change the alignment of the paragraph to justified.

k. Break the paragraph into two paragraphs beginning with the sentence "Our huge . . .". Insert a blank line between paragraphs.

l. Center the last three lines.

m. Add your name and the current date, left-aligned, four lines below the phone number.

n. Save your changes, preview the document and print it.

5. One of your job responsibilities at the National Potato Council is to think of ways to increase demand for potato chips. The following document is sure to do just that.

 a. Open a new document. Enter the following text:

Potato Chip Cookies

Potato chips give these cookies a crunchy texture and eliminate the need for baking soda.

Ingredients:

2 sticks of butter (softened)

1/2 c. dark brown sugar (firmly packed)

1/2 c. crushed potato chips

1 tsp. vanilla extract

1/2 c. sifted flour

Confectioner's sugar

Directions:

Cream the butter and brown sugar together.

Add vanilla, chips, and nuts.

Gradually add the flour. Mix thoroughly.

Cover and chill the dough for at least 1 hour.

Roll dough into 1" balls, and roll in confectioner's sugar.

Place 1" apart on greased cookie sheet.

Bake in 350 degree oven for 12–15 minutes.

This recipe makes about 3 1/2 dozen cookies.

 b. Center and bold the title. Change the font to Impact with a point size of 24.

 c. Add a color of your choice to the title text.

 d. Bold and increase the type size of the introductory sentence to 14 pt.

 e. Bold the word "Ingredients" and the colon that follows it.

 f. Bold the word "Directions" and the colon that follows it.

 g. Insert a blank line between the crushed potato chips and the vanilla extract items in the Ingredients list. Add "1/2 c. chopped pecans" to the list of ingredients.

 h. Insert four new blank lines between the Ingredients and Directions sections.

 i. Insert the graphic Chips from your data disk below the title.

 j. Size the graphic to be 2.5 by 2.5 inches and center it below the title.

 k. Correct any spelling and grammar errors.

l. Add your name and the current date two lines below the last line.

m. Save the document as Potato Chip Cookies.

n. Preview and print the document.

On Your Own

6. A career counselor wants to help you interview for a job you're interested in. To prepare for the career counseling session, you must write a one-paragraph description of your most recent job. Justify the paragraph. At the top of the page, write the name of the job, and bold and center it. Increase the font size of the title to 24 pt.

7. You are in charge of designing an invitation for an upcoming family reunion. The reunion will be held on July 26, 2001, at the Grand Hotel in Las Vegas. Design an invitation that includes all the information your relatives need to know to attend the event, including location, time, and family contacts. Be sure to use at least two colors of text, two sizes of text, two blank lines, and two kinds of paragraph alignment within your invitation.

8. Using Hands-On Practice Exercise 3 as a model, create a memo from yourself to the rest your class that explains the five most important rules to follow while working in the computer lab. Use a piece of clip art to liven up your memo. Format the document in the Arial typeface, 16 pt. Use different font colors for each rule.

9. Adventure Travel is also offering some great deals on trips to Holland. Using the formatting features of Word 2000 you have learned so far, create a flyer that will get your company off to a winning start. Include the graphic called Windmill on your data disk in your flyer.

10. You agreed to baby-sit your best friend's pet monkey, Pom-Pom. Everything was going well until Pom-Pom ran away. Write and design a poster to place around your neighborhood and attract as much attention as possible. You want to make sure people will contact you with any information they may have about Pom-Pom. Surf the Web to find a suitable graphic to accent your poster. You may want to do an Internet search on the word "monkey." Right-click on the image you located and use the Save Image As command to save it to your data disk. Insert and size the graphic appropriately.

TUTORIAL

2

Revising and Refining a Document

Competencies

After completing this tutorial, you will know how to:
1. Manually check spelling and grammar.
2. Move and copy text.
3. Use multiple documents.
4. Use the Find and Replace and Thesaurus features.
5. Insert the current date.
6. Zoom a document.
7. Change margins and line spacing.
8. Indent paragraphs.
9. Create a tabbed table and an itemized list.
10. Create and remove a hyperlink.
11. Use an AutoText entry.
12. Add an AutoShape.
13. Edit in Print Preview.

Case Study

After creating the rough draft of the trip announcement flyer, you showed the printed copy to your manager at Adventure Travel. The manager then made several suggestions on how to improve the flyer's style and appearance. In ad-

Revising text using spelling checker, Find and Replace, and the Thesaurus features makes it easy to produce professional appearing documents.

Formatting and page layout changes such as margin adjustments, indented paragraphs and tabbed tables help improve the readability and style of the document.

Graphic enhancements such as AutoShapes and additional color add interest to a document.

dition, you decided to write a letter to be sent to past clients along with your flyer. The letter briefly describes Adventure Travel's four new tours and invites clients to attend an informational presentation. Your manager likes the idea, but also wants the letter to include information about the new Adventure Travel Web site and a 10 percent discount for early booking.

In this tutorial, you will learn more about editing documents so you can reorganize and refine both your flyer and a rough draft of the letter to clients. You will also learn to use many more of the formatting features included in Word 2000 so you can add style and interest to your documents. Formatting features can greatly improve the appearance and design of any document you produce, so that it communicates its message more clearly. The completed letter and revised flyer are shown here.

January 10, 2001

Dear Adventure Traveler,

Imagine hiking and paddling your way through the rain forests of Costa Rica, camping under the stars in Africa, or following in the footsteps of the ancient Inca as you backpack along the Inca trail to Machu Picchu. Turn these dreams of adventure into memories you will cherish forever by joining us on one of our four new adventure tours.

To learn more about these exciting new adventures, we are offering several presentations. These presentations will focus on the features and cultures of the area. We will also show you pictures of places and activities you will participate in. Also presented is a detailed agenda and package costs. Plan on attending one of the following presentations:

Date	Time	Location	Room
January 5	7:00 PM	Town Center Hotel	Room 284B
February 3	7:30 PM	Airport Manor	Conference Room A
March 8	7:00 PM	Country Inn	Mountainside Room

In appreciation for your past patronage, we are pleased to offer you a 10% discount off the price of any of the new tour packages. You must book the trip at least 60 days prior to the departure date. Please turn in this letter to qualify for the discount.

Our vacation tours are professionally planned and designed solely for your enjoyment. Nearly everything is included in the price of your tour while giving you the best possible value for your dollar. All trips include:

- **Professional tour manager and local guides**
- **All accommodations and meals**
- **All entrance fees, excursions, transfers and tips**

We hope you will join us this year on another special Adventure Travel journey. Your memories of fascinating places and challenging physical adventures should linger for a long, long time. For reservations, please see your travel agent, or contact us directly at 1-800-777-0004. You can also visit us at our new Web site at www.AdventureTravelTours.com.

Best regards,

Student Name

Announcing
w Adventure Travel Tours

e introducing four new tours offering you a unique opportunity to nany different outdoor activities while exploring the world.

Hike the Inca trail to Machu Picchu
Camping Safari in Tanzania
Climb Mount Kilimanjaro
Explore the Costa Rican Rainforests

ture Travel presentation to learn about some of the earth's greatest ats and find out how you can experience the adventure of a lifetime.

n dates and times are January 5 at 7 PM, February 3 at 7:30 PM and at 7 PM. All presentations are held at convenient hotel locations. The are located in downtown Los Angeles, Santa Clara and at the airport.

1-800-777-0004 for presentation locations, a full color brochure, and itinerary information, costs, and trip dates.

Visit our
Web site at
AdventureTravelTours.com

Concept Overview

The following concepts will be introduced in this tutorial:

1 **Page Break**   There are two types of page breaks that can be used in a document: soft page breaks and hard page breaks.

2 **Find and Replace**   To make editing easier, you can use the Find and Replace feature to find text in a document and automatically replace it with other text.

3 **Thesaurus**   Word's Thesaurus is a reference tool that provides synonyms, antonyms, and related words for a selected word or phrase.

4 **Field**   A field is a placeholder that instructs Word to insert information into a document.

5 **Page Margins**   The margin is the blank space around the edge of the page. Standard single-sided documents have four margins: top, bottom, left, and right.

6 **Indents**   To help your reader find information quickly, you can indent paragraphs from the margins. Indenting paragraphs sets them off from the rest of the document.

7 **Tab Stop**   A tab stop is a stopping point along a line to which text will indent when you press [Tab].

8 **Bulleted and Numbered Lists**   Whenever possible, use bulleted or numbered lists to organize information and make your writing clear and easy to read.

Revising a Document

CHECKING SPELLING AND GRAMMAR MANUALLY

After speaking with the manager about the content to include in the letter you planned the basic topics that need to be included in the letter. They are to advertise the new tours, invite clients to the presentations, describe the early booking discount and promote the new Web site. You quickly entered the text for the letter and saved it as Tour Letter and printed out a hard copy. As you are reading the document again, you mark up the printout with the changes and corrections you want to make. The marked up copy is shown on the next page.

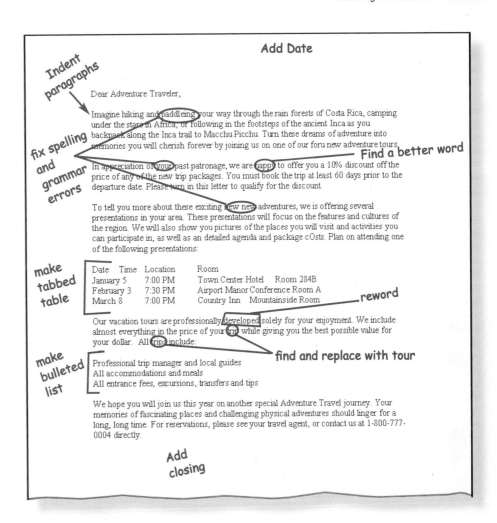

The first correction you want to make is to clean up the spelling and grammar errors that Word has identified.

1 Load Word 2000. Put your data disk in drive A (or the appropriate drive for your system).

Open the file Tour Letter.

If necessary, switch to Normal view.

Your screen should be similar to Figure 2-1.

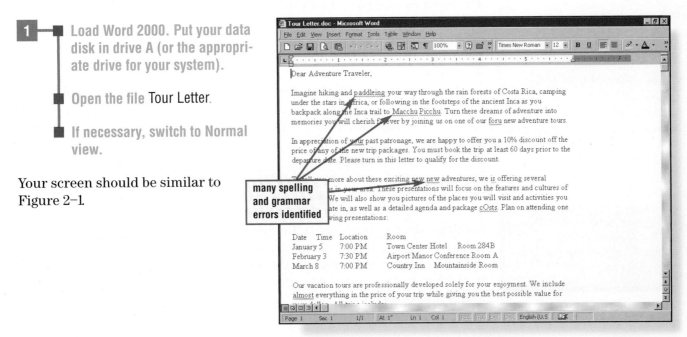

Figure 2-1

To correct the misspelled words and grammatical errors, you can use the shortcut menu to correct each individual word or error, as you learned in Tutorial 1. However, in many cases you may find it more efficient to wait until you are finished writing before you correct any spelling or grammatical errors. Rather than continually breaking your train of thought to correct errors as you type, you can manually turn on the Spelling and Grammar tool to check and correct all the words in the document at once.

2 ■ Click [ABC] Spelling and Grammar.

■ If necessary, select Check grammar to turn on grammar checking.

> The menu equivalent is **T**ools/**S**pelling and Grammar and the keyboard shortcut is [F7].

Your screen should be similar to Figure 2–2.

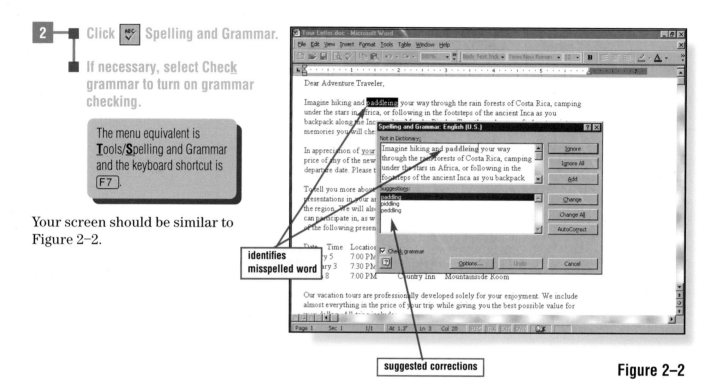

identifies misspelled word

suggested corrections

Figure 2–2

Additional Information

You can also double-click the Spelling and Grammar Status icon [icon] to move to the next spelling or grammar error and open the Spelling shortcut menu.

The [Change All] option replaces the same word throughout the document with the word you select in the suggestions list box.

The Spelling and Grammar dialog box is displayed, and the Spelling and Grammar tool has immediately located the first word that may be misspelled, "paddleling." The sentence with the misspelled word in red is displayed in the Not in Dictionary text box, and the word is highlighted in the document.

The Suggestions list box displays the words the Spelling tool has located in the dictionary that most closely match the misspelled word. The first word is highlighted. Sometimes the Spelling tool does not display any suggested replacements because it cannot locate any words in the dictionaries that are similar in spelling. If there are no suggestions, the Not in Dictionary text box simply displays the word that is highlighted in the text.

To change the spelling of the word to one of the suggested spellings, highlight the correct word in the list and then choose [Change]. If there were no suggested replacements, and you did not want to use any of the option buttons, you could edit the word yourself by typing the correction in the Not in Dictionary box. Because "paddling" is already highlighted and is the correct replacement,

3 ■ Click [Change] .

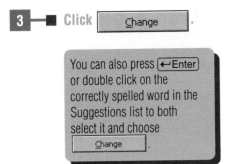

You can also press [←Enter] or double click on the correctly spelled word in the Suggestions list to both select it and choose [Change] .

Your screen should be similar to Figure 2–3.

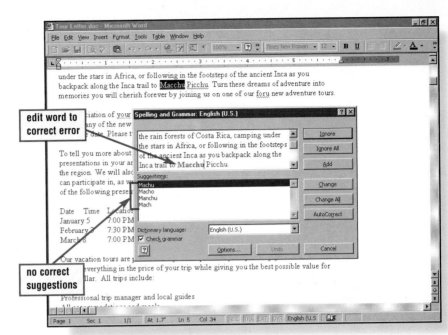

Figure 2–3

Additional Information

On your own computer system, you would want to add words to the custom dictionary that you use frequently and that are not included in the standard dictionary so they will be accepted when typed correctly and offered as a suggested replacement when not.

The Spelling Checker replaces the misspelled word with the selected suggested replacement and moves on to locate the next error. This time the error is the name of the Inca ruins at Machu Picchu. The word "Macchu" is spelled incorrectly; there is no correct suggestion, however, because the word is not found in the dictionary. You will correct the spelling of the word by editing it in the Not in Dictionary text box.

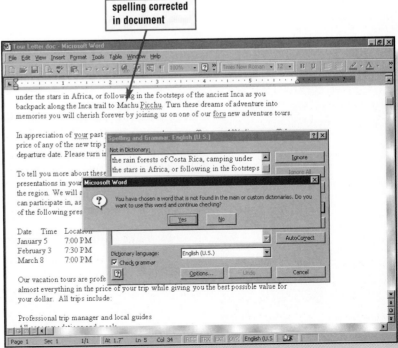

4 ■ Change the spelling of the word to Machu in the Not in Dictionary text box.

■ Click [Change] .

Your screen should be similar to Figure 2–4.

Additional Information

You can also edit words directly in the document and then click [Resume] to continue using the Spelling and Grammar checker.

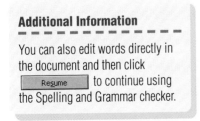

Figure 2–4

Word displays a question dialog box advising you that the correction to the word is not found in its dictionaries, and asking you to confirm that you want to continue.

5 Click  Yes .

Click Ignore All for the next located word, Picchu.

The spelling of the word Picchu is ignored, and the word is no longer identified as misspelled. The Ignore option accepts the error as correct for this occurrence only.

The next located error, "foru," is a typing error that you make frequently when typing the word four. The correct spelling is selected in the Suggestions list box. You want to change it to the suggested word and add it to the list of words that are automatically corrected.

6 Click AutoCorrect .

The word is corrected in the document. Because you also added it to the AutoCorrect list, in the future whenever you type this word incorrectly as "foru," it will automatically be changed to "four."

> If a dialog box appears telling you an AutoCorrect entry already exists for this word, simply click Yes to continue.

7 Continue to respond to the Spelling and Grammar checker by selecting the action shown below in response to the identified error:

Identified Error	Cause	Action	Result
your	Commonly confused words	Ignore	your
new	Repeated word	Delete	Duplicate word "new" is deleted
we is	Subject-verb disagreement	Change	we are
cOsts	Inconsistent capitalization	Change	costs
an detailed	Grammatical error	Change	a

There should be no other misspelled words or grammatical errors. However, if the Spelling and Grammar tool encounters others in your file, correct them as needed. When no others are located, a message appears telling you that the spelling and grammar check is complete.

5 Click  OK .

Move to the top of the document.

Moving Text

After looking over the letter, you decide to change the order of the paragraphs. You want the paragraph about the 10 percent discount (second paragraph) to follow the list of presentation dates. To do this, you will move the paragraph from its current location to the new location.

You can use several methods to move selections. One method is to use the Cut and Paste commands on the Edit menu. You will use the shortcut menu to select the Cut command. This menu displays options related to the current selection.

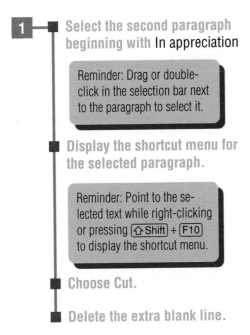

The Cut shortcuts are ✂ or Ctrl + X, the Copy shortcuts are 🖹 or Ctrl + C, and the Paste shortcuts are 📋 or Ctrl + V.

1 ■ Select the second paragraph beginning with In appreciation

> Reminder: Drag or double-click in the selection bar next to the paragraph to select it.

■ Display the shortcut menu for the selected paragraph.

> Reminder: Point to the selected text while right-clicking or pressing ⇧Shift + F10 to display the shortcut menu.

■ Choose Cut.

■ Delete the extra blank line.

Your screen should be similar to Figure 2–5.

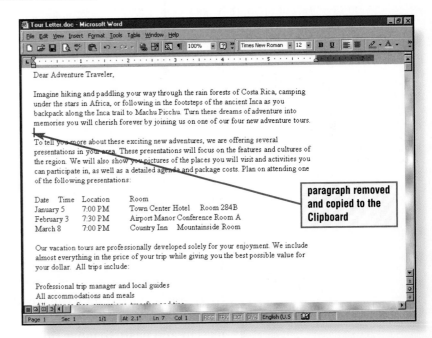

paragraph removed and copied to the Clipboard

Figure 2–5

Additional Information

The Clipboard is a temporary storage area in memory.

The selected paragraph is removed from the original location, called the **source**, and copied to the Clipboard. Next you need to move the insertion point to the location where the text will be inserted, called the **destination**, and paste the text into the document from the Clipboard.

2 ■ Move to the O in Our vacation tours (paragraph below list of presentation dates).

■ Click 📋 Paste.

> You can also choose Paste from the shortcut menu.

■ Press ⟵Enter to insert a blank line to separate the paragraphs.

Your screen should be similar to Figure 2–6.

paragraph copied from Clipboard and inserted into document

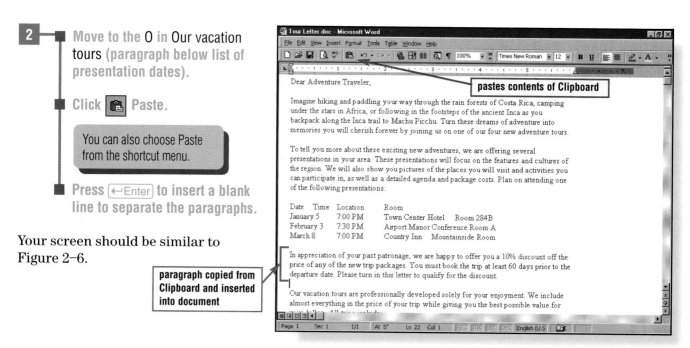

Figure 2–6

The deleted paragraph is reentered into the document at the insertion point location. That was a lot quicker than retyping the whole paragraph!

Using Drag and Drop Editing

> To use drag and drop to copy a selection, hold down Ctrl while dragging. The mouse pointer shape is 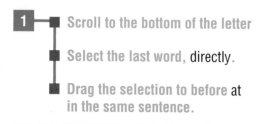.

Next you want to move the word "directly" in the last paragraph so that the sentence reads "... contact us directly at 1-888-777-0004." Rather than use cut and paste to move this text, you will use the **drag and drop** editing feature. This feature is most useful for copying or moving short distances in a document. To use drag and drop to move a selection, point to the selection and drag it to the location where you want the selection inserted. The mouse pointer appears as ⮂ as you drag, and a temporary insertion point shows you where the text will be placed when you release the mouse button.

1 ■ Scroll to the bottom of the letter

■ Select the last word, directly.

■ Drag the selection to before at in the same sentence.

Additional Information

You can also move and copy a selection by holding down the right mouse button while dragging. When you release the mouse button, a shortcut menu appears with the available move and copy options.

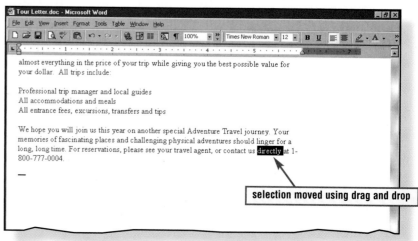

selection moved using drag and drop

Figure 2–7

Your screen should be similar to Figure 2–7.

Opening a Second Document

Next you want to open the flyer document so that you can copy the flyer into the letter document. You made several of the changes to the flyer suggested by the manager and saved it as Tour Flyer.

1 ■ Open the Tour Flyer document on your data disk.

Additional Information

Sometimes you may want to open several files at once. To do this you can select multiple files by holding down [Ctrl] while clicking on each file name. If the files are adjacent, you can click the first file name, hold down [⇧ Shift], and click on the name of the last file.

Your screen should be similar to Figure 2–8.

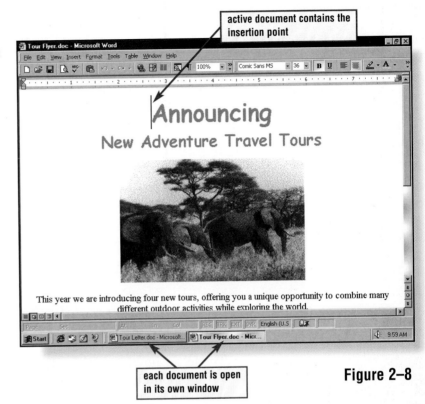

active document contains the insertion point

each document is open in its own window

Figure 2–8

You can also use [Alt] + [Tab] to switch from one open document window to another or use the Window menu.

The flyer document is opened and displayed in a separate window. It contains the insertion point which indicates that it is the active document or is the document you can work in. The taskbar displays a button for each open document window; it can be used to quickly switch from one window to the other.

Copying Between Documents

Additional Information

Office 2000 also includes an Office Clipboard that can store up to 12 items. This allows you to copy multiple items from various Office documents and paste all or part of the collection of copied items into another Office document.

You plan to modify the content included in the flyer, which will be mailed to clients with the letter. You also want to keep the flyer document in a separate file, because it will be handed out to clients when they come to the office. To include the flyer with the letter document, you will copy the flyer contents into the letter document. Copying is similar to moving, except that the original selection remains in the source and a duplicate is pasted into the destination.

1 — Select the entire flyer.

- Click 📋 Copy.

- Click 📄 Tour Letter.doc - Microsoft... in the taskbar.

- Move to the blank line below the last paragraph of the letter.

- Click 📋 Paste.

Your screen should be similar to Figure 2–9.

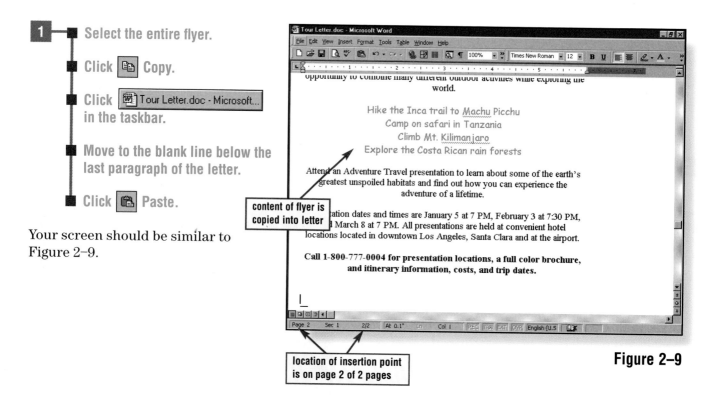

content of flyer is copied into letter

location of insertion point is on page 2 of 2 pages

Figure 2–9

Moving Through a Multiple-Page Document

The letter now consists of two pages. Notice the status bar shows the insertion point location is on page 2/2. You can move quickly through a document in large jumps by moving a window or a page at a time, moving to a specific page, or moving to the end or beginning of the document. The table below explains the various mouse and keyboard techniques that can be used to scroll a large document.

Mouse	Action
Click above/below scroll box	Scrolls the document window by window.
Drag scroll box	Moves multiple windows up/down.
Click ⬆	Go to top of previous page.
Click ⬇	Go to top of next page.
Click ⦾ Select Browse Object	Changes how you want the ⬆ and ⬇ buttons to browse through a document, such as by table or graphic. The default setting is by page.

Key	Action
Page Up	Top of window
Page Down	Bottom of window
Ctrl + Home	Beginning of document
Ctrl + End	End of document

To move up one full window in the document,

1 ◼ Press Page Up.

Your screen should be similar to Figure 2–10.

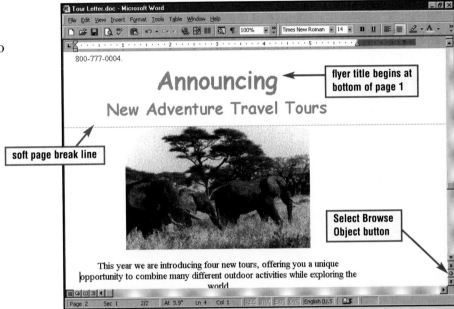

Figure 2–10

The document scrolled one full window of text upward. To show where one page ends and another begins, Word displays a dotted line across the page to mark the page break.

Inserting a Hard Page Break

Notice that the flyer title begins on the bottom of page 1. You want the entire flyer to print on a page by itself. To force a new page to begin at a specified location, you need to manually insert a page break.

Concept ① Page Break

There are two types of page breaks that can be used in a document: soft page breaks and hard page breaks. As you fill a page with text or graphics, Word inserts a **soft page break** automatically and starts a new page. As you add or remove text from a page, Word automatically readjusts the placement of the soft page break.

   Many times however, you may want to force a page break to occur at a specific location. To do this you can manually insert a **hard page break.** This instructs Word to begin a new page regardless of the amount of text on the previous page. Page breaks appear as a dotted line across the width of the page. Hard page breaks are distinguished by the words "Page Break" centered in the line.

When a hard page break is used, its location is never moved regardless of the changes that are made to the amount of text on the preceding page. All soft page breaks that precede or follow a hard page break continue to automatically adjust. Sometimes you may find that you have to remove the hard page break and reenter it at another location as you edit the document. To remove a hard page break, simply select the hard page break line and press [Delete].

1 ■ Move to the A in Announcing.

   ■ Choose **I**nsert/**B**reak.

Your screen should be similar to Figure 2–11.

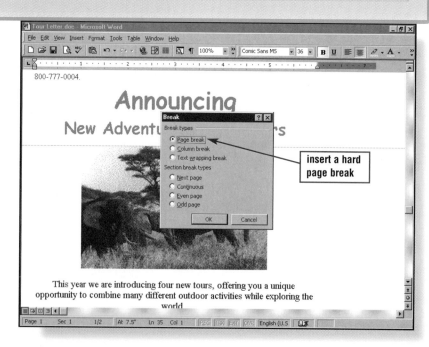

Figure 2–11

There are several different types of document breaks that can be inserted into a document. You will learn about the others in later tutorials.

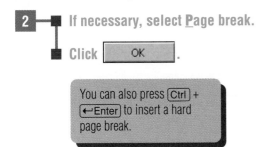

> **2** ■ If necessary, select <u>P</u>age break.
>
> ■ Click [OK] .

> You can also press (Ctrl) + (←Enter) to insert a hard page break.

Your screen should be similar to Figure 2–12.

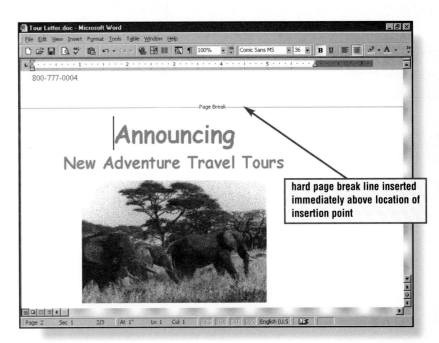

Figure 2–12

A dotted line containing the words "Page Break" appears across the page above the flyer title, indicating that a hard page break was entered at that position.

> **3** ■ Click [±] Previous Page to move to the top of the previous page.

Replacing Selected Text

As you continue checking the letter, you want to make several text changes suggested by the manager. First you will reword the first sentence of the fourth paragraph. You would like to replace the word "developed" with the words "planned and designed." Because the part you want to replace is shorter than the new text, Overtype mode will cut off some of the text you want to keep. By first selecting the text you want to remove and then typing in the new text, the part you want to keep will not be affected.

1 ■— ■ **Select** developed (first sentence of fourth paragraph).

 ■ **Type** planned and designed.

Your screen should be similar to Figure 2–13.

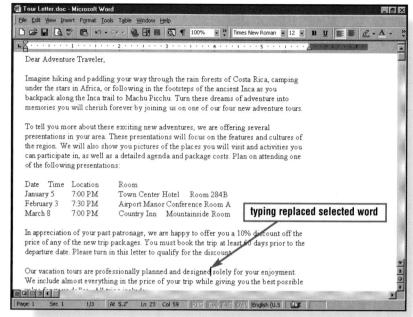

Figure 2–13

The selected text was deleted as soon as you began to type the new text.

Finding and Replacing Text

As you continue proofing the letter, you notice that you frequently used the word "trip." You think that the letter would read better if the word "tour" were used in place of "trip" in some instances. You want to find out how many times you actually used the word "trip," and then replace selected instances with "tour."

Concept ② Find and Replace

To make editing easier, you can use the Find and Replace feature to both find text in a document and replace it with other text as directed. For example, suppose you created a lengthy document describing the type of clothing and equipment needed to set up a world-class home gym, and then you decided to change "sneakers" to "athletic shoes." Instead of deleting every occurrence of "sneakers" and typing "athletic shoes," you can use the Find and Replace feature to perform the task automatically.

You can also find and replace occurrences of special formatting, such as replacing bold text with italicized text, and formatting marks. This feature is fast and accurate; however, use care when replacing so that you do not replace unintended matches.

First you will use the Find command to locate all occurrences of the word "trip" in the document.

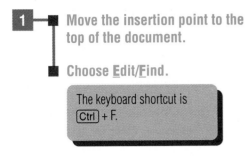

1 Move the insertion point to the top of the document.

Choose Edit/Find.

The keyboard shortcut is Ctrl + F.

Your screen should be similar to Figure 2–14.

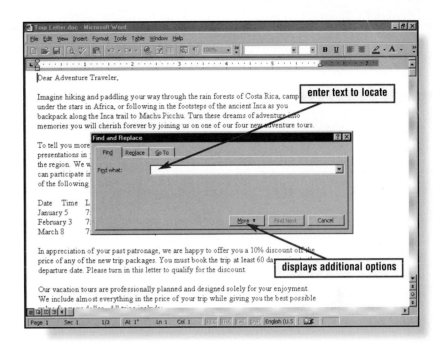

Figure 2–14

You can also open the Find and Replace dialog box by clicking the Select Browse Object button in the vertical scroll bar and selecting Find from the menu.

The Find and Replace dialog box is used to define the information you want to locate and replace. In the Find What text box, you enter the text you want to locate. In addition, you can use the search options to refine the search. To see these options,

2 Click More ≥.

Your screen should be similar to Figure 2–15.

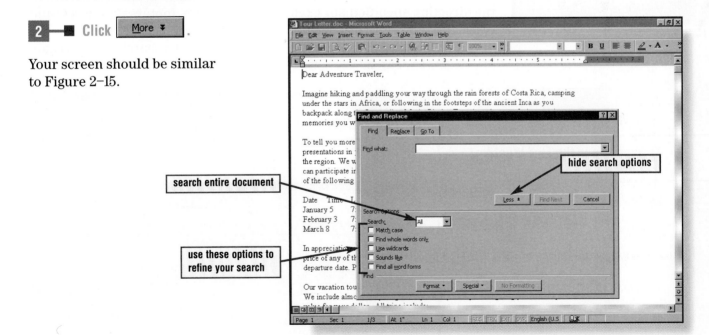

Figure 2–15

The additional options in the Find and Replace dialog box can be combined in many ways to help you find and replace text in documents. They are described in the table below.

Option	Effect on Text
Match case	Replaces words and retains the capitalization.
Find whole words only	For example, finds "cat" only and not "catastrophe" too.
Use wildcards	Fine-tunes a search; for example, c?t finds "cat" and "cot," while c*t finds "cat" and "catastrophe."
Sounds like	Finds words that sound like the word you type; very helpful if you do not know the correct spelling of the word you want to find.
Find all word forms	Finds and replaces all forms of a word; for example, "buy" will replace "purchase," and "bought" will replace "purchased."

When you enter the text to find, you can type everything lowercase, because the Match Case option is not selected. If Match Case is not selected, the search will not be **case sensitive**. This means that lowercase letters will match both upper- and lowercase letters in the text.

Also notice that the Search option default setting is All, which means Word will search the entire document, including headers and footers. You can also choose to search Up or Down the document, which searches in the direction specified but excludes the headers, footers, footnotes, and comments from the area to search. Because you want to search the entire document, All is the appropriate setting. To hide the search options again and begin the search,

You will learn about headers, footers, footnotes and comments in later tutorials.

3 Click [Less ↕] to close the advanced search options.

■ Type **trip** in the Find What text box.

■ Click [Find Next].

Your screen should be similar to Figure 2–16.

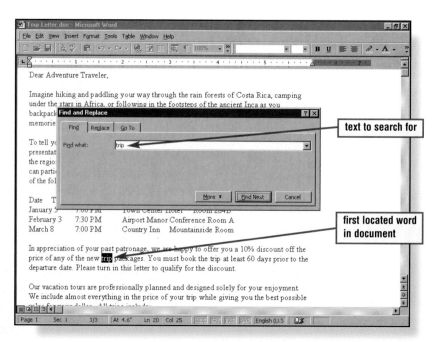

Figure 2–16

Word locates the first occurrence of the word "trip" and highlights it in the document.

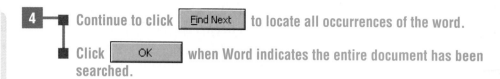

4 Continue to click [Find Next] to locate all occurrences of the word.

Click [OK] when Word indicates the entire document has been searched.

The word "trip" is used six times in the document. You decide to replace three occurrences of the word "trip" in the letter with "tour" where appropriate. To specify the text to enter as the replacement text,

5 Open the Replace tab.

Your screen should be similar to Figure 2–17.

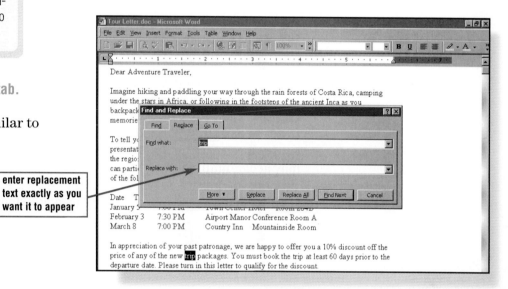

enter replacement text exactly as you want it to appear

Figure 2–17

The Replace tab includes a Replace With text box in which you enter the replacement text. This text must be entered exactly as you want it to appear in your document. To find and replace the first occurrence of the word "trip" with "tour,"

6 Type **tour** in the Replace With text box.

Click [Find Next].

Click [Replace].

Your screen should be similar to Figure 2–18.

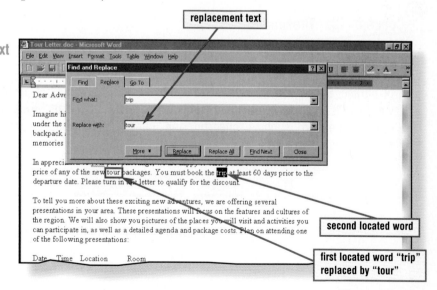

replacement text

second located word

first located word "trip" replaced by "tour"

Figure 2–18

Word replaced the first located word with "tour" and has highlighted the second occurrence of the word "trip." You do not want to replace this occurrence of the word. To tell the program to continue the search without replacing the highlighted text,

7 ─■ Click [Find Next] .

Word did not replace the located word and moved on to find the third occurrence of "trip."

8 ─■ Replace this occurrence.

─■ Continue to review the document, replacing every other occurrence of the word trip with tour.

If you wanted to change all the occurrences of the located text, it is much faster to use [Replace All] . Exercise care when using Replace All, however, because the search text you specify might be part of another word and you may accidentally replace text you want to keep.

9 ─■ Click [OK] to close the information dialog box.

─■ Click [Close] to close the Find and Replace dialog box.

Using the Thesaurus
- -

The next text change you want to make is to find a better word for "happy" in the sentence about the 10 percent discount. To help find a similar word, you will use the Thesaurus tool.

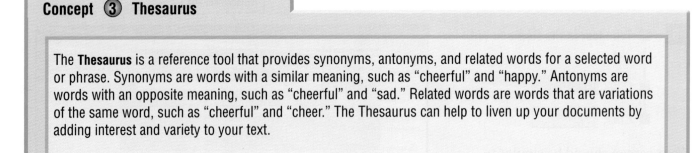

Concept ③ Thesaurus

The **Thesaurus** is a reference tool that provides synonyms, antonyms, and related words for a selected word or phrase. Synonyms are words with a similar meaning, such as "cheerful" and "happy." Antonyms are words with an opposite meaning, such as "cheerful" and "sad." Related words are words that are variations of the same word, such as "cheerful" and "cheer." The Thesaurus can help to liven up your documents by adding interest and variety to your text.

To identify the word you want looked up and to use the Thesaurus,

1 ■ Move to anywhere in the word **happy** (paragraph below tour dates).

■ Choose T̲ools/L̲anguage/T̲hesaurus.

> The keyboard shortcut is ⇧Shift + F7. You can also choose Sy̲nonyms from the shortcut menu and select a word from the list.

Your screen should be similar to Figure 2–19.

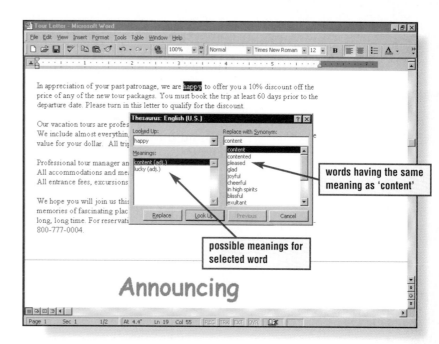

Figure 2–19

> If a synonym, antonym, or related word is not found, the Thesaurus displays an alphabetical list of entries that are similar in spelling to the selected word.

The Thesaurus dialog box displays a list of possible meanings for the selected word. From this list you can select the most appropriate meaning for the word. The currently selected meaning, "content," is appropriate for this sentence. The words in the Replace with Synonym box are synonyms for the word "happy" with a meaning of "content." The best choice from this list is "pleased." To replace "happy" with "pleased,"

2 ■ Select pleased.

■ Click .

Your screen should be similar to Figure 2–20.

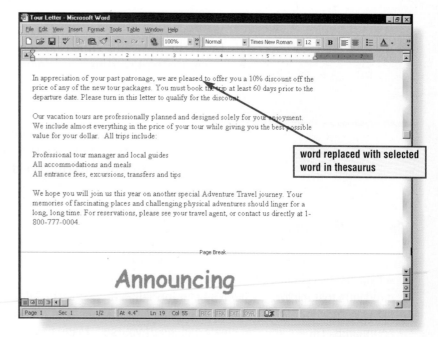

Figure 2–20

Word replaces the word "happy" with the word you selected from the Thesaurus.

Inserting the Current Date

- -

The last text change you need to make is to add the date to the letter. The Date and Time command on the Insert menu inserts the current date as maintained by your computer system into your document at the location of the insertion point. You want to enter the date on the first line of the letter, four lines above the salutation.

1 ▪ Move to the D in Dear at the top of the letter.

> Reminder: Use Ctrl + Home to quickly move to the top of a document.

▪ Insert four blank lines and move to the first blank line.

▪ Choose Insert/Date and Time.

Your screen should be similar to Figure 2–21.

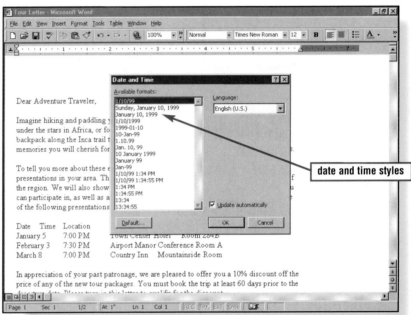

Figure 2–21

> The time as maintained by your system can also be inserted into a document using the same procedure.

From the Date and Time dialog box, you select the style in which you want the date displayed in your document. The Available Formats list box displays the format styles for the current date and time. You want to display the date in the format Month XX, 199X. This format is the third setting in the list.

You also want the date to be updated automatically whenever the letter is sent to new Adventure travelers. You use the Update Automatically option to do this by entering the date as a field.

Concept ④ Field

A **field** is a placeholder that instructs Word to insert information into a document. The **field code** contains the directions that tell Word what type of information to insert. The information that is displayed as a result of the field code is called the **field result**. Many field codes are automatically inserted when you use certain commands. Others you can create and insert yourself. Many fields update automatically when the document changes. Using fields makes it easier and faster to perform many common or repetitive tasks.

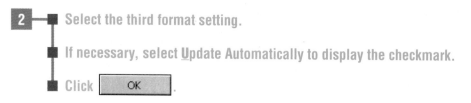

2 ■ Select the third format setting.

■ If necessary, select Update Automatically to display the checkmark.

■ Click OK.

The date is entered in the document in the format you selected. Although the date appears as text, it is a field. To see this,

3 ■ Press ←.

The date in Figure 2-22 will be different from the date that appears on your screen.

Your screen should be similar to Figure 2–22.

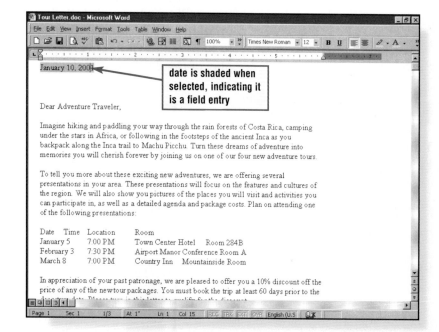

Figure 2–22

The entire date is shaded, indicating that the insertion point is positioned on a field entry. Whenever this file is printed, Word will print the current system date using this format.

The field code can be viewed by displaying the field's Shortcut menu and choosing Toggle Field Code.

Zooming the Document

Next the regional manager has suggested that you make several formatting changes to improve the appearance of the letter and flyer. One of the first changes you will make is to change the margin settings.

To make it easier to see how the margin setting changes you will make look on the page, you will first change the document view to Print Layout view. To see more of the text in the window at one time, you will also change the onscreen character size using the Zoom command.

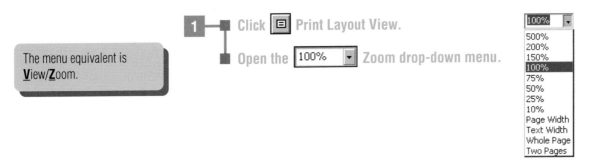

The menu equivalent is **V**iew/**Z**oom.

1 Click 🔲 Print Layout View.

Open the [100%] Zoom drop-down menu.

The default display, 100 percent, shows the characters the same size as they will be when printed. You can increase the onscreen character size up to five times normal display (500 percent) or reduce the character size to 10 percent. Changing the Zoom percent only affects the onscreen display of the document; it does not change font size.

2 Choose 75%.

Your screen should be similar to Figure 2–23.

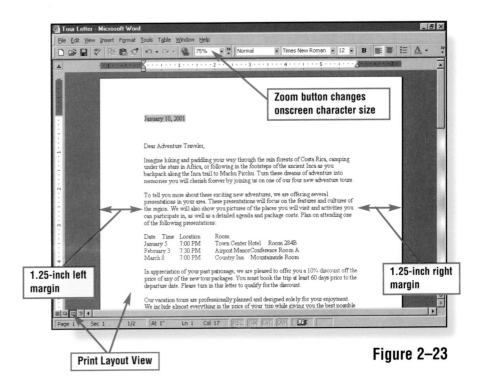

Figure 2–23

The page display is reduced by 25 percent, and three sides of the page are displayed. The current left and right margin settings of 1.25 inches are now easy to see. As you make changes to the margin settings next, you will be able to easily see the change in the layout of the document on the page.

Changing Margin Settings

You would like to see how the letter would look if you changed the right and left margin widths to 1 inch.

Concept ⑤ Page Margin

The **page margin** is the blank space around the edge of a page. Generally, the text you enter appears in the printable area inside the margins. However, some items can be positioned in the margin space. Standard single-sided documents have four margins: top, bottom, left, and right. Double-sided documents with facing pages, such as books and magazines, also have the four margins: top, bottom, inside, and outside. These documents typically use mirror margins in which the left page is a mirror image of the right page. This means that the inside margins are the same width and the outside margins are the same width.

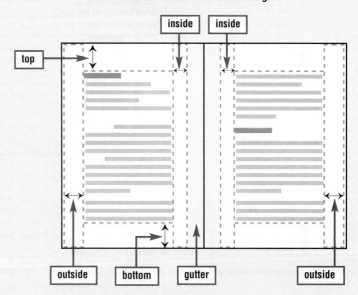

Single-Sided Document Margins

left

top

gutter   bottom   right

Double-Sided Document Margins

inside   inside

top

outside   bottom   gutter   outside

You can also set a "gutter" margin that reserves space on the left side of single-sided documents, or on the inside margin of double-sided documents, to accommodate binding. There are also special margin settings for headers and footers. (You will learn about these features in Tutorial 3.)

Word sets the default left and right margins in the Normal template at 1.25 inches, and the top and bottom margins at 1 inch. You can set different margin widths to alter the appearance of the document. However, because margin settings affect the entire document, changing the margin settings changes all paragraphs in the document.

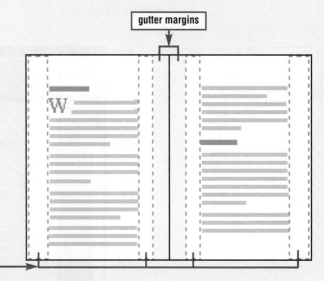

gutter margins

W

mirror margins

The Page Setup command on the File menu is used to change settings associated with the entire document.

1 ■ Choose File/Page Setup.

■ If necessary, open the Margins tab.

Your screen should be similar to Figure 2–24.

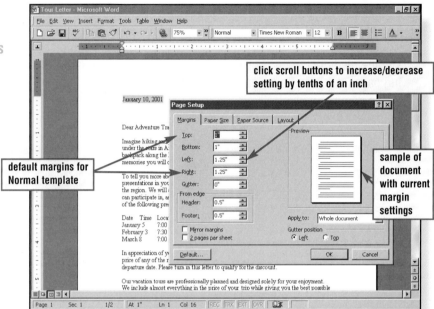

Figure 2–24

To set margins for double-sided documents, choose Mirror Margins.

The Margins tab of the Page Setup dialog box displays the default margin settings for a single-sided document. The Preview box shows how the current margin settings will appear on a page. New margin settings can be entered by typing the value in the text box, or by clicking the ▲ and ▼ scroll buttons or pressing the ↑ or ↓ keys to increase or decrease the setting by tenths of an inch.

2 ■ Using any of these methods, set the left and right margins to 1 inch.

■ Click   OK   .

Your screen should be similar to Figure 2–25.

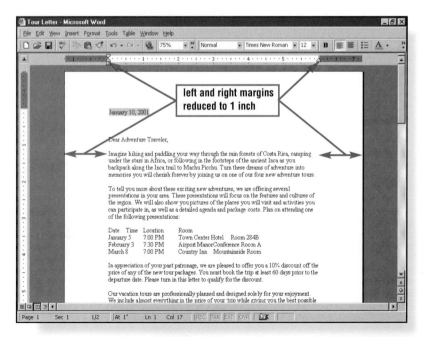

Figure 2–25

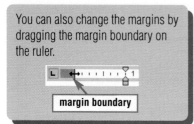

You can also change the margins by dragging the margin boundary on the ruler.

margin boundary

You can see that the letter has been reformatted to fit within the new margin settings. You would like to see what both pages look like at the same time.

3 ── Choose Two Pages from the Zoom drop-down menu.

Your screen should be similar to Figure 2–26.

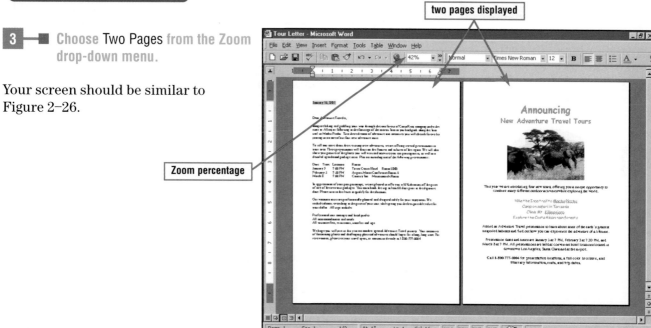

two pages displayed

Zoom percentage

Figure 2–26

Both pages are displayed in the workspace. The zoom percentage needed to display two pages of the document is automatically calculated by Word and displayed in the Zoom button. Although the text is difficult to read, you can easily see the layout of the pages.

4 ── Return the zoom percentage to 100%.

You can also change the zoom in Normal view.

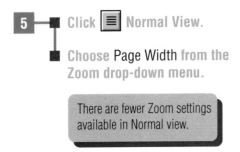

5   ● Click 📄 Normal View.

● Choose Page Width from the Zoom drop-down menu.

> There are fewer Zoom settings available in Normal view.

Your screen should be similar to Figure 2–27.

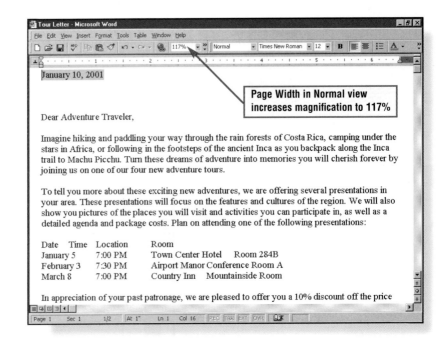

Figure 2–27

The onscreen character size has been increased 17 percent and the text is displayed across the width of the window.

Indenting Paragraphs

Business letters typically are either created using a block layout style or an indented layout style. In a block style, all parts of the letter, including the date, inside address, all paragraphs in the body, and closing lines, are evenly aligned with the left margin. This style has a very formal appearance. The indented layout style, on the other hand, has a more casual appearance. In this style, certain elements such as the date, all paragraphs in the body, and the closing lines are indented from the left margin. You want to change the letter style from the block paragraph style to an indented paragraph style.

Concept ⑥ Indents

To help your reader find information quickly, you can indent paragraphs from the margins. Indenting paragraphs sets them off from the rest of the document. There are four types of indents you can use to stylize your documents.

Indent		Effect on Text
Left	Left →	Indents the entire paragraph from the left margin. To extend the paragraph into the left margin, use a negative value for the left indent.
Right	← Right	Indents the entire paragraph from the right margin. To extend the paragraph into the right margin, use a negative value for the right indent.
First Line	First line	Indents the first line of the paragraph. All following lines are aligned with the left margin.
Hanging	Hanging	Indents all lines after the first line of the paragraph. The first line is aligned with the left margin. A hanging indent typically is used for bulleted and numbered lists.

You will begin by indenting the first line of the first paragraph.

1 Move to the **I** in **Imagine** (first sentence, first paragraph).

Choose **F**ormat/**P**aragraph

If necessary, open the **I**ndents and Spacing tab.

Your screen should be similar to Figure 2–28.

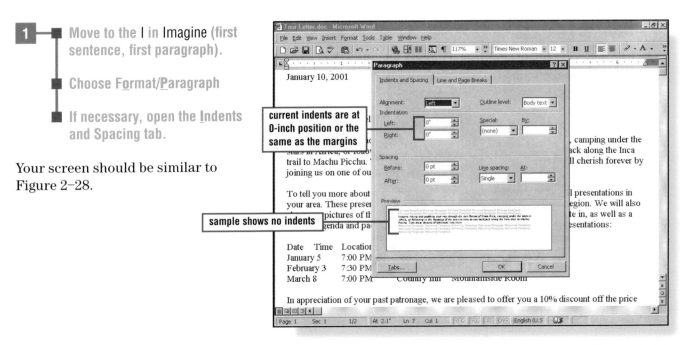

Figure 2–28

The Indents and Spacing tab shows that the left and right indentation settings for the current paragraph are 0. This setting aligns each line of the paragraph with the margin setting. Specifying an indent value would indent each line of the selected paragraph the specified amount from the margin. However, you only want to indent the first line of the paragraph. To do this,

2 Select **First Line** from the **S**pecial drop-down list box.

Your screen should be similar to Figure 2–29.

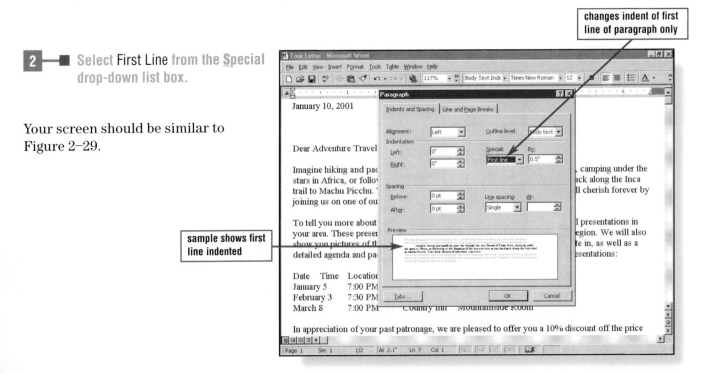

Figure 2–29

The default first line indent setting of 0.5-inch displayed in the By text box is acceptable. The Preview area shows how this setting will affect a paragraph.

3 ■ Click [OK].

Your screen should be similar to Figure 2–30.

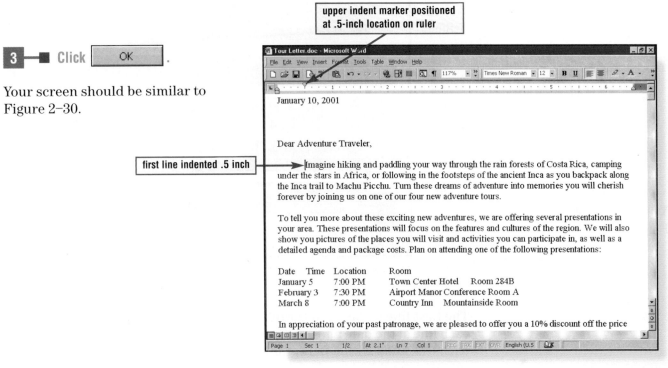

Figure 2–30

The first line of the paragraph indents a half inch from the left margin to the first tab setting. The text in the paragraph wraps as needed, and the text on the following line begins at the left margin. Notice that the upper indent marker on the ruler moved to the 0.5-inch position. This marker controls the location of the first line of text in the paragraph.

A much quicker way to indent the first line of a paragraph is to press [Tab ⇥] at the beginning of the paragraph. Pressing [Tab ⇥] indents the first line of the paragraph to the first tab stop from the left margin.

> You will learn about setting custom tabs later in this tutorial.

4 ■ Move to the beginning of the second paragraph.

■ Press [Tab ⇥].

Additional Information

A quick way to select a large area of text is to click at the beginning of the selection, scroll to the end of the selection using the scroll bar, and press [⇧ Shift] while clicking at the end of the area.

You can indent the remaining paragraphs individually, or you can select the paragraphs and indent them simultaneously by either using the Format menu or dragging the upper indent marker ▽ on the ruler.

5 ■ Select the remaining text on page 1.

■ Drag the upper indent marker on the ruler to the 0.5-inch position.

> A dotted vertical line is displayed as you drag to show where the indent will appear in the text.

> When you point to the indent marker, a ScreenTip is displayed to help identify the different markers.

Your screen should be similar to Figure 2-31.

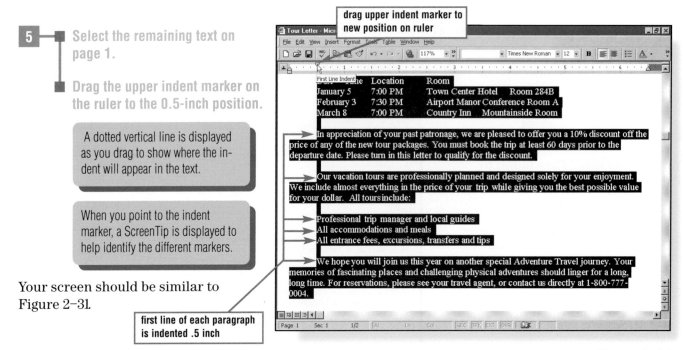

> drag upper indent marker to new position on ruler

> first line of each paragraph is indented .5 inch

Figure 2-31

The first line of each paragraph in the selection is indented. Notice that each line of the date and time information is also indented. This is because each line ends with a paragraph mark. Word considers each line a separate paragraph.

Setting Tab Stops

Next you want to improve the appearance of the list of presentation times and dates.

1 ■ Move to the top of the letter.

■ Move to the word **Date** in the list of presentation dates and times.

Your screen should be similar to Figure 2-32.

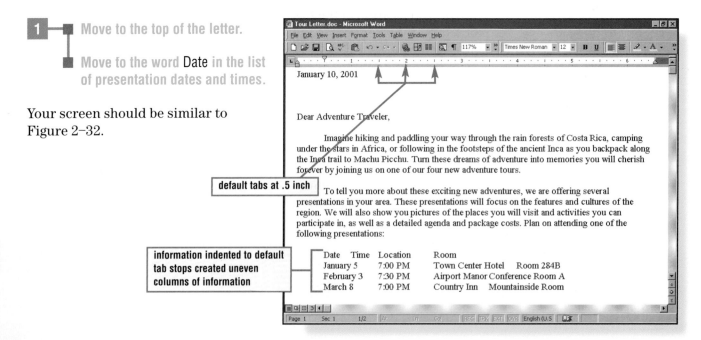

> default tabs at .5 inch

> information indented to default tab stops created uneven columns of information

Figure 2-32

The date and time information was entered using tabs to separate the different columns of information. However, because the default tab stops are set at every 0.5 inch, the columns are not evenly spaced. You want to reformat this information to appear as a tabbed table of information so that it is easier to read as shown in the figure below.

Date	Time	Location	Room
January 5 ------7:00 PM-----------Town Center Hotel --------Room 284B
February 3 ----7:30 PM-----------Airport Manor-------------Conference Room A
March 8 -------7:00 PM-----------Country Inn----------------Mountainside Room

To improve the appearance of the data, you will create custom tab stops that will align the data in evenly spaced columns.

Concept ⑦ Tab Stop

A **tab stop** is a stopping point along a line to which text will indent when you press [Tab⇄]. The default tab stops of every 0.5 inch are visible on the ruler as light vertical lines below the numbers. As with other default settings, you can change the location of tab stops in the document. You can also select from five different types of tab stops that control how characters are positioned or aligned with the tab stop. The following table explains the five tab types, the alignment tab marks which appear in the tab alignment selector box on the horizontal ruler, and the effects on the text.

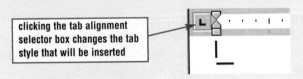

clicking the tab alignment selector box changes the tab style that will be inserted

Alignment	Tab Mark	How It Affects Text	Example
Left	⌞	Extends text to right from tab stop	left
Center	⊥	Aligns text centered on tab stop	center
Right	⌟	Extends text to left from tab stop	right
Decimal	⊥	Aligns text with decimal point	35.78
Bar	Ⅰ	Draws a vertical line through text at tab stop	text

When setting custom tab stops, the new settings affect the current paragraph or selected paragraphs; all default tab stops to the left of the custom tab stop are deleted.

Setting different types of tab stops is helpful for aligning text or numeric data vertically in columns. Using tab stops ensures that the text will indent to the same set location. Setting custom tab stops instead of pressing [Tab⇄] or [⇧Shift] repeatedly is a more professional way to format a document, as well as faster and more accurate. It also makes editing easier because you can change the tab stop settings for several paragraphs at once.

To remove a custom tab stop, simply drag it off the ruler.

To align the data, you will place three left tab stops at the 1.5-inch, 3-inch and 4.5-inch positions. You can quickly specify custom tab stop locations and types using the ruler. To select a type of tab stop, click the tab alignment selector box on the left end of the ruler to cycle through the types. Then, to specify where to place the selected tab stop type, click on the location in the ruler. As you specify the new tab stop settings, the table data will align to the new settings.

2 ■ Select the line of table headings and the three lines of data.

■ If necessary, click the tab alignment selector box until the left tab icon **L** appears.

■ Click the 1.5-inch position on the ruler.

■ Click the 2.75-inch and the 4.5-inch positions on the ruler.

The menu equivalent is Format/Tabs/1.5/2.75/4.5/Left.

Your screen should be similar to Figure 2–33.

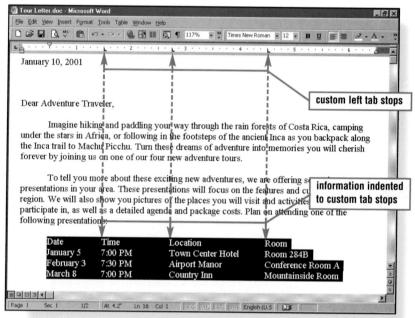

Figure 2–33

The three tabbed columns appropriately align with the new tab stops. All default tabs to the left of the new tab stops are cleared. After looking at the columns, you decide the column headings would look better centered over the columns of data. To make this change,

3 ■ Move to anywhere in the heading line.

■ Drag the three left tab stop marks off the ruler.

■ Click the tab alignment selector box until the center tab icon **⊥** appears.

■ Set a center tab stop at the .75-inch, 1.75-inch, 3.25-inch, and 5-inch positions.

The menu equivalent is Format/Tabs/.75/1.75/3.25/Center.

Your screen should be similar to Figure 2–34.

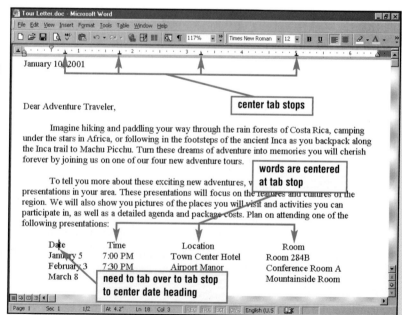

Figure 2–34

The Time, Location and Room headings are appropriately centered on the tab stops. However, the Date heading still needs to be indented to the .75 tab stop position by pressing (Tab↹).

5 ─ If necessary, move to the D in Date.

Press (Tab↹).

The Date heading is now centered at the .75-inch tab stop.

Adding Tab Leaders

- -

To make the presentation times and location data even easier to read, you will add tab leaders to the table. **Leader characters** are solid, dotted, or dashed lines that fill the blank space between tab stops. They help the reader's eye move across the blank space between the information aligned at the tab stops.

1 ─ Select the three lines of presentation information, excluding the heading line.

Choose F**o**rmat/**T**abs.

Your screen should be similar to Figure 2–35.

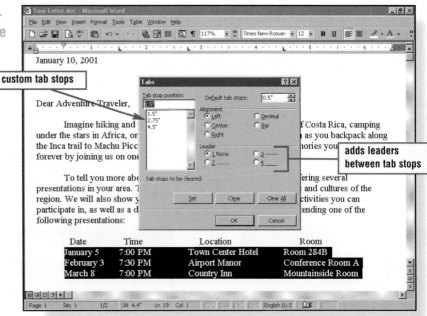

Figure 2–35

Notice that the Tabs dialog box displays the custom tabs you set on the ruler. You can set tab positions in the dialog box by entering the tab positions in the text box. The current tab leader setting is set to None for the 1.5-inch tab stop. You can select from three styles of tab leaders. You will use the third tab leader style, a series of dashed lines. Each tab stop needs to have the leader individually set.

2
- Select 3 ---
- Click **Set** .
- Select the 2.75-inch tab stop setting from the Tab Stop Position list box.
- Select 3 ---
- Click **Set** .
- In a similar manner, set the tab leader for the 4.5-inch tab.
- Click **OK** .
- Clear the highlight.

Your screen should be similar to Figure 2-36.

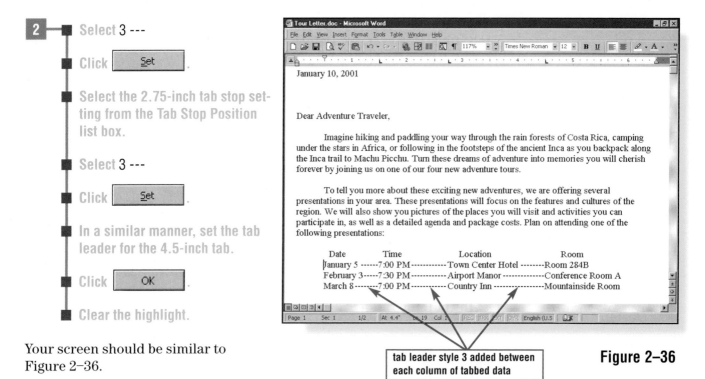

tab leader style 3 added between each column of tabbed data

Figure 2-36

The selected leader style has been added to the blank space between each column of tabbed text.

Underlining Text

Finally, you will bold and underline the headings. In addition to the default single underline style, there are eight other types of underlines.

1
- Select the heading Date.
- Click **B** Bold.
- Choose Format/Font.
- If necessary, open the Font tab.
- Open the Underline style drop-down list box.

Your screen should be similar to Figure 2-37.

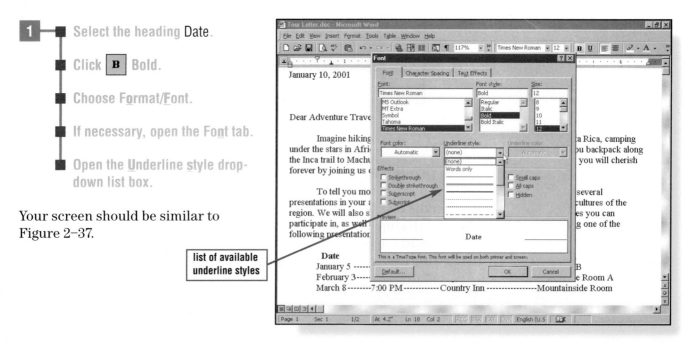

list of available underline styles

Figure 2-37

2 ■ Select several underline styles and look at how they appear in the Preview box.

■ Select a style of your choice.

> The keyboard shortcut for the single underline style is [Ctrl] + U.

■ Click [OK] .

■ Clear the selection.

Your screen should be similar to Figure 2–38.

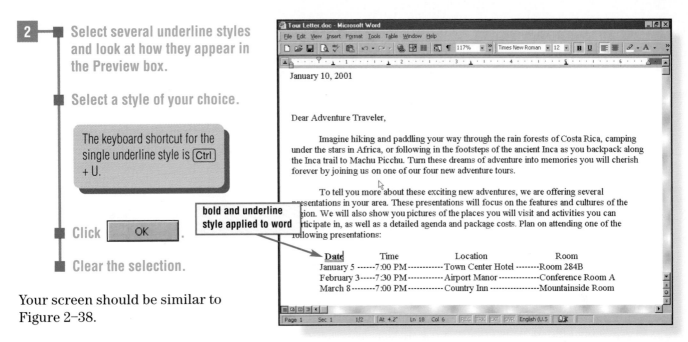

Figure 2–38

Using Format Painter

You want to quickly apply the same formats to the other headings. To do this you can use the **Format Painter**. This feature applies the formats associated with the current selection to new selections. If the selection is a paragraph (including the paragraph mark), the formatting is applied to the entire paragraph. If the selection is a character, the format is applied to a character, word, or selection you specify. To turn on the feature, move the insertion point to the text whose formats you want to copy and click the Format Painter button. Then you select the text you want the formats applied to. The format is automatically applied to an entire word simply by clicking on the word. To apply the format to more or less text, you must select the area. If you double-click the Format Painter button you can apply the format multiple times.

> When Format Painter is on, the mouse pointer appears as [brush].

1 ■ If necessary, move to anywhere in Date.

■ Double-click [brush].

■ Click on the three other headings.

■ Click [brush] to turn off Format Painter.

> You can also press [Esc] to turn off Format Painter.

Changing Line Spacing

You also want to increase the line spacing in the table to make the presentation data even easier to read. Line spacing is the vertical space between lines of text. The default setting of single line spacing accommodates the largest font in that line, plus a small amount of extra space.

Line spacing is a paragraph format setting, therefore it affects the paragraph containing the insertion point or all paragraphs in a selection.

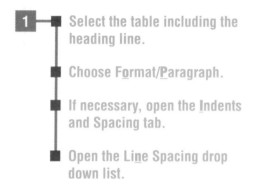

- Select the table including the heading line.

- Choose Format/Paragraph.

- If necessary, open the Indents and Spacing tab.

- Open the Line Spacing drop down list.

Your screen should be similar to Figure 2–39.

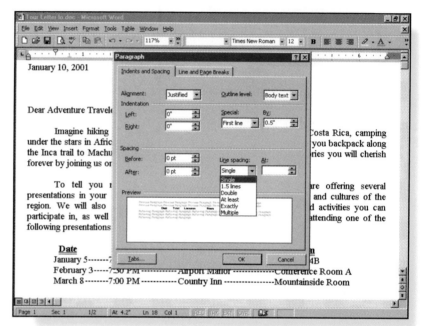

Figure 2–39

The line spacing options are described in the table below.

Spacing	Effect
1.5 lines	Spacing is one and a half times that of single line spacing.
Double	Spacing is twice that of single line spacing.
At least	Uses a value specified in points in the At text box as the minimum line spacing amount that can accommodate larger font sizes or graphics that would not otherwise fit within the specified spacing.
Exactly	Uses a value specified in points in the At text box as a fixed line spacing amount that is not changed, making all lines evenly spaced.
Multiple	Uses a percentage value in the At text box as the amount to increase or decrease line spacing. For example, entering 1.3 will increase the spacing by 33 percent.

2

Choose 1.5 lines from the Line Spacing drop-down list.

Click OK .

Clear the highlight.

Your screen should be similar to Figure 2–40.

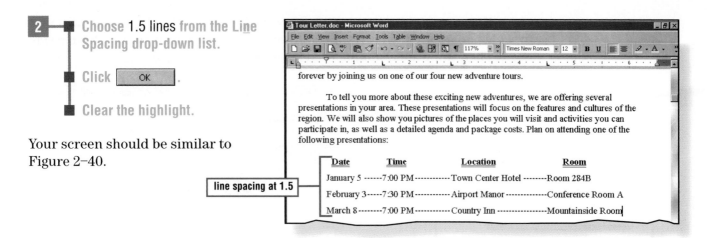

line spacing at 1.5

Figure 2–40

The line spacing within the selection has increased to 1.5 spaces.

Creating an Itemized List

Next you want to display the three lines of information about tour features as a bulleted list so that they stand out better from the surrounding text.

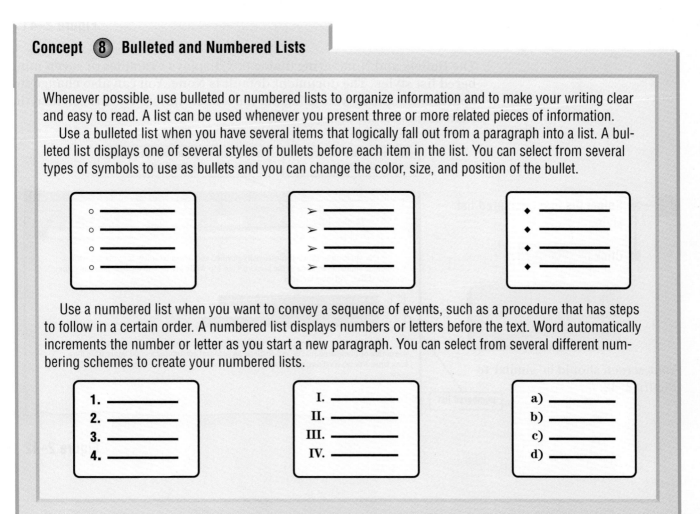

Concept ⑧ Bulleted and Numbered Lists

Whenever possible, use bulleted or numbered lists to organize information and to make your writing clear and easy to read. A list can be used whenever you present three or more related pieces of information.

Use a bulleted list when you have several items that logically fall out from a paragraph into a list. A bulleted list displays one of several styles of bullets before each item in the list. You can select from several types of symbols to use as bullets and you can change the color, size, and position of the bullet.

Use a numbered list when you want to convey a sequence of events, such as a procedure that has steps to follow in a certain order. A numbered list displays numbers or letters before the text. Word automatically increments the number or letter as you start a new paragraph. You can select from several different numbering schemes to create your numbered lists.

Because both bullet and number styles automatically indent the item when applied, you first need to remove the indent from the three items. Then you will try a numbered list style to see how it looks.

1
- Move to the P in Professional.

- Press Backspace.

  > You can also drag the upper indent marker on the ruler back to the margin boundary to remove the indent setting.

- In a similar manner, remove the indent from the other two lines.

- Select the three items.

- Choose F̲ormat/Bullets and Numbering.

- Open the N̲umbered tab.

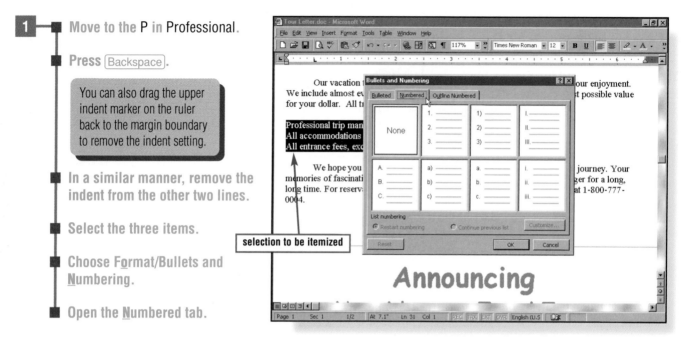

Your screen should be similar to Figure 2–41.

Figure 2–41

The Bullets and Numbering dialog box displays examples of seven numbered list styles. The document default is None. You can also change the appearance of the styles using the Customize option. The first style to the right of None is the style you will use.

2
- Select the first numbered list style.

- Click [OK].

  > You can also click ⊞ Numbering to insert the last used numbering style.

Your screen should be similar to Figure 2–42.

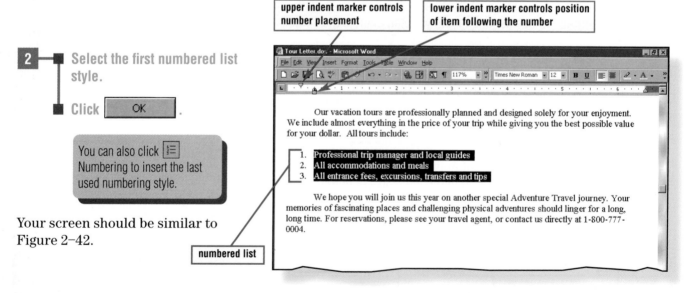

Figure 2–42

A number is inserted at the 0.25-inch position before each line, and the text following the number is indented to the 0.5-inch position. In an itemized list, the upper indent marker on the ruler controls the position of the number or bullet, and the lower indent marker controls the position of the item following the number or bullet. The lower indent marker creates a hanging indent. If the text following each bullet were longer than a line, the text on the following lines would also be indented to the 0.5-inch position.

After looking at the list you decide it really would be more appropriate if it was a bulleted list instead of a numbered list. To change the list to the bullet style,

3 ■ Click ▤ **Bullets.**

■ **Clear the highlight.**

Your screen should be similar to Figure 2–43.

applies last used numbered list style

applies last used bullet style

default bullet style applied to selection

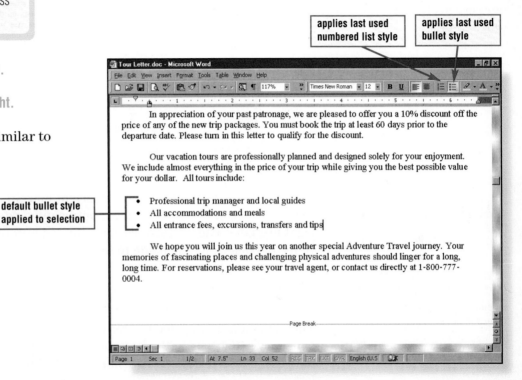

Figure 2–43

The last used bullet style replaces the number.

Justifying Paragraphs

The final formatting change you want to make to the letter is to change the alignment of all paragraphs in the letter from the default of left-aligned to justified.

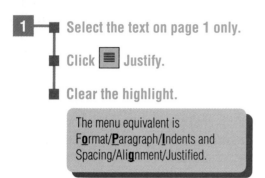

1 Select the text on page 1 only.

■ Click 🔳 Justify.

■ Clear the highlight.

> The menu equivalent is Format/Paragraph/Indents and Spacing/Alignment/Justified.

Your screen should be similar to Figure 2–44.

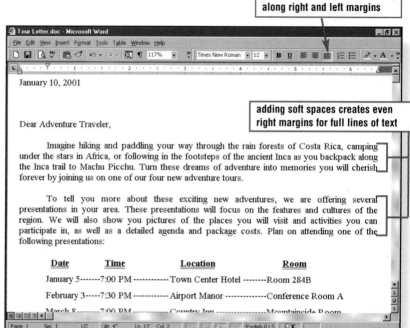

Figure 2–44

Additional Information

The alignment settings can also be specified before typing in new text. As you type, the text is aligned according to your selection until the alignment setting is changed to another setting.

All full lines now end even with the right margin. To do this, Word inserts extra spaces, called **soft spaces,** between words to push the text to the right margins. The soft spaces are adjusted automatically whenever additions and deletions are made to the text.

Creating and Removing a Hyperlink

The next change you need to make is to add some information about the company's Web site to the letter and flyer. First you will add the Web site address, called a **URL** (Uniform Resource Locator) to the last line of the letter.

1 Add the following sentence after the phone number in the last paragraph: **You can also visit us at our new Web site www.AdventureTravelTours.com.**

■ Press ⏎Enter twice.

Your screen should be similar to Figure 2–45.

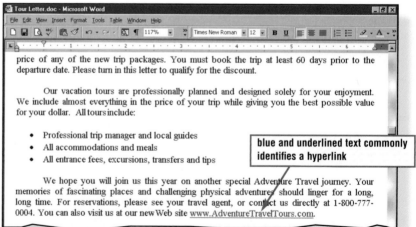

Figure 2–45

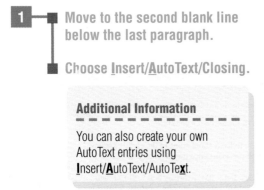

The mouse pointer shape changes to 🖑 when pointing to a hyperlink.

You could also click 🔄 Undo to remove the hyperlink autoformatting.

Notice that when you type the Web address, the text appears in blue and underlined. This indicates that Word has automatically formatted the text to a hyperlink. A **hyperlink** is a connection to a location in the current document, another document, or to a Web site. It allows the reader to jump to the referenced location by clicking on the hyperlink text when reading the document on the screen.

Word's **AutoFormat** feature makes certain formatting changes to your document as you type. These formats include such things as replacing ordinals (1st) with superscript (1st), fractions (1/2) with fraction characters ($\frac{1}{2}$) and applying a bulleted list format to a list if you type an asterisk (*) followed by a space at the beginning of a paragraph. Since this is a printed document you do not want the text displayed as a link.

2 ■ Right-click on the hyperlink and select **H**yperlink from the shortcut menu.

■ Choose **R**emove Hyperlink.

The Web address now appears as normal text.

Using an AutoText Entry

While looking at the letter, you realize that the closing lines have not been added to the document. You can quickly add standard phrases such as a closing to a document using the AutoText feature.

1 ■ Move to the second blank line below the last paragraph.

■ Choose **I**nsert/**A**utoText/**C**losing.

Additional Information

You can also create your own AutoText entries using **I**nsert/**A**utoText/AutoTe**x**t.

Your screen should be similar to Figure 2–46.

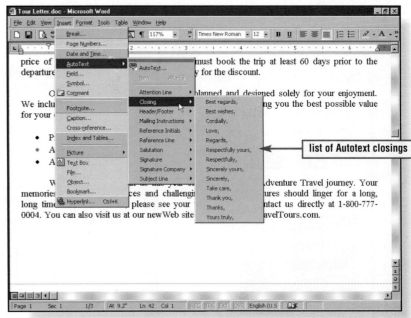

Figure 2-46

The menu includes a list of standard closing lines. You think "Best regards" is the best closing for this document.

2
- Choose **Best regards**.

- Press ⏎Enter four times.

- Type **Your name**.

- Finally, indent both closing lines to the 3.5-inch position.

Your screen should be similar to Figure 2–47.

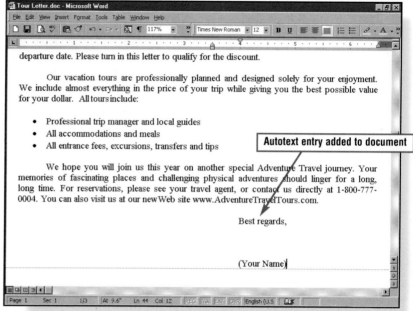

Figure 2–47

Adding an AutoShape

You want to add a special graphic to the flyer containing information about the Web site to catch the reader's attention. To quickly add a shape, you will use one of the ready-made shapes called **AutoShapes** that are supplied with Word. These include such basic shapes as rectangles and circles, a variety of lines, block arrows, flowchart symbols, stars and banners, and callouts.

1
- Move to the bottom of the flyer.

- Click 🖉 Drawing to display the Drawing toolbar.

- Click AutoShapes ▾.

- Select Stars and Banners.

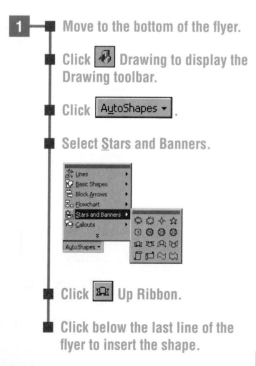

- Click 🏳 Up Ribbon.

- Click below the last line of the flyer to insert the shape.

Your screen should be similar to Figure 2–48.

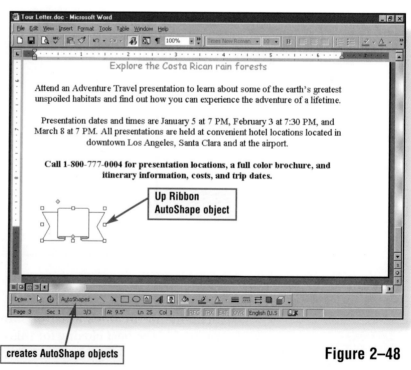

Figure 2–48

The AutoShape graphic object you selected is inserted into the document. It can be sized and moved just like a picture object. It can also be enhanced using many of the features on the drawing toolbar. First you will increase its size, then you will add color.

> The menu equivalent is **I**nsert/**P**icture/**A**utoShapes.

2 Drag to increase the AutoShape size to that shown in Figure 2–49.

> To maintain the height and width proportions of the AutoShape hold down ⇧Shift while you drag.

Open the 🖌▾ Fill Color drop-down menu.

Select a fill color of your choice.

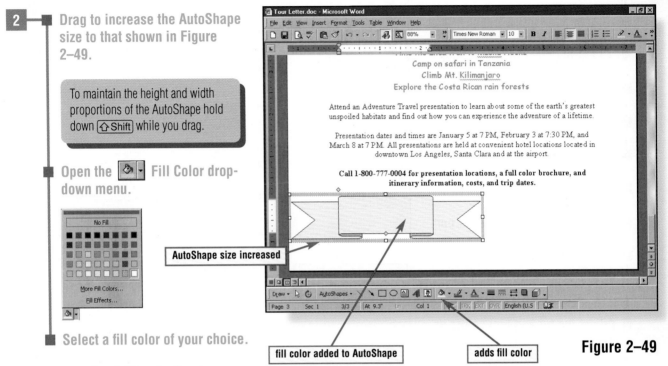

Figure 2–49

Your screen should be similar to Figure 2–49.

Next you will add text to the drawing.

3 ■ Right-click on the shape to open the shortcut menu.

■ Click Add Te**x**t.

■ Change the font settings to Arial, size 12, bold, italic, centered, and a font color of your choice.

■ Type **Visit our**

■ Press ⏎Enter.

■ Type **Web site at**

■ Press ⏎Enter.

■ Type **AdventureTravelTours.com**

■ If necessary, adjust the AutoShape size until the text appears on three lines.

■ Adjust the fill and font colors as needed.

■ Zoom to Page Width.

■ Drag to move and center the object between the margins.

■ Clear the selection.

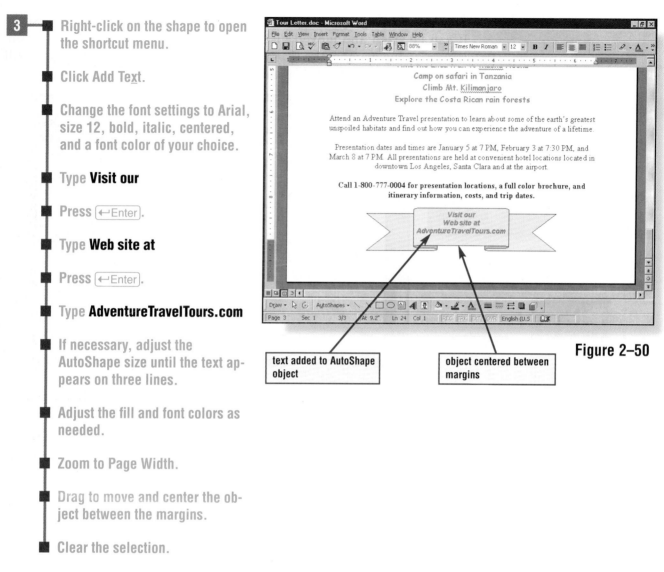

Figure 2–50

text added to AutoShape object

object centered between margins

Your screen should be similar to Figure 2–50.

Editing in Print Preview

You would like to save the edited version of the tour letter as Revised Tour Letter. This will allow the original file, Tour Letter, to remain unchanged in case you want to repeat the lab for practice.

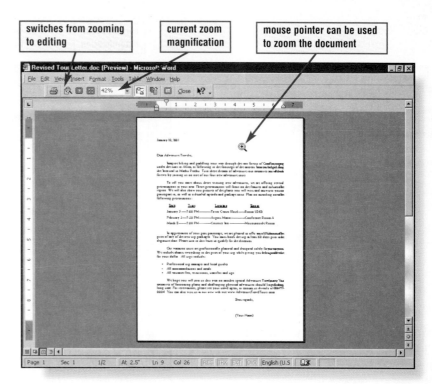

Figure 2–51

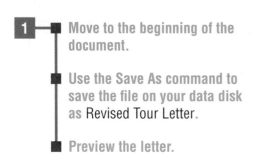

1 Move to the beginning of the document.

Use the Save As command to save the file on your data disk as Revised Tour Letter.

Preview the letter.

Your screen should be similar to Figure 2–51.

Now that you can see the entire letter, you decide that the date would look better at the 3.5-inch tab position. While in Print Preview, you can edit and format text. Notice that the mouse pointer is a magnifying glass [115] when it is positioned on text in the window. This indicates that when you click on a document, the screen will toggle between the whole page view you currently see and 100 percent magnification.

2 To edit the date in the Print Preview window, point to the top of the letter and click the mouse button.

The text is displayed in the size it will appear when printed (100 percent zoom). Then, to switch between zooming the document and editing it,

3 Click Magnifier.

When positioned near text, the mouse pointer changes to an I-beam and the insertion point is displayed. Now you can edit the document as in Normal view.

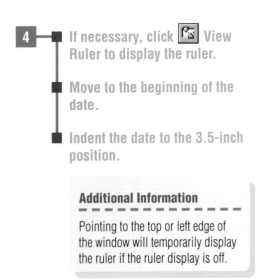

4 ■ If necessary, click [img] View Ruler to display the ruler.

■ Move to the beginning of the date.

■ Indent the date to the 3.5-inch position.

Additional Information

Pointing to the top or left edge of the window will temporarily display the ruler if the ruler display is off.

Your screen should be similar to Figure 2–52.

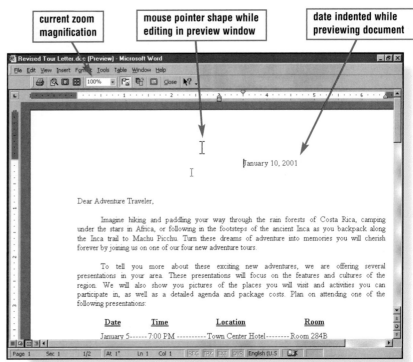

current zoom magnification

mouse pointer shape while editing in preview window

date indented while previewing document

Figure 2–52

To switch back to zooming the document and restore it to the original preview size,

5 ■ Click [img] Magnifier.

■ Click the document.

While looking at the document, you decide to emphasize some of the text by adding bold and underlines. Because you are using Print Preview, the Formatting toolbar buttons are not displayed. You could display the Formatting toolbar or you could use the Format menu to change the text. Another quick way, however, is to use the keyboard shortcut. To magnify the document again and add bold to the bulleted items,

6 ■ Click on the bulleted list area.

■ Click [img] Magnifier.

■ Select the three bulleted items.

■ Press Ctrl + B.

■ Click [img] Magnifier.

■ Click the document.

The [100% ▾] Zoom button can also be used to specify the magnification.

Now that the document has been edited and formatted the way you want, you will print a copy of the letter from the Print Preview window using the default print settings.

> If you need to specify a different printer, you will need to close the Preview window and use the Print command on the File menu.

> Make sure your printer is on and ready to print.

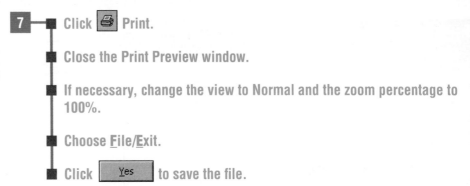

7 ■ Click 🖨 Print.

■ Close the Print Preview window.

■ If necessary, change the view to Normal and the zoom percentage to 100%.

■ Choose File/Exit.

■ Click [Yes] to save the file.

Concept Summary

Tutorial 2: Revising and Refining a Document

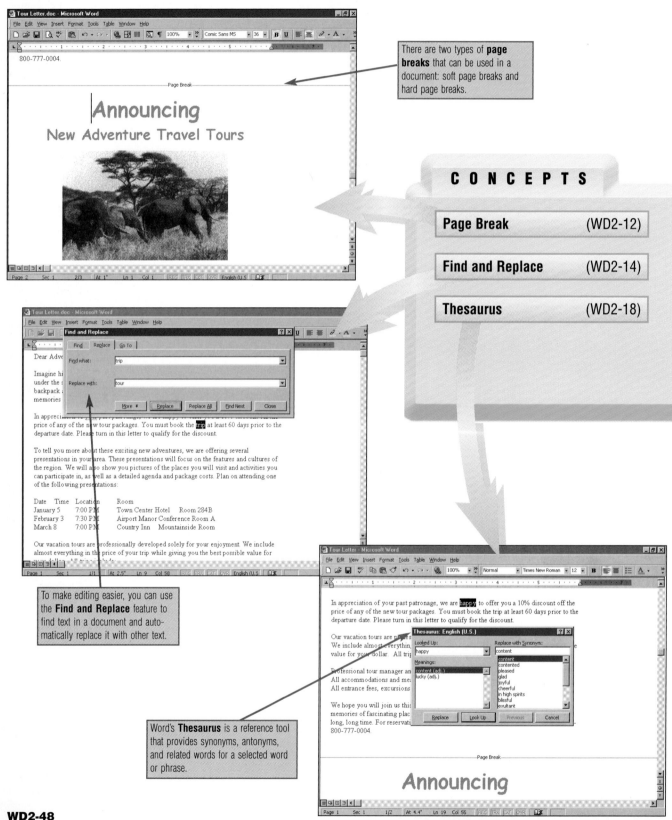

There are two types of **page breaks** that can be used in a document: soft page breaks and hard page breaks.

C O N C E P T S

Page Break	(WD2-12)
Find and Replace	(WD2-14)
Thesaurus	(WD2-18)

To make editing easier, you can use the **Find and Replace** feature to find text in a document and automatically replace it with other text.

Word's **Thesaurus** is a reference tool that provides synonyms, antonyms, and related words for a selected word or phrase.

The **page margin** is the blank space around the edge of the page. Standard single-sided documents have four margins: top, bottom, left, and right.

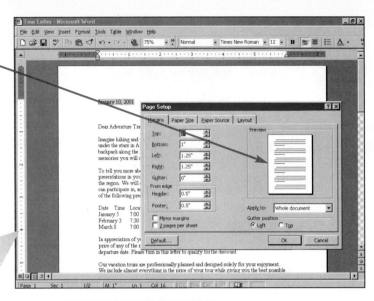

To help your reader find information quickly, you can **indent** paragraphs from the margins. Indenting paragraphs sets them off from the rest of the document.

A **field** is a placeholder that instructs Word to insert information into a document.

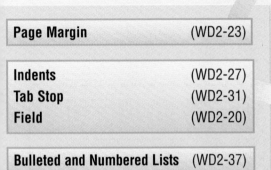

A **tab stop** is a stopping point along a line to which text will indent when you press Tab.

Whenever possible, use **bulleted** or **numbered lists** to organize information and make your writing clear and easy to read.

Tutorial Review

Key Terms

AutoFormat WD2-41	field code WD2-20	page margin WD2-23
AutoShape WD2-42	field results WD2-20	soft page break WD2-12
case sensitive WD2-16	Format Painter WD2-135	soft space WD2-40
destination WD2-7	hard page break WD2-12	source WD2-7
drag and drop WD2-8	hyperlink WD2-41	Thesaurus WD2-18
field WD2-20	leader character WD2-33	URL WD2-40

Command Summary

Command	Shortcut Keys	Button	Action
File/Page Setup			Changes layout of page including margins, paper size, and paper source
Edit/Cut	Ctrl + X	🗋	Cuts selected text to Clipboard
Edit/Copy	Ctrl + C	📑	Copies selected text to Clipboard
Edit/Paste	Ctrl + V	📋	Pastes text from Clipboard
Edit/Find	Ctrl + F		Locates specified text
Edit/Replace	Ctrl + H		Locates and replaces specified text
View/Zoom			Changes onscreen character size
View/Zoom/Whole Page			Displays entire page onscreen
Insert/Break/Pagebreak	Ctrl + Enter		Inserts hard page break
Insert/Date and Time			Inserts current date or time, maintained by computer system, in selected format
Insert/AutoText			Enters predefined text at insertion point
Insert/Picture/Autoshapes		AutoShapes ▾	Inserts selected AutoShape
Format/Font/Font/Underline style/Single	Ctrl + U	U	Underlines selected text with a single line
Format/Paragraph/Indents and Spacing/ Special/First Line			Indents first line of paragraph from left margin
Format/Paragraph/Indents and Spacing/ Alignment/Justified	Ctrl + J	≡	Aligns text equally between left and right margins
Format/Paragraph/Indents and Spacing/ Alignment/Line Spacing			Changes amount of white space between lines

Command	Shortcut Keys	Button	Action
F**o**rmat/**B**ullets and **N**umbering			Creates a bulleted or numbered list
F**o**rmat /**T**abs			Specifies types and position of tab stops
Tools/**S**pelling and Grammar	F7		Starts Spelling and Grammar tool
Tools/**L**anguage/**T**hesaurus	⇧Shift + F7		Starts Thesaurus tool

Screen Identification

1. In the following Word screen, letters identify elements. Enter the correct term for each screen element in the space provided.

a. _____   e. _____

b. _____   f. _____

c. _____   g. _____

d. _____   h. _____

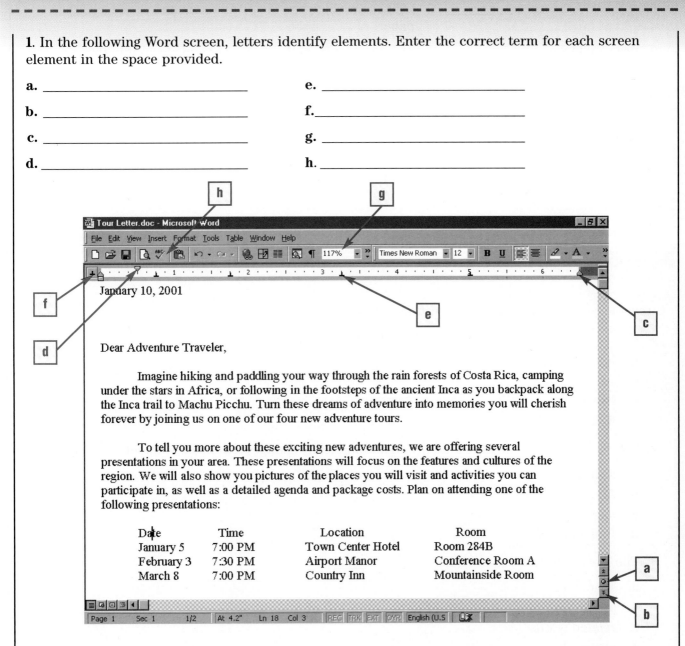

Matching

Match the letter on the right to the item in the numbered list on the left.

1. justified _____ **a.** suggests synonyms and antonyms
2. date field _____ **b.** used to spell- and grammar-check the document
3. [≡] _____ **c.** shortcut for the bold command
4. margins _____ **d.** used to copy or move a selection
5. [Ctrl] + B _____ **e.** text that has even left and right margins
6. [ABC✓] _____ **f.** white space between the printed text and the edge of the paper
7. drag and drop _____ **g.** removes text from the document and stores it in the Clipboard
8. Thesaurus _____ **h.** quickly locates specified text
9. [▯] _____ **i.** creates a bulleted list
10. Find _____ **j.** a code that instructs Word to insert the current date in the document using the selected format whenever the document is printed

Multiple Choice

Circle the correct response to the questions below.

1. A _____ page break is inserted manually by the user.
   a. hard
   b. soft
   c. fixed
   d. floating

2. The _____ feature locates and automatically changes text in a document.
   a. search and replace
   b. find and change
   c. locate and change
   d. find and replace

3. The Thesaurus in Word provides _____ .
   a. synonyms
   b. antonyms
   c. related words
   d. all the above

4. The field _____ contains the directions that tell Word what type of information to insert.

   a. results
   b. code
   c. placeholder
   d. format

5. The distance from the edge of the page to the text is called the _____ .

   a. gutter
   b. indent
   c. margin
   d. white space

6. The _____ indent positions the first line of a paragraph at the left margin with all following lines indented.

   a. left
   b. right
   c. first line
   d. hanging

7. To convey a sequence of events in a document, you should consider using a _____ .

   a. bulleted list
   b. numbered list
   c. organization list
   d. paragraph list

8. A tab stop is the_____ point along a line to which text will indent when you press
   Tab ⇤.

   a. starting
   b. stopping
   c. beginning
   d. ending

9. The feature most useful for copying or moving short distances in a document is _____
   .

   a. drag and drop
   b. drop and drag
   c. move and place
   d. drag and place

10. _____ are solid, dotted, or dashed lines that fill the blank space between tab stops.

   a. tab leaders
   b. leader characters
   c. leader tabs
   d. tab characters

True/False

Circle the correct answer to the following questions.

1. The white space between the text and the edge of the paper is the margin.   True   False

2. A bulleted list conveys a sequence of events.   True   False

3. Indents are used to set paragraphs off from the rest of the text.   True   False

4. Tab leaders are used to separate columns of text.   True   False

5. The Spelling Checker identifies synonyms for common words.   True   False

6. The Find and Replace feature is used to find misspelled words in a document.   True   False

7. Soft page breaks are automatically inserted whenever the text reaches the bottom margin.   True   False

8. Field placeholders define the information to be inserted in a document.   True   False

9. Hyperlinks are usually colored and underlined in Word documents.   True   False

10. Formatting and text editing can be done in the Print Preview window.   True   False

Discussion Questions

1. Use Help for more information about the AutoFormatting feature. Discuss how the AutoFormatting feature works and the two ways it can be used.

2. Discuss how the AutoText feature works. When might you want to consider adding words to the AutoText feature? Will added words be recognized in other documents?

3. Discuss the different ways information can be moved within a document. Explain which method is most appropriate in certain circumstances.

4. Discuss how field codes are used in Word documents. What other field codes are available (list several)? Why are field codes important in documents that are reused?

5. Discuss the problems that can be associated with finding and replacing text. What can you do to avoid some of these problems?

Hands-On Practice Exercises

Step by Step

☆

1. You are thinking about starting your own business and you need to make a number of decisions first. To help organize the process, you decide to create a list of the main categories of decisions you will have to make.

   a. Open a new document and set line spacing to 1.5.

   b. Enter a title of New Business Decisions. Bold, color, and increase the font size to 14.

   c. Two blank lines below the title, enter the following list of items:

Product list
Type of business
Ownership
Management
Location of business
Source of capital

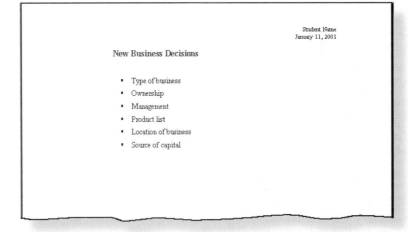

   d. Select the six lines of text and create an itemized list using the solid square bullet style.

   e. Set the indentation of the entire list to the 1-inch position. Center the title over the list.

   f. Use drag and drop to move the "Product list" item to the fourth item in the list.

   g. Add your name and the current date several lines below the list.

   h. Save the document on your data disk as Decision List. Print the document.

2. In addition to coffee beverages, the Downtown Internet Cafe also sells fresh roast coffee. You want to create a document describing the roast coffee varieties and prices. Using tab settings, create a table of coffee varieties and prices according to the following specifications.

   a. Open a new document and set the line spacing to double.

   b. Enter the title DownTown Internet Cafe centered on the first line.

   c. Enter a second title, Roast Coffee, centered below the title.

   d. Apply formats of your choice to both title lines.

e.   Place left tab stops at .75 and 2.5 inches and a center tab at 5.25 inches on the ruler.

f.   Enter the word Coffee at the first tab stop, Description at the second tab stop, and Cost/Pound at the third tab stop.

g.   Enter the rest of the information shown here in the final document.

h.   Add tab leaders between the data in the table.

i.   Increase the font to 14 point. Add bold, color, and an underline style of your choice to the table headings.

j.   Add your name and the current date using the Date and Time command several lines below the table.

k.   Save the document as Coffee Table on your data disk and print it.

3. To complete this exercise, you must have completed Practice Exercise 5 in Tutorial 1. You are still working on the potato chip cookie recipe for the National Potato Council. They have decided to publish a booklet of potato recipes and want to include this recipe.

a.   Open the file Potato Chip Cookies from your data disk.

b.   Change the top margin to 1.5 inches. Change the right and left margins to 1 inch.

c.   Indent the list of ingredients 0.5 inches.

d.   Change the directions to an itemized numbered list. Indent the itemized list 0.5 inches from the left.

e.   Use the Find and Replace feature to replace every occurrence of the abbreviation "c." with the full word "cup".

f.   Preview, then print the document.

g.   Save the document using the same file name.

Potato Chip Cookies

Potato chips give these cookies a crunchy texture and eliminate the need for baking soda.

Ingredients:

    2 sticks of butter (softened)
    1/2 cup dark brown sugar (fiirmly packed)
    1/2 cup crushed potato chips
    1/2 cup chopped pecans
    1 tsp. vanilla extract
    1/2 cup sifted fllour
    Confectioner's sugar

Directions:

1. Cream the butter and brown sugar together.
2. Add vanilla, chips, and nuts.
3. Gradually add the fllour. Mix thoroughly.
4. Cover and chill the dough for at least 1 hour.
5. Roll dough into 1-inch balls, and roll in confectioner's sugar.
6. Place 1" apart on greased cookie sheet.
7. Bake in 350 degree oven for 12-15 minutes.

This recipe makes about 3 1/2 dozen cookies.

Student Name
Current Date

☆ ☆ ☆

4. To complete this exercise, you must have completed Practice Exercise 1 in this tutorial. You plan to share your great idea for a business with a colleague in the hopes of getting some to help with your plans. You have quickly written a draft of the letter, but now realize you need to revise it to fix mistakes and add more details of what you would like to discuss with your colleague.

a. Open the file Cafe Proposal from your data disk.

b. Select the words [Current Date] and insert a date field using the Date and Time command. Be sure to use the form of the date shown in the final document.

c. Move paragraph 2 (beginning with "I would like to talk") below paragraph 3 (beginning with "As you also know").

d. Add the following new sentence as a new paragraph just before the last paragraph.

Here is a list of topics we would need to discuss before we could start this business.

Insert new lines as necessary to keep an empty line between every paragraph.

e. Open the file Decision List from your data disk that you created in Practice Exercise 1 above. Copy the list of items into the space beneath your new paragraph in the letter. Adjust the spacing around the list as needed.

---

123 Fourth Street
New York, NY 10012

February 3, 1999

Kyle Lewis
234 Fifth Street
New York, NY 10012

Dear Mr. Lewis:

I'm writing to see if I can interest you in a very exciting idea that I have. As you know, the number of people who use and are familiar with the Internet is increasing by leaps and bounds every year. This trend will only continue as the cost of personal computers continues to drop. It will also continue as the amount of useful information and services people can fiind on th Internet continues to grow.

As you also know, coffee shops have really become a big business in the last few years. People like to study, read, or just meet and talk at their local coffee shop while they enjoy a latte or mocha. A coffee shop is a gathering place for all kinds of people.

I would like to talk to you about the possibility of opening an Internet Café here in the city. An Internet Café joins two very popular trends into a business venture with a very good chance of success. In fact, there are already a number of successful models for this kind of business that we can follow.

Here is a list of topics we would need to discuss before we could start this business.

- Form of business
- Ownership
- Management
- Product list
- Location
- Source of capital

Please call me at your earliest convenience to discuss this business ide**a**. You can reach me at 555-6789.

Sincerely,

Student Name
Student Name

---

f. You want to change the word "type" in the first bulleted item in your list to another similar word. Use the Thesaurus to find a suitable synonym.

g. Change the left and right margins to 1 inch.

h. Using the Autotext feature to insert a closing on the second line under the last paragraph.

i. Replace [Student Name] with your name in the closing.

j. Perform a Spelling and Grammar check to eliminate errors.

k. Save your letter as Cafe Proposal Revised and print it. Sign it just above your name.

☆ ☆ ☆

5. To complete this exercise, you must have completed Practice Exercise 2 in this tutorial. Your business partner has written the text for a flyer to promote a sale on roast coffee, but has asked you to create the final design for the mailer and put it into its final form. You will need to add formatting features to turn your partner's words into a two-page informational flyer.

a.   Open the file Coffee Flyer.

b.   Insert a hard page break after the second line of text.

c.   Center the first line, make it brown, and change the font size to 72 pt.

d.   Center the second line, make it brown, and change the font size to 22 pt.

e.   Tab the first line of text on the second page of your flyer to 2.5 inches. Change the font size of this line to 24 pt.

f.   Use AutoShapes to insert a right-facing block arrow to the left of this line, sized to be 2 inches in length. Fill the block arrow with red.

g.   Copy the table of coffee descriptions and prices you created in the file Coffee Table to after the first two paragraphs.

h.   Indent the first line of each of the three full paragraphs on the second page to 0.5 inch.

i.   Use Find and Replace to quickly replace the single word "sale" with "Internet Coffee Sale" in the first and last full paragraphs on the second page.

j.   Add your name to the bottom of the second page. Print the flyer.

k.   Save the flyer as Coffee Flyer2.

The Internet Coffee Sale

Visit *www.somecoffee.com* for unbeatable prices!

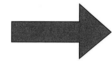 This way to great coffee!

Tired of brewing a wimpy cup of coffee that just doesn't have the punch you crave? Then point your Web browser to www.somecoffee.com for our huge Internet Coffee Sale, and have our high-powered java delivered right to your front door. You'll never buy bland supermarket coffee again.

Our Web-based business allows us to sell our wonderful blends to you at low prices, because we have lower overhead costs than the mega-chains. Check out the low prices available to you by ordering from us via the Internet.

DownTown Internet Café

Roast Coffee

Coffee	Description	Cost/Pound
Columbian Blend	Classic body and aroma	$11
French Roast	Sophisticated taste	$10
Kenyan	Robust and deep flavor	$12
Arabian Blend	Strong yet subtle	$11

Through January, take $2 off the regular coffee prices shown above.

Visit *www.somecoffee.com* today, and tomorrow you'll be enjoying the best coffee you've ever had. But hurry, our Internet Coffee Sale won't last forever.

On Your Own

6. Write a business letter requesting information on a reporting internship at Newsworthy Publishers. Include their address, which is 356 Haste Street, Berkeley, CA 94705. Tell the Internship Director, Christine Kent, why you are interested in reporting and three skills you can offer Newsworthy Publishers as a reporter. Include your skills in the form of a bulleted list. Be sure to also include the date, a salutation, two justified paragraphs, a closing, and your name as a signature. Use the business letter in Practice Exercise 4 as a model.

7. Using center tabs at 1.5 and 3 inches, create a tabbed table with the following information on maximum suggested daily fat intake for various daily calorie intakes. Bold and underline the column heads. Add style 2 tab leaders to the table entries. Include a paragraph describing the table contents.

Calories	Total Fat (in grams)	Total Saturated Fat (in grams)
1600	53 or less	18 or less
2000	65 or less	20 or less
2200	73 or less	24 or less
2500	80 or less	25 or less

8. Many people create lists of things they need to do each day or each week. In this problem you will create a list of things you need to do for the week.

- Create a numbered "to do" list of all the things you have to do this week (or all the things you would like to do this week) either in order of importance or in chronological order.

- Add a title that includes your name and the current date. Use the formatting techniques you have learned to improve the appearance of the list.

- Save the document as To Do List. Print the document.

9. Adventure Travel has recently hired a new sales representative, Amity Zeh, and you need to write a memo to let the rest of the sales staff know. Address the memo to the sales staff and add appropriate From, Date, and RE: lines. Using a bulleted list, describe Amity Zeh's past experience as an assistant manager at a movie theater and the skills you think she learned there. Describe as well her new function of selling Adventure Travel tours. Justify your paragraphs and indent the first lines. Add two AutoShapes to accent your memo.

10. Create a flyer to advertise something you have for sale (used car, used stereo, and so on). Integrate the following features into the flyer:

- Different fonts in different sizes, colors, and styles

- Bulleted or numbered list

- Indents

- An AutoShape

- A graphic from the Web

- A tabbed table with tab leaders

Creating Reports and Tables

Competencies

After completing this tutorial, you will know how to:

1. Create and modify an outline.
2. Apply styles.
3. Use Click and Type.
4. Hide spelling and grammar errors.
5. Create and update a table of contents.
6. Center a page vertically.
7. Create footnotes.
8. Use Document Map.
9. Wrap text around graphics.
10. Create a simple table.
11. Add captions and cross-references.
12. Sort a list.
13. Add headers, footers, and page numbers.
14. Print selected pages.

Case Study

Adventure Travel gives out information on their tours in a variety of forms. Travel brochures, for instance, contain basic tour information in a promotional format and are designed to entice potential clients to sign up for a tour. More detailed regional information packets are given to people who have already signed up for a tour, so they can prepare for their vacation. These packets include facts about each region's climate, geography, and culture. Additional informational formats include pages on Adventure Travel's Web site and scheduled group presentations.

Using Outline view helps you organize the topics in a document.

A table of contents listing can be created quickly from heading styles you have used in the document.

Tables, footnotes, and headers and footers, are among many Word features that can be used to create a report.

Part of your responsibility as advertising coordinator is to gather the information that Adventure Travel will publicize about each regional tour. Specifically, you have been asked to provide information for two of the new tours: the Tanzania Safari and the Machu Picchu Hike. Because this information is used in a variety of formats, your research needs to be easily adapted. You will therefore present your facts in the form of a general report on Tanzania and Peru.

In this tutorial, you will learn to use many of the features of Word 2000 that make it easy to create an attractive and well-organized report. A portion of the completed report is shown here.

Tanzania and Peru

Table of Contents

Stu...
Janua...

Tanzania

Geography and Climate

"In the midst of a great wilderness, full of wild be... a dazzlingly white cloud (qtd. in Cole 56). This is... the splendor of Africa's highest mountain, describ... white clouds he "fancied" he saw were the dense...

Tanzania is prima... the country's five... Nearly three-qua... that the Swahili w... "wasteland." Wit... Valley, which fo... Several of these... vegetation. Contr... coastal areas, wh... plateau slopes dra...

Figure 1-Serengeti Plains

Ngorongoro Conservation Area

Some of Tanzania's most distinguishing geograph... Conservation Area.[2] The park is composed of m... and plains. Among these features is the area's na... huge expanse, covering more than one hundred s... blend into swamps, lakes, rivers, and woodland.... is the Olduvai Gorge, commonly referred to as th... tools of prehistoric man were found. This find su... of humans who lived 1.75 million years ago.

Serengeti Plain

Adjacent to the western edge of the Ngorongoro Conservation Area is the Serengeti Plain. Its area is approximately 5,700 square miles, and its central savanna supports many grazing animals with plentiful water and lush grasses. Its southern portion is dry, receiving an average of only twenty inches of rainfall annually. The north is wooded grassland with watercourses and tributaries to larger rivers. Only two seasons occur on the Serengeti: dry and wet. The dry season occurs between June and October and the wet season between November to May.

[1] Kilimanjaro is 19,340 feet high, making it the fourth tallest mountain in the world.
[2] The Conservation Area is a national preserve spanning 3,196 square miles.

Created on 1/15/01 2:1...

Student Name 5

Works Cited

Camerapix Publishers International. <u>Spectrum Guide to Tanzania</u>. Edison: Hunter, 1992.

Cole, Tom. <u>Geographic Expeditions</u>. San Francisco: Geographic Expeditions, 1999.

Hudson, Rex A., ed. "Peru : A Country Study." <u>The Library of Congress – Country Studies</u>. 1992. <http://lcweb2.loc.gov/frd/cs/petoc.html#pe0049> (11 Jan. 2000).

"The Living Edens: Manu – Peru's Hidden Rainforest." <u>PBS Online</u>. <http://www.pbs.org/edens/manu> (11 Jan. 2000).

Valdizan, Mónica V. "Virtual Peru." 9 Jan. 1999. <http://www.xs4all.nl/~govertme/visitperu/> (11 Jan. 2000).

Concept Overview

The following concepts will be introduced in this tutorial:

1 **Style**   A style is a set of formats that is assigned a name.

2 **Section Break**   A section break divides a document into sections so that they can be formatted differently.

3 **Footnote and Endnote**   A footnote is a source reference or text offering additional explanation that is placed at the bottom of a page. An endnote is also a source reference or long comment that typically appears at the end of a document.

4 **Text Wrapping**   You can control how text appears around a graphic object by specifying the text wrapping style.

5 **Caption**   A caption is a title or explanation for a table, picture, or graph.

6 **Cross-Reference**   A cross-reference is a reference from one part of your document to related information in another part.

7 **Table**   A table is used to organize information into an easy-to-read format.

8 **Sorting**   Word can quickly arrange or sort paragraphs in alphabetical, numeric, or date order based on the first character in each paragraph.

9 **Header and Footer**   A header is a line or several lines of text at the top of each page just below the top margin. A footer is text at the bottom of every page just above the bottom margin.

Creating and Modifying an Outline

After several days of research, you have gathered many notes from various sources, including books, magazines and the WWW. However, the notes are very disorganized and you are having some difficulty getting started on writing the report.

Often the best way to start is by creating an outline of the main topics using Outline view. Outline view shows the hierarchy of topics in a document by displaying the different heading levels indented to represent their level in the document's structure. The arrangement of headings in a hierarchy of importance quickly shows the relationship between topics.

You can use Outline view to help you create a new document or to view and reorganize the topics in an existing document. You will create the organization of your research report using Outline view.

1 Open a blank new Word
document.

Click ▤ Outline View.

Your screen should be similar to
Figure 3–1.

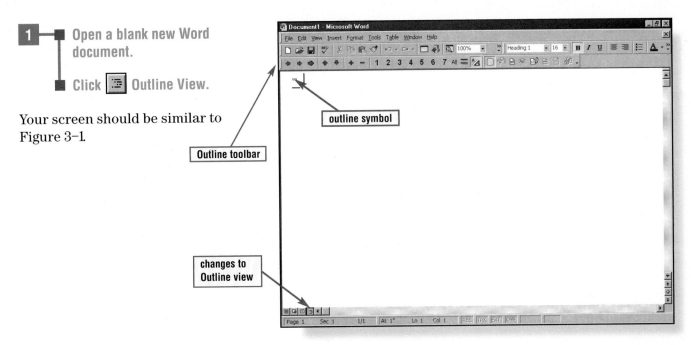

Figure 3–1

The Outline toolbar is displayed. It contains buttons that make it easy to
modify the outline. The first line of the blank document displays an outline symbol. There are three different outline symbols (▭ , ✛ , and ▪)
that are used to identify the levels of topics in the outline and to quickly
reorganize topics. You will begin by entering the main topic headings for
the report.

2 Type the following headings,
pressing ◁—Enter after each
except the last:

Tanzania
Climate
Geography
Animal Life
Peru
Culture
Historical Culture
Machu Picchu
Current Culture
Geography and Climate
La Costa
La Sierra
La Selva
Animal Life (do not press
◁—Enter))

Your screen should be similar to
Figure 3–2.

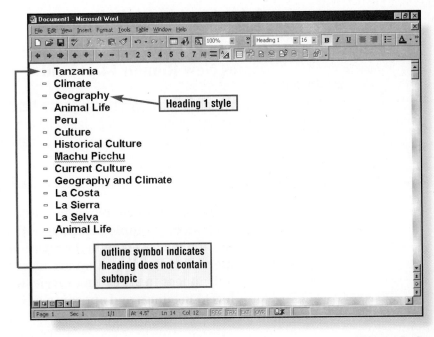

Figure 3–2

Each heading is preceded with the ▭ outline symbol. This symbol indicates the heading does not contain subtopics. As you create a new document in Outline view, Word automatically applies built-in heading styles to the text as it is entered in the outline.

Concept (1) Style

A **style** is a set of formats that is assigned a name. Word includes 75 predefined styles, or you can create your own custom styles. Many styles are automatically applied when certain features, such as footnotes, are used. Others must be applied manually to selected text.

Styles can be applied to characters or paragraphs. **Character styles** consist of a combination of any character formats in the Fonts dialog box that affect selected text. **Paragraph styles** are a combination of any character formats and paragraph formats that affect all text in a paragraph. A paragraph style can include all the font settings that apply to characters, as well as tab settings, indents, and line settings that apply to paragraphs. The default paragraph style is Normal, and it includes character settings of Times New Roman 12 pt and paragraph settings of left indent at 0, single line spacing, and left alignment. The Styles drop-down list box in the Formatting toolbar displays the style of the current selection.

In addition, many paragraph styles are designed to affect specific text elements such as headings, captions, and footnotes. One of the most commonly used styles is a heading style, which is designed to identify different levels of headings in a document. Heading styles include combinations of fonts, type sizes, bold, and italics. The first four heading styles and the formats associated with each are shown below:

Heading Level	Appearance
Heading 1	**Arial 16 pt bold**
Heading 2	***Arial 14 pt bold, italic***
Heading 3	**Arial 13 pt bold**
Heading 4	**Times New Roman 14 pt bold**

The most important heading in a document should be assigned a Heading 1 style. This style is the largest and most prominent. The next most important heading should be assigned the Heading 2 style, and so on. Headings give your reader another visual cue about how the information is grouped in your document.

Each topic you entered is initially formatted with a Heading 1 style. As you rearrange the topic headings and subheadings, different heading styles are applied based upon the position or level of the topic within the outline hierarchy. Headings that are level 1 appear as the top level of the outline and appear in a Heading 1 style, level 2 headings appear indented below level 1 headings and appear in a Heading 2 style, and so on.

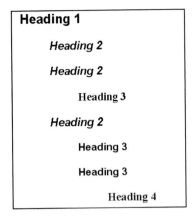

Next you need to arrange the headings by outline levels. The outline symbols are used to select and move the heading to a new location or level within the document. Dragging the outline symbol to the right or left changes the level. To demote a heading to a lower level, drag the symbol to the right; to promote a heading to a higher level, drag the symbol to the left. As you drag the symbol, a vertical dotted line appears at each outline level to show where the heading will be placed. First you will make the Climate topic heading a subtopic below the main heading of Tanzania.

Additional Information

In an existing document, you need to apply the heading style levels before viewing the document in Outline view.

3 ■ Drag the ▭ symbol of the Climate heading to the right one level.

The mouse pointer changes to ✛, indicating dragging it will move the heading.

You can also click ⬅ Promote and ➡ Demote to change outline levels.

Your screen should be similar to Figure 3–3.

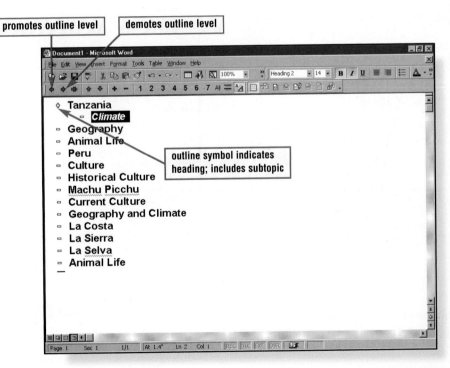

Figure 3–3

The Climate heading has changed to a Heading 2 style, and the heading is indented one level to show it is subordinate to the heading above it. The Tanzania heading now displays a ✛ outline symbol, which indicates the topic heading includes subtopics.

4 ■ Demote the Geography heading two levels.

Your screen should be similar to Figure 3–4.

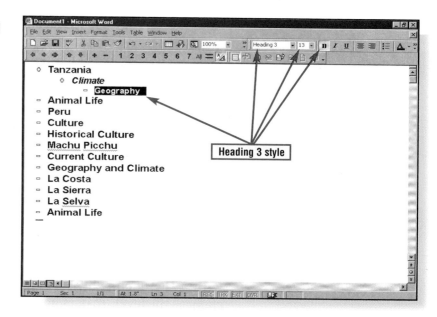

Figure 3–4

The Geography heading is now a Heading 3 style and is indented two levels in the outline.

5 ■ Demote the remaining topics to the heading levels shown below.

Animal Life	Level 2
Culture	Level 2
Historical Culture	Level 3
Machu Picchu	Level 4
Current Culture	Level 3
Geography and Climate	Level 2
La Costa	Level 3
La Sierra	Level 3
La Selva	Level 3
Animal Life	Level 2

Your screen should be similar to Figure 3–5.

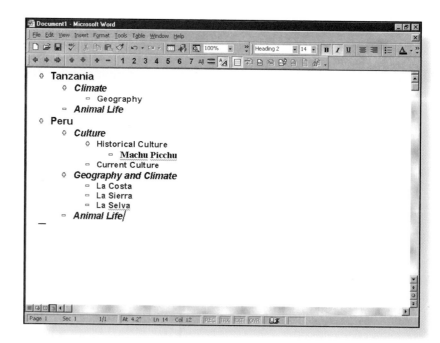

Figure 3–5

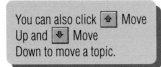

You can also click ⬆ Move Up and ⬇ Move Down to move a topic.

Next you want to change the order of topics. To move a heading to a different location, drag the outline symbol up or down. As you drag, a horizontal line shows where the heading will be placed when you release the mouse button.

6 Drag the Geography heading up above the Climate heading.

Promote the Geography heading to a level 2.

Demote the Climate heading to a level 3.

Your screen should be similar to Figure 3–6.

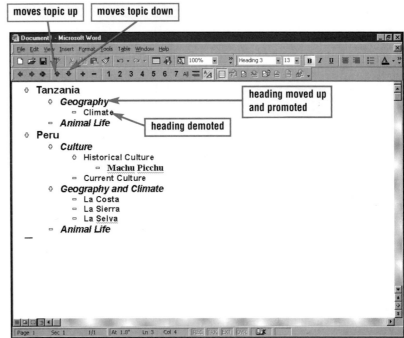

Figure 3–6

As you check the outline, you realize you forgot a heading for Culture under Tanzania.

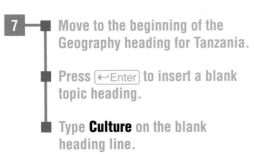

7 Move to the beginning of the Geography heading for Tanzania.

Press ⏎Enter to insert a blank topic heading.

Type **Culture** on the blank heading line.

Your screen should be similar to Figure 3–7.

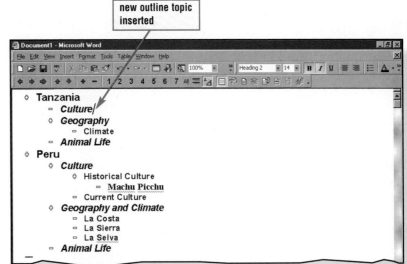

Figure 3–7

When you're satisfied with the organization, you can switch to Normal view or Page Layout view to add detailed body text and graphics.

8 ■ Switch to Normal view.

Your screen should be similar to Figure 3-8.

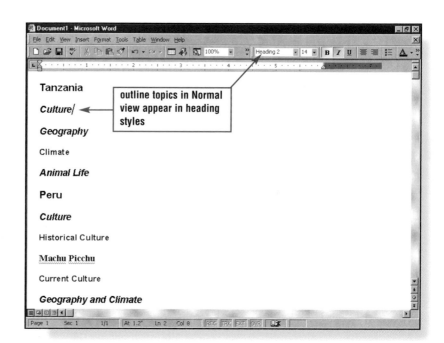

Figure 3-8

The topic headings appear left-aligned on the page in the style that was applied to the text as you created the outline.

Saving to a New Folder

Next you will save the outline you have created in a folder on your data disk that you will use to hold files related to the report. You can create a new folder at the same time you save a file.

1 ■ Choose File/Save As.

■ Change the Save In location to A: (or the appropriate location for your data files).

■ Click ⬜ Create New Folder.

Your screen should be similar to Figure 3-9.

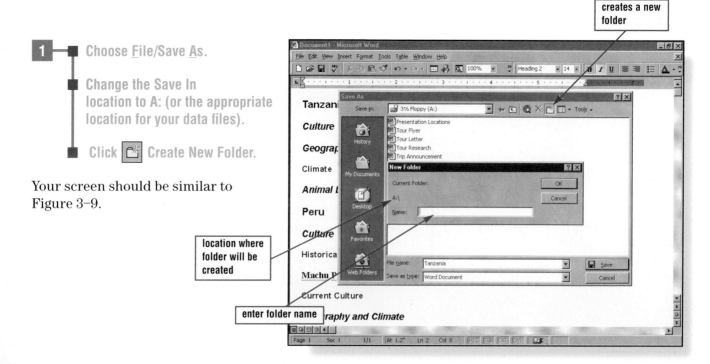

Figure 3-9

The new Folder dialog box displays the path of the active directory. This should be the location of your data disk (A:\). The new folder will be created as a subfolder in the active directory.

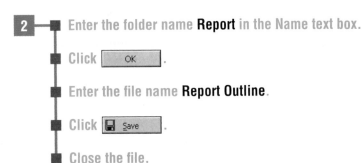

2 ■ Enter the folder name **Report** in the Name text box.

■ Click [OK].

■ Enter the file name **Report Outline**.

■ Click [🖫 S̲ave].

■ Close the file.

> **Additional Information**
>
> The rules for naming folders are the same as for naming filenames, except they typically do not include an extension.

The document is saved in the newly created folder, Report.

Hiding Spelling and Grammar Errors

You have continued to work on the report during the day and have entered most of the body information for the different topics. To see the information that has been added to the report,

1 ■ Open the file Tour Research from your data disk.

> Click 🖻 in the Open dialog box to move up one level into the root directory of your data disk.

■ Switch to Outline view.

■ Scroll the window to view the entire document outline.

■ Return to the top of the document.

Your screen should be similar to Figure 3–10.

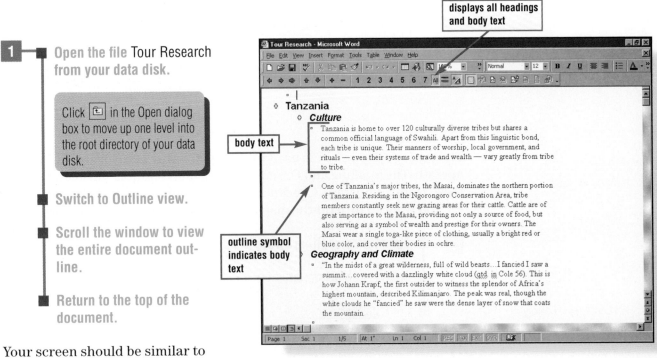

Figure 3–10

> Your outline may display less text than in Figure 3–10. This is because Outline view reflects the settings that were in effect on your computer when this feature was last used.

The document is displayed as an outline with the topic headings indented appropriately. The body text appears below the appropriate heading. Any text not identified with a heading style is considered body text. The small square to the left of a paragraph identifies it as body text.

As you scrolled the document, you noticed that many spelling and grammar errors were identified. They were mostly for words that are not in the dictionary. While working on a document, you can turn off the display of these errors so that they are not distracting as you work.

2 — ■ Choose <u>T</u>ools/<u>O</u>ptions.

■ Open the Spelling & Grammar tab.

Your screen should be similar to Figure 3–11.

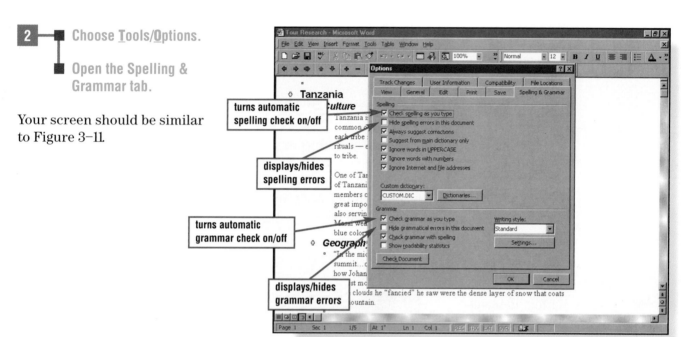

Figure 3–11

The Options dialog box is used to change the way many features in Word operate. The Spelling and Grammar tab displays options that control how these features operate. Checkmarks next to options indicate the setting is on. You want to turn off the display of spelling and grammar errors.

3 — ■ Select Hide <u>s</u>pelling errors in this document.

■ Select Hide gra<u>m</u>matical errors in this document.

■ Click [OK] .

The red and green wavy lines are no longer displayed. You can still run spelling and grammar checking manually to check errors at any time.

Collapsing and Expanding the Outline

In Outline view you can display as much or as little of the document text as you want. To make it easier to view and reorganize the document's structure, you can "collapse" the document to show just the headings you want. Alternatively, you can display part of the body text below each heading or the entire body text. You can then easily move the headings around until the order is logical, and the body text will follow the heading. The table below shows how you can collapse and expand the amount of text displayed in Outline view.2

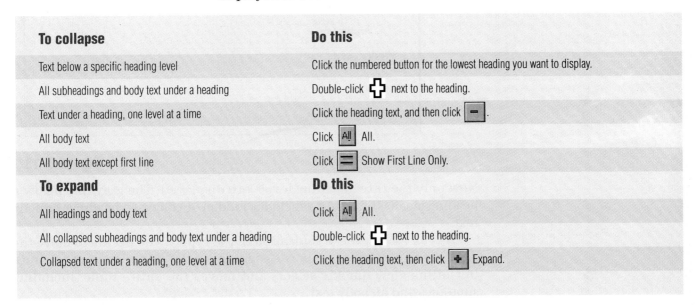

To collapse	Do this
Text below a specific heading level	Click the numbered button for the lowest heading you want to display.
All subheadings and body text under a heading	Double-click ✛ next to the heading.
Text under a heading, one level at a time	Click the heading text, and then click ⊟ .
All body text	Click All All.
All body text except first line	Click ☰ Show First Line Only.
To expand	**Do this**
All headings and body text	Click All All.
All collapsed subheadings and body text under a heading	Double-click ✛ next to the heading.
Collapsed text under a heading, one level at a time	Click the heading text, then click ⊞ Expand.

To see more of the outline, you will collapse the display of the text under the Geography and Climate heading.

1 ▪ Double-click ✛ of the Geography and Climate heading.

Your screen should be similar to Figure 3–12.

heading is collapsed and no body text is displayed

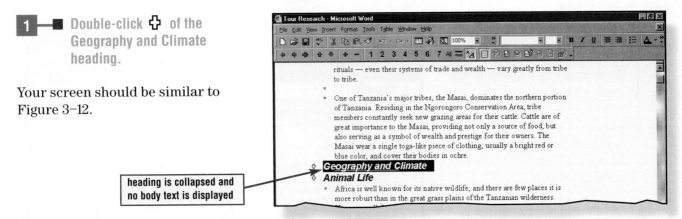

Figure 3–12

All the body text below this heading is hidden. You would like to see only the three heading levels of the document, not the body text, so you can quickly check its organization.

2 ■ Click **3** Show Heading 3.

Your screen should be similar to Figure 3–13.

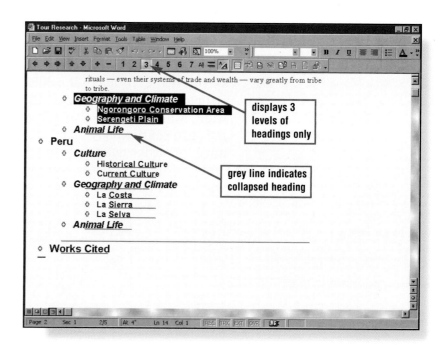

Figure 3–13

Now only the three heading levels are displayed. The gray line below a heading means the heading includes hidden or collapsed headings or body text.

As you look at the organization of the report, you decide to move the discussion of culture to follow Geography and Climate. Moving headings in Outline view quickly selects and moves the entire topic, including subtopics and all body text.

3 ■ Drag the Culture heading in the Tanzania section down to above the Animal Life heading in the same section.

■ Drag the Culture heading in the Peru section down to above the Animal Life heading in the same section.

Your screen should be similar to Figure 3–14.

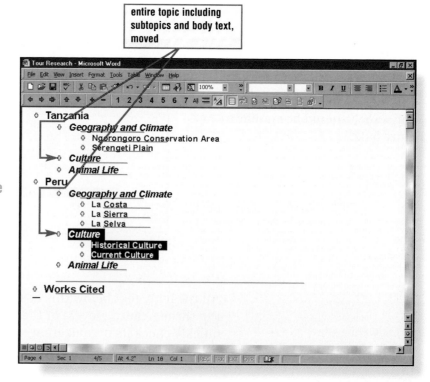

Figure 3–14

When you move or change the level of a heading that includes collapsed subordinate text, the collapsed text is also selected. Any changes you make to the heading, such as moving, copying, or deleting it, also affect the collapsed text. To verify this, you will display all body text again.

4 ■ Click ▣ Show All Headings.

■ Scroll the outline to see the top of the Peru section.

Your screen should be similar to Figure 3–15.

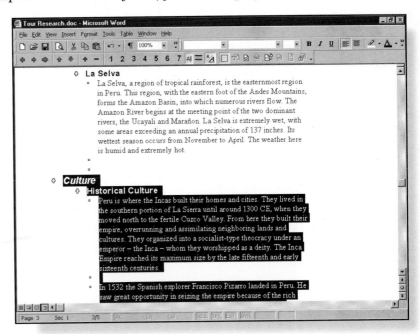

Figure 3–15

The subtopics and body text appear below the heading you moved.

Using Click and Type

Now that you are finished reorganizing the report, you want to add a title page. Generally, this page includes information such as the report title, the name of the author, and the date. You also want this page to include a table of contents list.

When preparing research reports, two styles of report formatting are commonly used: MLA (Modern Language Association) and APA (American Psychological Association). Although they require the same basic information, they differ in how this information is presented. For example, MLA style does not include a separate title page, but APA style does. The report you will create in this tutorial will use many of style requirements of the MLA. However, because this report is not a formal report to be presented at a conference or other academic proceeding, some liberties have been taken with the style to demonstrate features in Word.

You will create a new page above the first report topic and enter the title information in Print Layout view using the Click and Type feature. This feature, available only in Print Layout view, is used to quickly insert text, graphics, and other items in a blank area of a document, avoiding the need to enter blank lines.

Additional Information

For specific information about the MLA and APA style requirements, visit our Web site at www.mhhe.com/cit/apps/oleary.

1 ■ Switch to Print Layout view.

■ Press Ctrl + Home to move to the top of the document.

■ Press Ctrl + ←Enter to insert a hard page break and create a blank page above it.

■ Move to the top of the blank new page.

■ Move the mouse pointer from left to right across the page and observe the change in the mouse pointer.

Your screen should be similar to Figure 3–16.

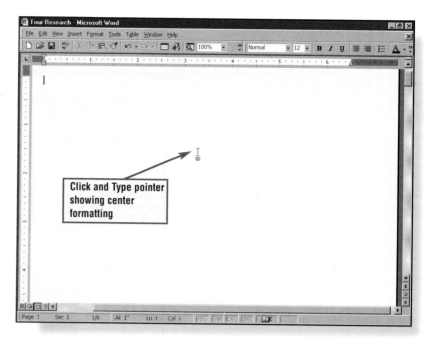

Figure 3–16

Print Layout view includes formatting "zones" that control the formatting that will be applied. As you move the mouse pointer through the zones, the I-beam pointer displays an icon that indicates which formatting will be applied when you double-click at that location. This is the Click and Type pointer. It also automatically applies several paragraph formatting and styles to the text as you type based upon the location of the pointer. Double-clicking on the location in the page moves the insertion point to that location and applies the formatting to the entry. You will enter the report title centered on the page.

2 ■ Point to the center of the page at the .5-inch vertical ruler position.

■ Double-click at this location while the mouse pointer is a I .

■ Type the report title, **Tanzania and Peru**

■ Click on the page to redisplay the Click and Type pointer.

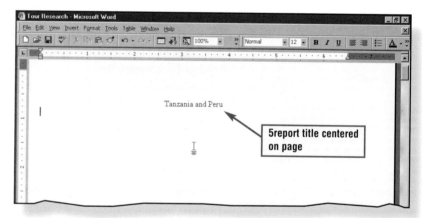

Figure 3–17

Your screen should be similar to Figure 3–17.

Next you will add a heading for the table of contents listing you will create, and you will enter your name and date at the bottom of the title page.

3 Double-click on the center of the page at the 1.5-inch vertical ruler position while the mouse pointer is a 🍷.

Enter the title **Table of Contents**

Click on the page to redisplay the Click and Type mouse pointer.

Type **Your name** centered at the 3-inch vertical ruler position.

Press ⏎Enter.

Type the current date centered below your name.

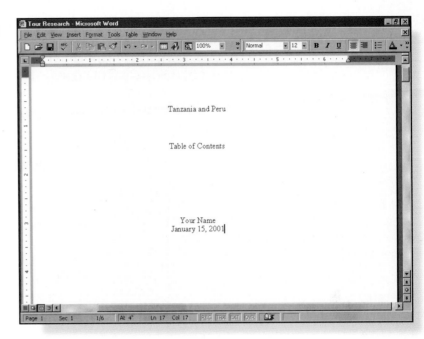

Your screen should be similar to Figure 3–18.

Figure 3–18

Applying Styles

Next you want to improve the appearance of the main title. You can do this quickly by applying a style to the title.

shows how paragraph will look if you apply the selected style

1 Move to anywhere in the Tanzania and Peru heading.

Choose F**o**rmat/S**t**yle.

If necessary, select All styles from the **L**ist drop-down list box.

If you accidentally apply the wrong style, reselect the text and select the correct style. To return the style to the default, select Normal.

Your screen should be similar to Figure 3–19.

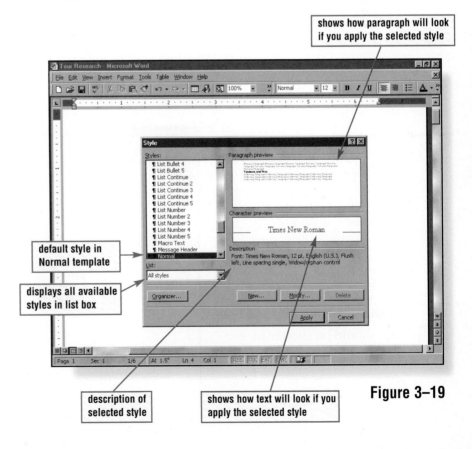

default style in Normal template

displays all available styles in list box

description of selected style

shows how text will look if you apply the selected style

Figure 3–19

The Style dialog box displays the names of all the preset styles in the Styles list box in alphabetical order. The style applied to the current selection, Normal, is highlighted, and the Preview areas show how text formatted in this style will appear. The specific format settings included in the currently selected style are displayed in the Description box. You will apply the Title style to the text.

2 ■ Select Title.

■ Click [Apply].

Your screen should be similar to Figure 3–20.

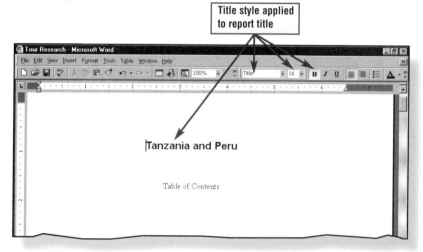

Figure 3–20

Notice that the entire heading appears in the selected style. This is because a Title style is a paragraph style, affecting the entire paragraph that the insertion point is on. Also notice that the Styles drop-down list box in the Formatting toolbar now displays "Title" as the style applied to the selection. This style includes formatting settings of Arial, 16 pt, and bold.

You want to apply a subtitle style to the Table of Contents heading next. Another way to select a style is from the Style button. The Style menu displays the names of the basic styles used in a document as well as those that have been applied already.

3 ■ Move the insertion point to anywhere in the Table of Contents heading.

■ Hold down ⟨⇧Shift⟩ while clicking [Normal ▼] Style.

> Clicking [Normal ▼] without holding ⟨⇧Shift⟩ displays the most commonly used styles only.

Your screen should be similar to Figure 3–21.

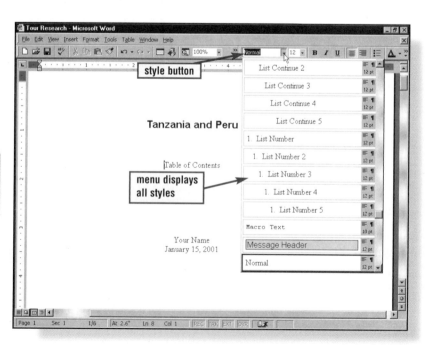

Figure 3–21

The Styles drop-down menu displays all available styles. The style name appears formatted in that style.

4 ─■ Choose Subtitle.

Your screen should be similar to Figure 3–22.

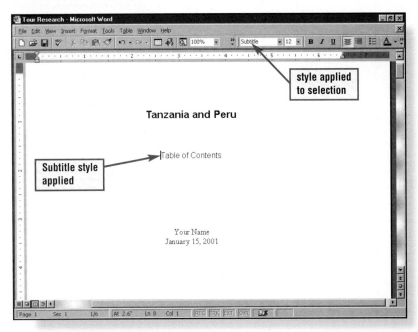

Figure 3–22

Creating a Table of Contents

- -

Now you are ready to create the table of contents. A table of contents is a listing of the topics that appear in a document and their associated page references. It shows the reader at a glance what topics are included in the document and makes it easier for the reader to locate information. Word can generate a table of contents automatically once you have applied heading styles to the document headings.

You want the table of contents listing to be displayed several lines below the subtitle heading on the title page. To create the table of contents,

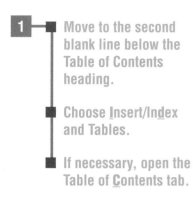

1 Move to the second blank line below the Table of Contents heading.

Choose Insert/Index and Tables.

If necessary, open the Table of Contents tab.

Your screen should be similar to Figure 3–23.

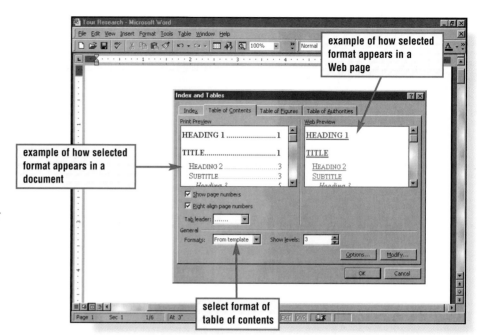

Figure 3–23

From the Index and Tables dialog box, you first need to select the format or design of the table of contents. The Formats drop-down list box displays the name of the default table of contents style, From Template, that is supplied with the Normal template. The Preview boxes display an example of how the selected format will look in a normal printed document or in a document when viewed in a Web browser. The From Template format option is used to design your own table of contents and save it as a template by modifying the existing format.

2 ▪ **Open the Formats drop-down list box.**

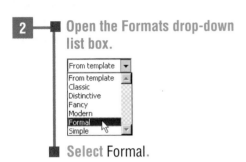

▪ **Select** Formal.

Your screen should be similar to Figure 3–24.

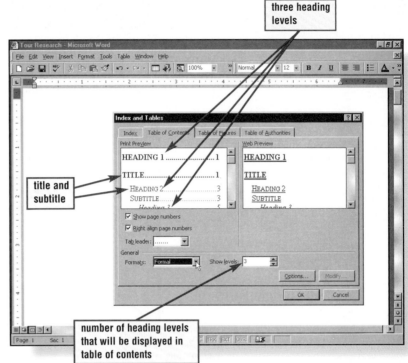

Figure 3–24

The Print Preview area shows this style will display the page numbers flush with the right margin, and with a series of tab leaders between the heading and the page number. This format will display all entries in the document that are formatted with Headings 1, 2, and 3, and Title and Subtitle styles in the table of contents. You want the table of contents to include topics formatted with the Heading 4 styles but to exclude those formatted with the Title and Subtitle headings. You will modify the settings for the Formal format and turn off the use of these styles.

3 ▪ **Change the level number in the Show Levels text box to 4.**

▪ **Click** Options... .

Your screen should be similar to Figure 3–25.

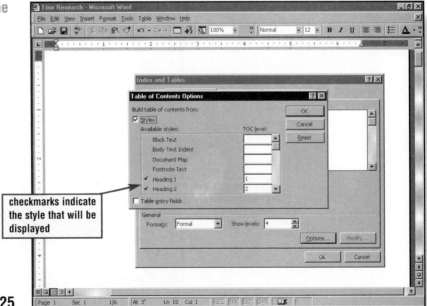

Figure 3–25

The Table of Contents Options dialog box shows the styles that are used to build the table of contents. The checkmark indicates which styles Word will look for in the document to use as items to include in the table of contents, and the number indicates the level at which they will be displayed. To clear a style selection, simply delete the number from the TOC level text box.

4 ■ Scroll the Available Styles list to see the Subtitle and Title selections.

■ Delete the numbers from the Subtitle and Title text boxes to clear the checkmarks.

■ Click **OK** .

Your screen should be similar to Figure 3–26.

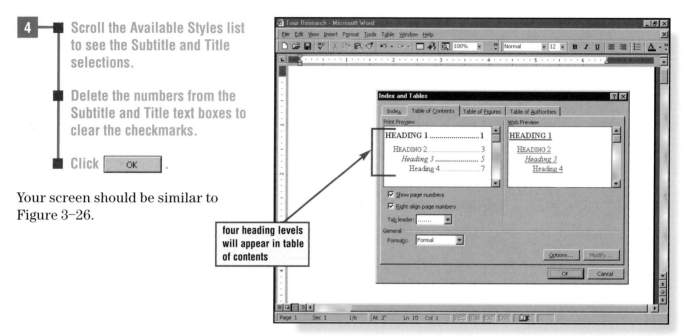

four heading levels will appear in table of contents

Figure 3–26

The Print Preview area now shows that four levels of headings will be reflected in the table of contents listing, and the title and subtitle will not be included. To generate the listing,

5 ■ Click **OK** .

Your screen should be similar to Figure 3–27.

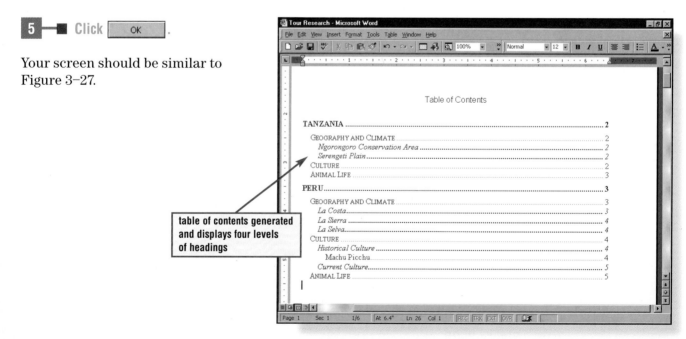

table of contents generated and displays four levels of headings

Figure 3–27

Word searches for headings with the specified styles, sorts them by heading level, references their page numbers, and displays the table of contents in the document. The headings that were assigned a Heading 1 style are aligned with the left margin, and subordinate heading levels are indented as appropriate.

6 Use the directional keys to move the insertion point anywhere in the table of contents list.

Your screen should be similar to Figure 3–28.

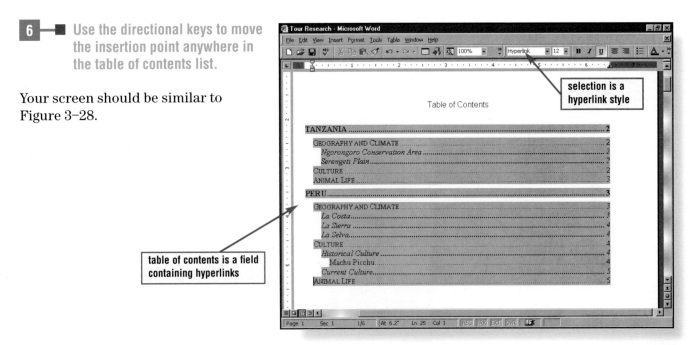

Figure 3–28

Notice that the text in the table of contents is shaded, indicating it is a field. This means it can be updated to reflect changes you may make at a later time in your document. Also notice that the Style button displays "Hyperlink." Each line in the table of contents has been changed to a hyperlink. Now simply clicking on a line will move you directly to that location in the document.

The mouse pointer shape changes to a 🖑 when pointing to a hyperlink.

7 Click the Peru table of contents line.

The insertion point jumps to that location in the document.

8 Return to the title page.

Centering a Page Vertically

Finally, you want the information on the title page to be centered vertically. To do this,

1. ■ Zoom to Whole Page.

   ■ Select the entire title page by dragging, starting at the very top of the page through the line below the date (see Figure 3–29).

   ■ Choose File/Page Setup.

   ■ If necessary, open the Layout tab.

Your screen should be similar to Figure 3–29.

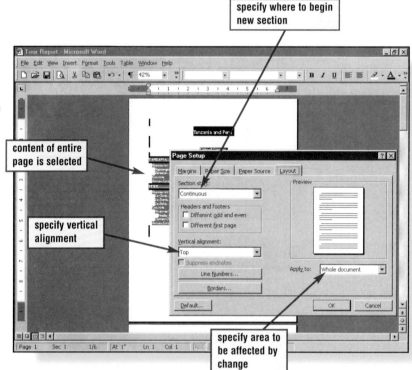

Figure 3–29

From the Vertical Alignment list box you specify how the text is to be aligned on the page vertically. In addition, in the Apply To list box you need to specify what part of the text you want to be aligned to the new setting. Because you will be applying a format to one page that is different than the rest of the document, you also need to create a section break after this page.

Concept ② Section Break

A **section break** divides a document into sections so that they can be formatted differently. The section break identifies the end of a section and stores the format settings, such as margins and page layout, associated with that section of the document. The section break mark is a double dotted line that contains the words "Section Break" followed by the type of section break.

There are three types of section break you can insert: New Page, Continuous, and Odd or Even page. The different types control the location where text following the section break begins.

Option	Action
New Page	Starts the new section on the next page.
Continuous	Starts the new section on the same page.
Odd or Even	Starts new section on the next odd or even numbered page.

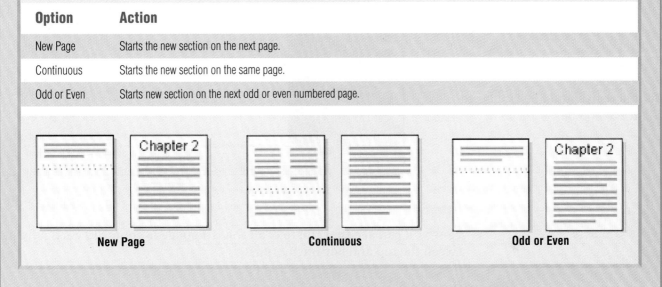

New Page   Continuous   Odd or Even

Word automatically inserts section breaks for you if you change the formatting of selected text, such as inserting columns or centering selected text vertically on a page. You can also manually enter section breaks using Insert/Break.

To center the selected text vertically on the page,

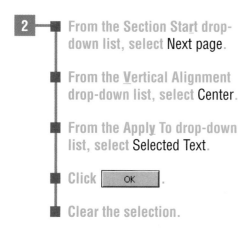

2
- From the Section Start drop-down list, select **Next page**.
- From the <u>V</u>ertical Alignment drop-down list, select **Center**.
- From the Appl<u>y</u> To drop-down list, select **Selected Text**.
- Click   OK   .
- Clear the selection.

Your screen should be similar to Figure 3–30.

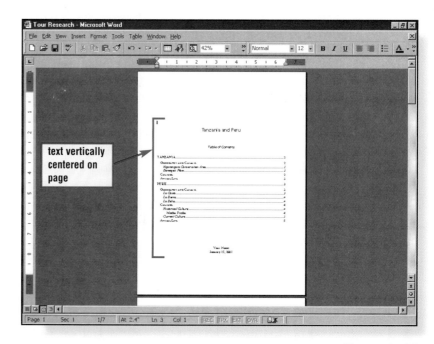

Figure 3–30

Now you can see that the text on the title page is centered vertically between the top and bottom margins.

3 ■ Change to Normal view and scroll to the bottom of page 1.

Your screen should be similar to Figure 3–31.

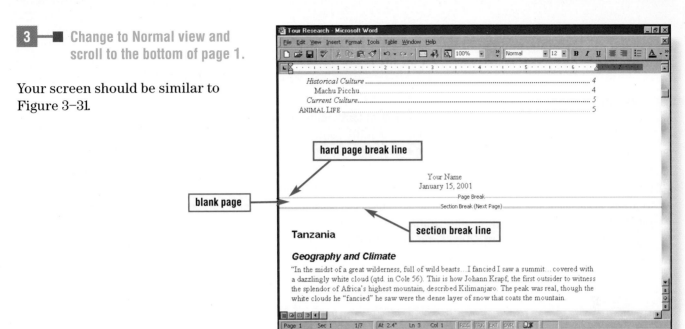

Figure 3–31

A double dotted line containing the words "Section Break" identifies the type of document break that was inserted. Word requires a section break at this location because a different page format, in this case vertical alignment, was used in the title page than the rest of the document. This type of section break starts the next page of the document on a new page. Therefore the page break you added earlier, if left in the document, would cause a blank page to be printed.

> To remove a hard page break, select the page break line and press Delete.

4 ■ Delete the hard page break line.

■ Delete the blank line above the Tanzania heading.

Adding Footnotes

Next you need to add several footnotes to the document.

Concept ③ Footnote and Endnote

A **footnote** is a source reference or text offering additional explanation that is placed at the bottom of a page. An **endnote** is also a source reference or long comment that typically appears at the end of a document. You can have both footnotes and endnotes in the same document.

Footnotes and endnotes consist of two parts, the note reference mark and the note text. The **note reference mark** is commonly a superscript number appearing in the document at the end of the material being referenced (for example, text[1]). It can also be a character or combination of characters. The **note text** for a footnote appears at the bottom of the page on which the reference mark appears. The footnote text is separated from the document text by a horizontal line called the **note separator.** Endnote text appears as a listing at the end of the document. The Footnote command on the Insert menu will automatically number and place footnotes and endnotes in a document.

This document already includes parenthetical source references entered according to the MLA style for research papers. However, you still have several reference notes you want to add to help clarify some information included in the report. The first reference you want to add is the height of Mt. Kilimanjaro. This note will follow the reference to the mountain at the end of the first paragraph in the Geography and Climate section for Tanzania. Before using the Footnote command, the insertion point must be positioned where the footnote number is to be displayed.

1 ■ Move to the end of the first paragraph after the word mountain.

■ Choose Insert/Footnote.

> The keyboard shortcut to insert a footnote using the default settings is [Alt]+[Ctrl]+F.

Your screen should be similar to Figure 3–32.

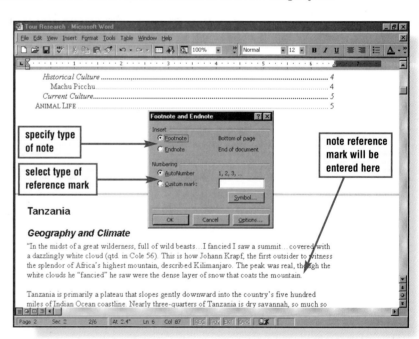

Figure 3–32

In the Footnote and Endnote dialog box, you specify whether you want to create footnotes or endnotes and the type of reference mark you want to appear in the document: a numbered mark or a custom mark. A custom mark can be any nonnumeric character, such as an asterisk, that you enter in the text box. You want to create numbered footnotes, so the default settings of Footnote and AutoNumber are acceptable.

2 ▬ Click [OK].

Your screen should be similar to Figure 3–33.

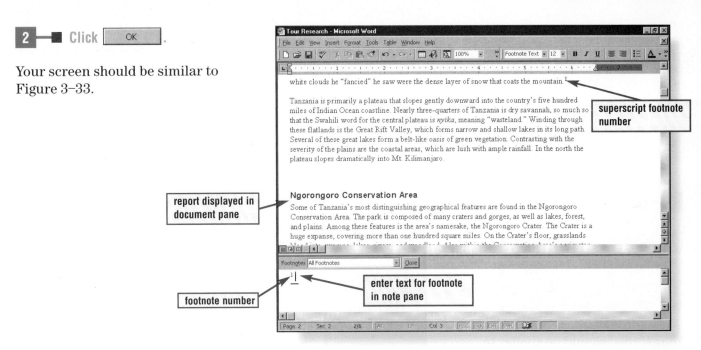

superscript footnote number

report displayed in document pane

footnote number

enter text for footnote in note pane

Figure 3–33

The workspace is now horizontally divided into upper and lower panes. A pane is a split window and area that you can view and scroll independently. The report is displayed in the document pane. The footnote number, 1, appears as a superscript in the document where the insertion point was positioned when the footnote was created. The note pane displays the footnote number and the insertion point. This is where you enter the text for the footnote. When you enter a footnote, you can use the same menus, commands, and features as you would in the document window. Any commands that are not available are dimmed.

3 ▬ Type **Mt. Kilimanjaro is 19,340 feet high, making it the fourth tallest mountain in the world.**

Your screen should be similar to Figure 3–34.

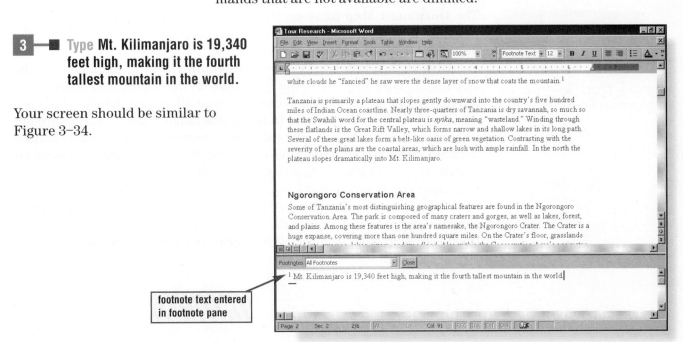

footnote text entered in footnote pane

Figure 3–34

Using the Document Map

The second footnote you want to add is in the Geography and Climate section under Peru. To quickly move to that location in the document, you can use the Document Map feature. Document Map is used to quickly navigate through the document and keep track of your location in it.

1 ■ Click 🔍 Document Map.

🔍 Document Map is on the Standard toolbar. The menu equivalent is **V**iew/**D**ocument Map.

Your screen should be similar to Figure 3–35.

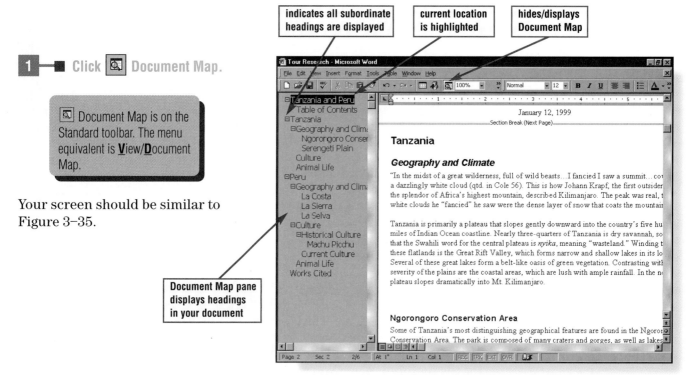

Figure 3–35

The Document Map can be displayed in all views.

The **Document Map pane** on the left edge of the window displays the headings in your document. The document pane on the right displays the document in Normal view.

All text that is formatted with a heading style is displayed in the Document Map pane. Notice the ▬ symbol to the left of many of the headings in the Document Map; this indicates that all subordinate headings are displayed. A ➕ symbol would indicate that subordinate headings are not displayed. When your document does not contain any headings formatted with heading styles, the program automatically searches the document for paragraphs that look like headings (for example, short lines with a larger font size) and displays them in the Document Map. If it cannot find any such headings, the Document Map is blank. The highlighted heading shows your location in the document. Clicking on a heading in the Document Map quickly jumps to that location in the document.

2 Change the zoom to Page Width.

Click on La Sierra in the Document Map.

Your screen should be similar to Figure 3–36.

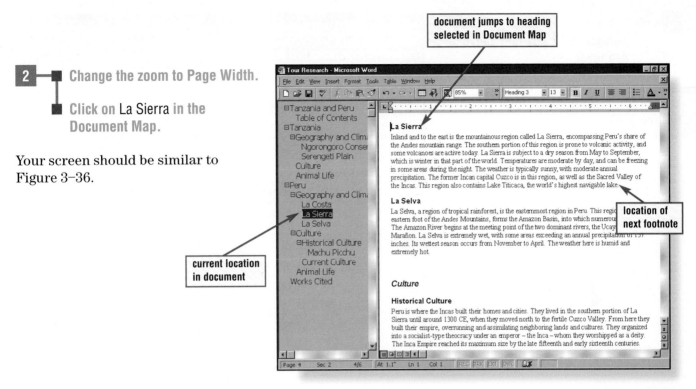

document jumps to heading selected in Document Map

location of next footnote

current location in document

Figure 3–36

The selected heading is displayed at the top of the window and highlighted in the Document Map. You can now quickly locate the text you want to reference. You want to add a note about Lake Titicaca.

3 Click at the end of the paragraph following the word lake to place the insertion point for the footnote.

Choose <u>I</u>nsert/Foot<u>n</u>ote/  .

The footnote number 2 is entered at the insertion point location. The note pane is active again, so you can enter the text for the second footnote. The Document Map pane is temporarily hidden while the note pane is displayed. When you close the note pane, the Document Map pane will be displayed again.

4 In the footnote pane type **Lake Titicaca is 12,507 feet above sea level.**

Your screen should be similar to Figure 3–37.

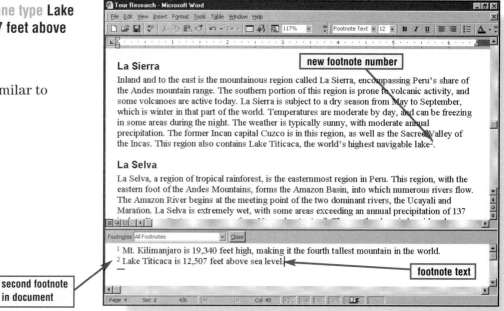

second footnote in document

Figure 3–37

5 Click Close.

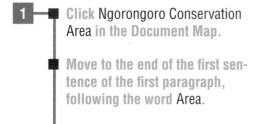

To delete a footnote or endnote, highlight the reference mark and press Delete. The reference mark and associated note text are removed, and the following footnotes are renumbered.

Now you realize that you forgot to enter a footnote earlier in the text, on page 2.

1 Click Ngorongoro Conservation Area in the Document Map.

Move to the end of the first sentence of the first paragraph, following the word Area.

Insert a footnote at this location.

Your screen should be similar to Figure 3–38.

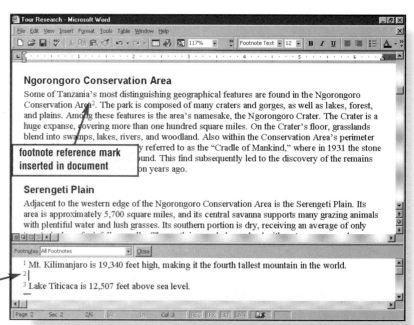

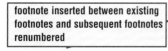

footnote inserted between existing footnotes and subsequent footnotes renumbered

Figure 3–38

Notice that this footnote is now number 2 in the document, and a blank footnote line has been entered in the note pane for the footnote text. Word automatically adjusted the footnote numbers when the new footnote was inserted.

2 ■ In the footnote pane, type **The Conservation Area is a national preserve spanning 3,196 square miles.**

You are finished entering footnotes for now.

3 ■ Click Close .

■ Click on Tanzania in the Document Map.

■ Click Document Map.

Viewing Footnotes

In Normal view you can see the footnote associated with a note reference mark by pointing to the note reference mark. The footnote will be displayed as a ScreenTip.

1 ■ Point to note reference mark 1 in the document.

Your screen should be similar to Figure 3–39.

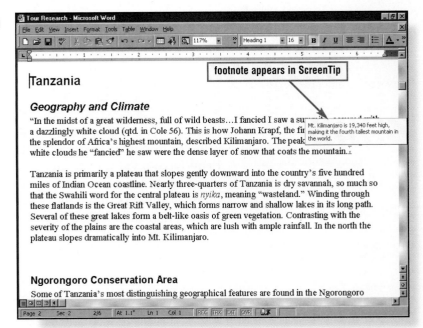

Figure 3–39

Finally, you want to see how the footnotes will actually appear when the document is printed.

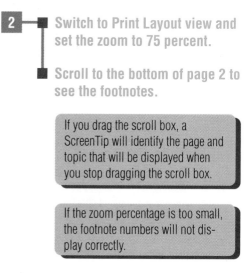

2 Switch to Print Layout view and set the zoom to 75 percent.

■ Scroll to the bottom of page 2 to see the footnotes.

If you drag the scroll box, a ScreenTip will identify the page and topic that will be displayed when you stop dragging the scroll box.

If the zoom percentage is too small, the footnote numbers will not display correctly.

Your screen should be similar to Figure 3–40.

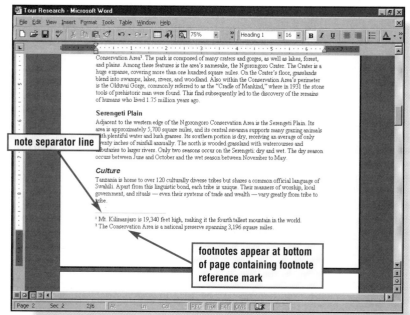

Figure 3–40

The footnotes are displayed immediately above the bottom margin separated from the text by the note separator line. They appear at the bottom of the page containing the footnote reference mark.

3 Scroll to the bottom of page 4 to see the third footnote.

Inserting a Footnote in Print Layout View

While looking at this page, you decide you want to explain the CE abbreviation following the date 1300 in the Historical Culture section. While in Print Layout view, you can insert, edit, and format footnotes just like any other text. After using the command to insert a footnote, the footnote number appears in the footnote area at the bottom of the page, ready for you to enter the footnote text.

1 Move the insertion point following CE in the first sentence below Historical Culture.

Insert a footnote at this location.

Type **Common Era (CE) is the period dating from the birth of Christ.**

Your screen should be similar to Figure 3–41.

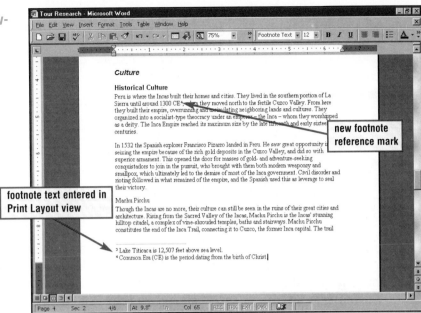

Figure 3–41

2 Check the other footnotes. If you see any other errors, correct them.

Wrapping Text Around Graphics

Next you want to add a picture of the Tanzania landscape to the report that will complement the subject of the first topic. You would like the picture to appear after the fourth paragraph on page 2.

1 Use the Document Map to move to the Geography and Climate head under Tanzania.

Move to the beginning of the second paragraph.

Close the Document Map and change the zoom to Text Width.

Insert the picture Serengeti from your data disk.

Adjust the size of the picture to approximately 2 by 2 inches.

If necessary, display the Picture toolbar.

> Dragging the corner handle maintains the original proportions of the picture.

Your screen should be similar to Figure 3–42.

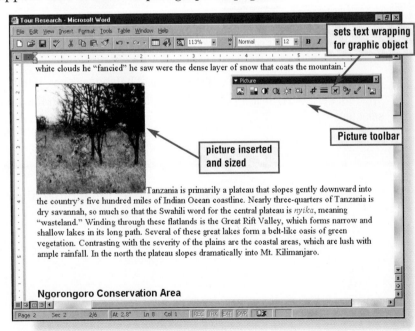

Figure 3–42

Next you want to have the text wrap around the graphic object.

Concept ④ Text Wrapping

You can control how text appears around a graphic object by specifying the text wrapping style. The text in the paragraph may wrap around the object in different ways. The text wrapping styles are shown below.

Inline with Text **Square** **Tight** **Through** **Top and Bottom** **Behind Text** **In Front of Text**

By default, pictures are inserted into Word documents as an **inline object.** This means it is positioned directly in the text at the position of the insertion point. It becomes part of the paragraph, and any paragraph alignment settings that apply to the paragraph also apply to the picture.

A graphic can be changed to a **floating object** that is inserted in the drawing layer. The drawing layer is a separate layer from the text and allows graphic objects to be positioned precisely on the page, including in front of and behind other objects including the text. You can change an inline image to a floating picture by changing the wrapping style of the object. As floating objects are added to a document, they stack in layers and may overlap. You can move floating objects up or down within a stack using the O<u>r</u>der option on the D<u>r</u>aw button of the Drawing toolbar.

Triangle is on top of stack   **Triangle is sent to the back**   **Square is brought to the front**

Sometimes it is easy to lose a floating object behind another. If this happens you can press ⎯Tab⎯ to cycle forward or ⇧Shift + ⎯Tab⎯ to cycle backward through the stacked objects until the one you want is selected.

You want the text to wrap to the right side of the picture.

2 Click 🖼 Text Wrapping.

Choose 🖼 Square.

> The menu equivalent is
> Format/Picture/Layout/Square

If necessary, resize the picture until the text wraps around it as in Figure 3–43.

Clear the selection by clicking anywhere outside the graphic object.

Your screen should be similar to Figure 3–43.

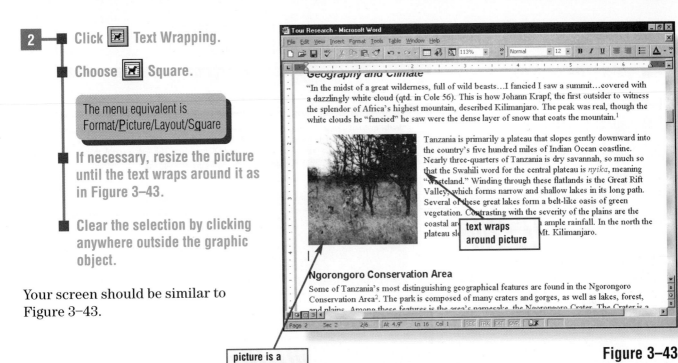

picture is a floating object

Figure 3–43

The picture is now a floating object. Because the picture is aligned with the left margin, the text wraps to the right side of the object. If you moved the picture, the text would wrap around the object on all sides.

Adding a Figure Caption

Next you want to add a caption below the picture.

Concept ⑤ Caption

A **caption** is a title or explanation for a table, picture, or graph. Captions aid the reader in quickly finding information in a document. Word can automatically add captions to graphic objects as they are inserted, or you can add them manually. The caption label can be changed to reflect the type of object to which it refers, such as a table, chart, or figure. In addition, Word automatically numbers graphic objects and adjusts numbering when objects of the same type are added or deleted.

1 Move to the blank line below the picture.

Choose Insert/Caption.

Your screen should be similar to Figure 3–44.

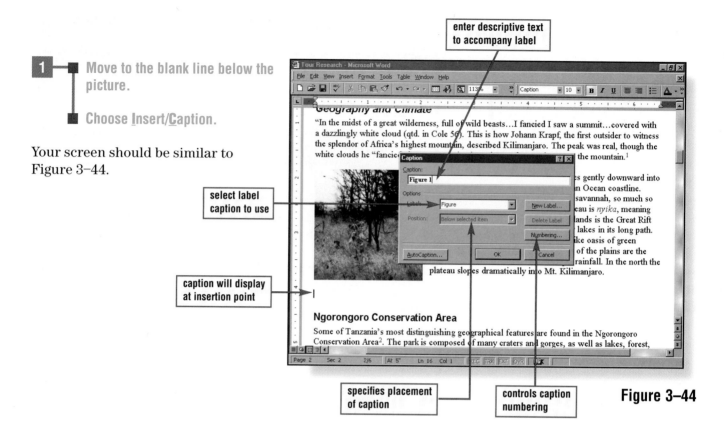

Figure 3–44

The Caption options are described in the table below.

Option	Description
Label	Select from one of three default captions: Table, Figure, or Equation.
Position	Specify the location of the caption, either above or below a selected item. When an item is selected, the Position option is available.
New Label	Create your own captions.
Numbering	Specify the numbering format and starting number for your caption.
AutoCaption	Turns on the automatic insertion of a caption (label and number only) when you insert selected items into your document.

The most recently selected caption label and number appear in the Caption text box. You want the caption to be Figure 1, and you want to add additional descriptive text.

2 In the Caption text box following "Figure 1," type **- Serengeti Plain**.

Click [OK].

Your screen should be similar to Figure 3–45.

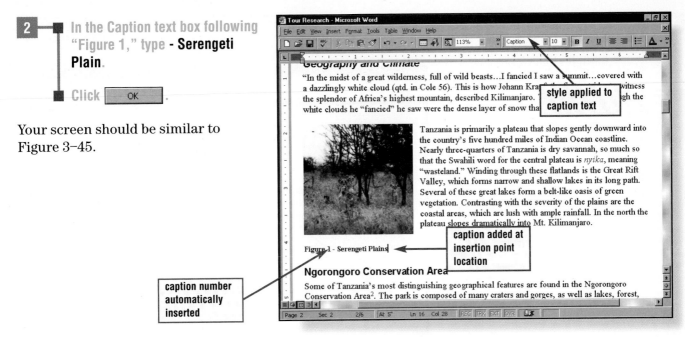

Figure 3–45

The caption label appears below the figure. It can be moved like any other text.

Adding a Cross-Reference

In the Animal section of the report, you discuss the animals found in the Serengeti Plain. You want to include a cross-reference to the picture at this location.

Concept 6 Cross-Reference

A **cross-reference** is a reference from one part of your document to related information in another part. Once you have captions you can also include cross-references. For example, if you have a graph in one part of the document that you would like to refer to in another section, you can add a cross-reference that tells the reader what page the graph is on. A cross-reference can also be inserted as a hyperlink, allowing you to jump to another location in the same document or in another document.

1
Move to following the word prey in the third paragraph in the Animal Life section (page 3).

Press [Spacebar].

Type **(see**

Press [Spacebar].

Choose Insert/Cross-reference.

Your screen should be similar to Figure 3–46.

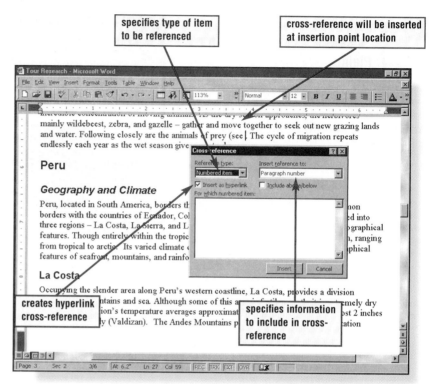

specifies type of item to be referenced

cross-reference will be inserted at insertion point location

creates hyperlink cross-reference

specifies information to include in cross-reference

Figure 3–46

In the Cross-reference dialog box, you need to specify the type of item you are referencing and how you want the reference to appear. You want to reference the Serengeti picture, and you want only the label "Figure 1" entered in the document.

cross-reference is to a figure

displays label and number only of referenced item

2
From the Reference Type drop-down list box, select Figure.

From the Insert Reference To list box, select Only label and number.

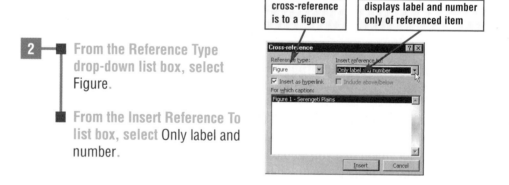

Because there is only one figure in this document, the Refers To list box correctly selects the figure to refer to. If there were multiple figures in the document, you would need to select the appropriate figure. Notice that the Insert as Hyperlink option is selected by default. This option creates a hyperlink between the cross-reference and the caption. The default setting is appropriate.

3 ● Click [Insert].

● Click [Close].

● Type **)**.

Your screen should be similar to Figure 3–47.

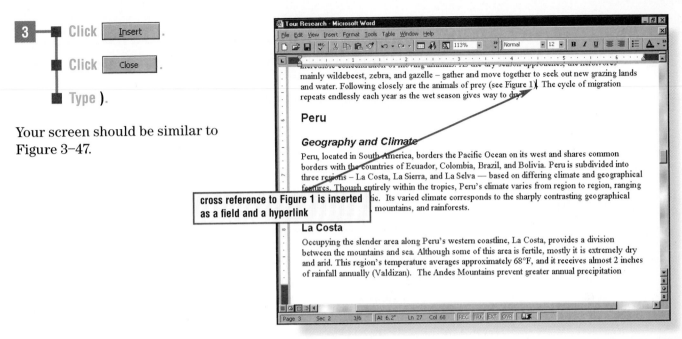

cross reference to Figure 1 is inserted as a field and a hyperlink

Figure 3–47

A cross-reference is entered into the document as a field. Therefore, if you insert another picture, the captions and cross-references will renumber automatically. When you are working on a long document with several figures, tables, and graphs, this feature is very helpful.

To use a cross-reference hyperlink to jump to the source it references, simply click on it.

4 ● Click on the Figure 1 cross-reference.

The document automatically jumps to the caption beneath the figure. The Web toolbar is automatically displayed, because many hyperlinks are to items on the World Wide Web.

> The mouse pointer shape changes to a 🖑 when pointing to a hyperlink to show that the cross-reference is a hyperlink.

5 ● Close the Web toolbar.

Creating a Simple Table

Next you want to add a table comparing the rainfall and temperature data for the three regions of Peru.

Concept 7 Table

A table is used to organize information into an easy-to-read format. A table displays information in horizontal rows and vertical columns. The insertion of a row and column creates a cell in which you can enter data or other information.

Cells in a table are identified by a letter and number, called a table reference. Columns are identified from left to right beginning with the letter A, and rows are numbered from top to bottom beginning with the number 1. The table reference of the top leftmost cell is A1 because it is in the first column (A) and first row (1) of the table. The second column is cell B2. The fourth cell in column 3 is C4.

	A	B	C	D
1	Cell A1			
2		Cell B2		Cell D2
3				
4			Cell C4	
5				
6				

column B → (points to column B)

row 3 → (points to row 3)

Tables are a very effective method for presenting information. The table layout organizes the information for the reader and greatly reduces the number of words they have to read to interpret the data. Use tables whenever you can to make your documents easier to read.

The table you want to create will display the rainfall and temperature data for the three regions in the columns. The rows will display the data for the each region. Your completed table will be similar to the one shown below.

Region	Annual Rainfall (Inches)	Average Temperature (Fahrenheit)
La Costa	2	68
La Sierra	35	54
La Selva	137	80

Word includes several different methods you can use to create tables. One method (Table/Convert Text to Table) will quickly convert text that is arranged in columns into a table. Another method uses the Table/Insert/Table command to create a simple table consisting of the same number of rows and columns. Finally, table/Draw Table is used to create any type of table, but is most useful for creating complex tables that contain cells of different heights or a varying number of columns per row. You will use the Draw Table feature in later tutorials.

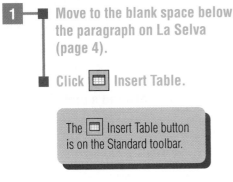

1 Move to the blank space below the paragraph on La Selva (page 4).

Click Insert Table.

The Insert Table button is on the Standard toolbar.

Your screen should be similar to Figure 3-48.

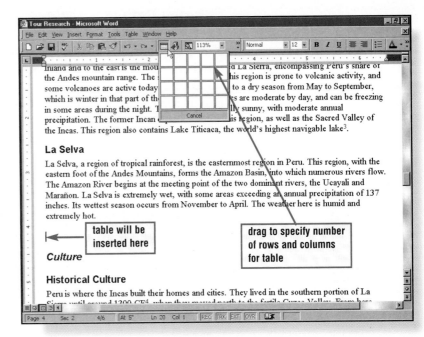

Figure 3-48

The Insert Table drop-down menu displays a grid in which you specify the number of rows and columns for the table. Moving the mouse pointer over the grid highlights the boxes in the grid and defines the table size. The dimensions are reflected in the bottom of the grid.

2 Select a 3-by-3 table.

Click on the lower right corner of the selection.

Your screen should be similar to Figure 3-49.

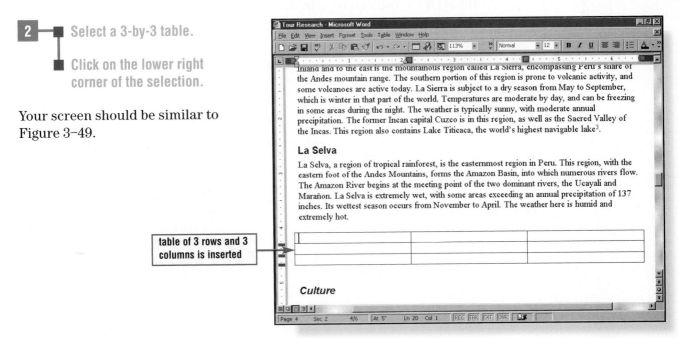

Figure 3-49

A table the full width of the page is drawn. It has equal sized columns and is surrounded by a black borderline.

Entering Data in a Table

- -

Now you are ready to enter information in the table. Each cell contains a single line space where you can enter data. You can move from one cell to another by using the arrow keys or by clicking on the cell. In addition, you can use the keys shown in the table below to move around a table.

To move to	Press
Next cell in a row	Tab ⇥
Previous cell in row	⇧ Shift + Tab ⇥
First cell in row	Alt + Home
Last cell in row	Alt + End
First cell in column	Alt + Page Up
Last cell in column	Alt + Page Down
Previous row	↑
Next row	↓

The mouse pointer may also appear as an arrow ⬇ when positioned in the table. When it is an arrow and you click on a cell, the entire cell is highlighted, indicating that it is selected. You will learn more about this feature shortly.

You will begin by entering the information for La Costa in cells A1 through C1. You can type in the cell as you would anywhere in a normal document.

1 ■ If necessary, click cell A1.

■ Type **La Costa**

■ Press Tab ⇥.

■ In the same manner, type **2** in cell B1 and **68** in cell C1.

■ Click cell A2 and continue entering the information shown on the right.

Cell	Entry
A2	La Sierra
B2	35
C2	54
A3	La Selva
B3	137
C3	80

Your screen should be similar to Figure 3–50.

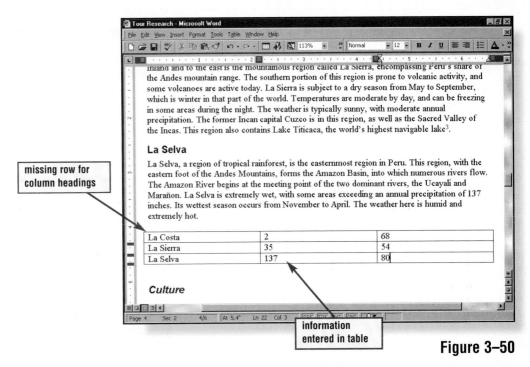

missing row for column headings

information entered in table

Figure 3–50

Inserting a Row

After looking at the table, you realize you forgot to include a row above the data to display the column headings.

1 ■ Move to any cell in row 1.

■ Choose T<u>a</u>ble/<u>I</u>nsert/Rows <u>A</u>bove.

■ Click in the new row to clear the highlight.

Your screen should be similar to Figure 3–51.

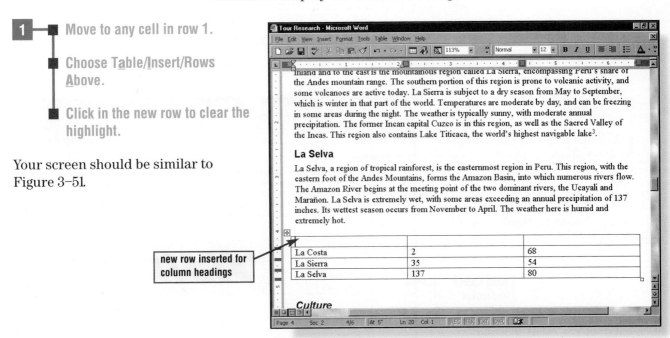

new row inserted for column headings

Figure 3–51

Now you are ready to add the text for the headings.

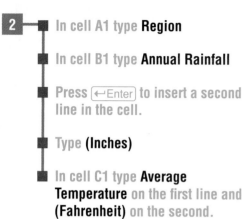

2
- In cell A1 type **Region**
- In cell B1 type **Annual Rainfall**
- Press ⟨←Enter⟩ to insert a second line in the cell.
- Type **(Inches)**
- In cell C1 type **Average Temperature** on the first line and **(Fahrenheit)** on the second.

Your screen should be similar to Figure 3–52.

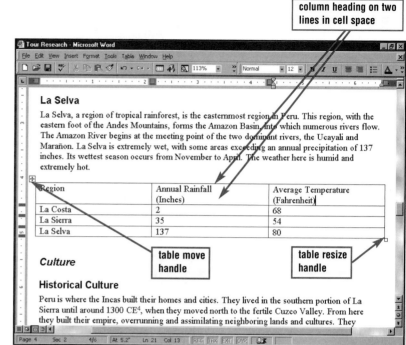

Figure 3–52

Sizing a Table

The table is much larger than it needs to be. To quickly reduce the overall table size, you can drag the resize handle ☐. This handle appears whenever the mouse pointer rests over the table. Once the table is smaller, you then want to center it between the margins. The ⊞ move handle is used to move the table.

1
- Drag the ☐ resize handle to decrease the width of the table to 5 inches (see Figure 3–53).
- Drag the ⊞ move handle to center the table.

Your screen should be similar to Figure 3–53.

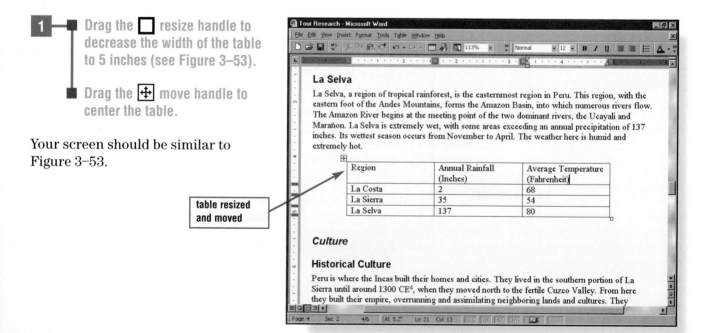

Figure 3–53

Formatting the Table

To enhance the appearance of the table, you can apply many different formats to the cells. This is similar to adding formatting to a document, except the formatting affects the selected cells only.

You want the entries in the cells A1 through C1, and B2 through C4, to be centered in their cell spaces. As you continue to modify the table, many cells can be selected and changed at the same time. You can select areas of a table using the Select command on the Table menu. However, it is often faster to use the procedures described in the table below.

Area to Select	Procedure
Cell	Click the left edge of the cell when the pointer is ⇗.
Row	Click to the left of the row when the pointer is ⇗.
Column	Click the top of the column when the pointer is ↓.
Multiple cells, rows, or columns	Drag through the cells, rows, or columns, or select the first cell, row, or column and hold down ⇧Shift while clicking on another cell, row, or column.
Contents of next cell	Press Tab⇥.
Contents of previous cell	Press ⇧Shift + Tab⇥.
Entire table	Press Alt + 5 (on the numeric keypad with NumLock off) or click ✛.

1 Select cells B2 through C4.

Click  Center.

In the same manner, center cells A1 through C1.

Your screen should be similar to Figure 3–54.

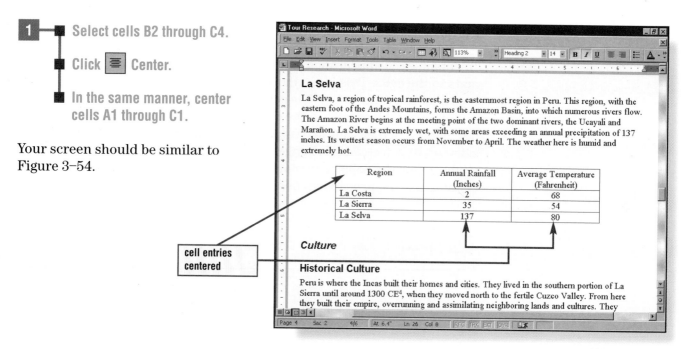

Figure 3–54

A quicker way to apply formats to a table is to use the table AutoFormat feature. This feature includes built-in combinations of formats that can be applied to a table. The AutoFormats consist of a combination of fonts, colors, patterns, borders, and alignment settings.

2 Move to any cell of the table.

Choose T<u>a</u>ble/Table Auto<u>F</u>ormat.

Your screen should be similar to Figure 3–55.

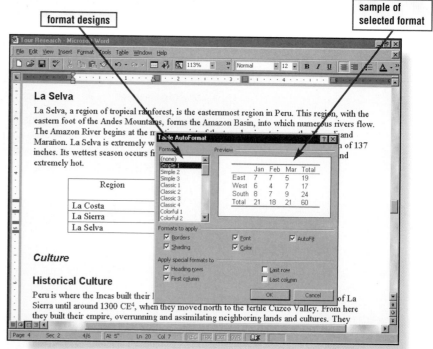

Figure 3–55

From the AutoFormat dialog box, you select the format design you want to apply to the table. The Preview area shows how the selected format will look.

The None AutoFormat option removes an existing AutoFormat.

3 To preview the AutoFormats, highlight several names in the Formats list and look at the table layout in the Preview box.

You think the Classic 4 format would enhance that appearance of the table nicely.

4 Select Classic 4.

Click OK.

Center the table again.

Your screen should be similar to Figure 3–56.

AutoFormat applied to table includes color shading and font changes

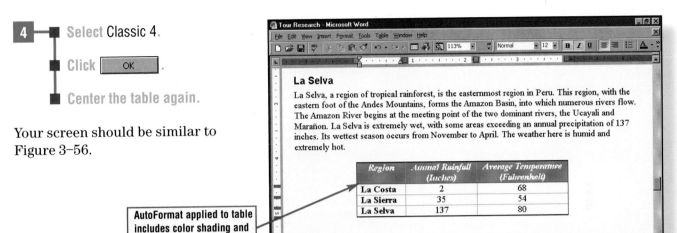

Figure 3–56

The table is reformatted to the new design. The table lines now appear gray, indicating they will not print and are only displayed to help you while entering data on screen. Color shading is applied to the top row along with a change in the text color and italics. Using AutoFormat was much faster than applying these features individually.

Updating the Table of Contents

You have made many modifications to the report since generating the table of contents, so you want to update the page references in the listing. Because the table of contents is a field, if you add or remove headings, rearrange topics, or make other changes that affect the table of contents listing, you can quickly update the table of contents using the Update Field command on the shortcut menu.

You can also press F9 to quickly update a field.

1 Right-click on the table of contents to display the shortcut menu.

Choose Update Field.

From the Update Table of Contents dialog box, you specify the part of the table of contents that needs updating. You need to update the page references.

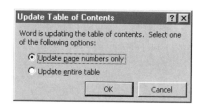

2 ■ If necessary, choose Update page numbers only.

■ Click OK.

Your screen should be similar to Figure 3–57.

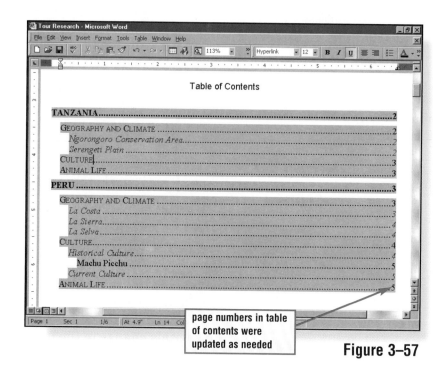

page numbers in table of contents were updated as needed

Figure 3–57

The page numbers referenced by each table of contents hyperlink have been updated as needed.

Sorting a List

The last page of the report contains the list of works cited in the report. According to the MLA style, each work directly referenced in the paper must appear in alphabetical order by author's last name. The first line is even with the left margin, and subsequent lines of the same work are indented .5 inch. This page needs to be alphabetized and formatted.

To quickly arrange the references in alphabetical order, you can sort the list.

Concept ⑧ Sorting

Word can quickly arrange or **sort** paragraphs in alphabetical, numeric, or date order based on the first character in each paragraph. The sort order can be ascending (A to Z, 0 to 9, or earliest to latest date) or descending (Z to A, 9 to 0, or latest to earliest date). The table below describes the rules that are used when sorting.

Sort by	Rules
Text	First, items beginning with punctuation marks or symbols (such as !, #, $, %, or &) are sorted.
	Second, items beginning with numbers are sorted. Dates are treated as three-digit numbers.
	Third, items beginning with letters are sorted.
Numbers	All characters except numbers are ignored. The numbers can be in any location in a paragraph.
Date	Valid date separators include hyphens, forward slashes (/), commas, and periods. Colons (:) are valid time separators. If unable to recognize a date or time, Word places the item at the beginning or end of the list (depending on whether you are sorting in ascending or descending order).
Field results	If an entire field (such as a last name) is the same for two items, Word next evaluates subsequent fields (such as a first name) according to the specified sort options.

When a tie occurs, Word uses the first non-identical character in each item to determine which item should come first.

---

1 ⎯ Move to the last page of the document.

■ Select the list of references.

■ Choose T**a**ble/**S**ort

Your screen should be similar to Figure 3–58.

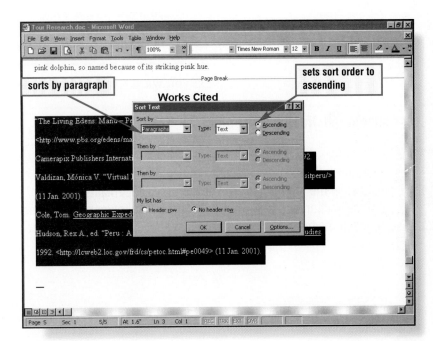

Figure 3–58

The default Sort Text settings will sort by text and paragraphs in ascending order.

2
- Click [OK].

- Drag the Hanging Indent marker to the .5-inch tab stop on the ruler.

- Clear the selection.

> need to move to correct alphabetical location

Your screen should be similar to Figure 3–59.

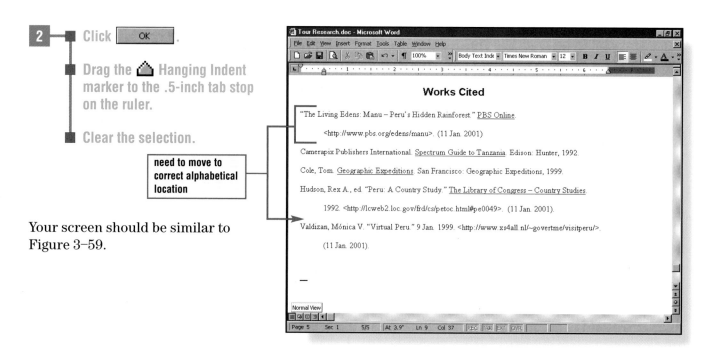

Figure 3–59

The list is in ascending alphabetical order. Entries that are longer than one line appear with a hanging indent. Notice however that the citation for "The Living Edens . . ." is still at the top of this list. This is because Word sorts punctuation first. You will need to move this item to below the citation for Hudson.

3
- Select the entire "The Living Edens . . ." citation and drag it to below the Hudson citation.

Adding Headers and Footers

Next you want to add a header to the report.

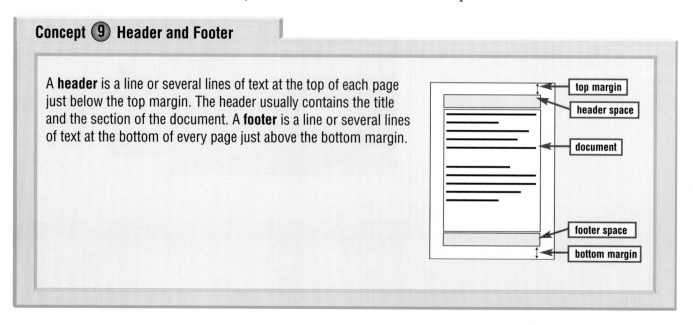

Concept 9 Header and Footer

A **header** is a line or several lines of text at the top of each page just below the top margin. The header usually contains the title and the section of the document. A **footer** is a line or several lines of text at the bottom of every page just above the bottom margin.

top margin

header space

document

footer space

bottom margin

You want the header to display your name and the page number.

1 Move to the Tanzania heading on page 2.

Choose <u>V</u>iew/<u>H</u>eader and Footer.

Your screen should be similar to Figure 3–60.

Additional Information

MLA style requires that headers and footers be placed .5 inch from the top and bottom of the page. The header must include the page number preceded by the author's name.

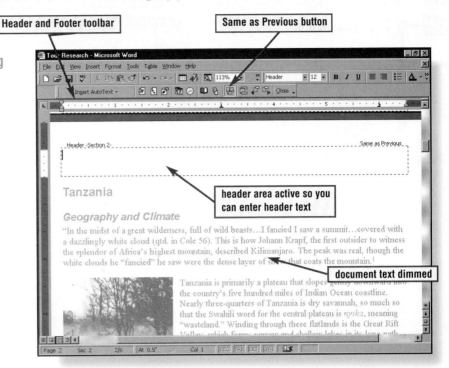

Header and Footer toolbar

Same as Previous button

header area active so you can enter header text

document text dimmed

Figure 3–60

The document dims, the header area becomes active, and the Header and Footer toolbar is displayed.

You could also double-click in the header or footer area to activate it.

Refer to the Introduction to Common Office 2000 Features section for directions to dock a toolbar.

2 If necessary, dock the Header and Footer toolbar below the Standard and Formatting toolbars.

Notice that you are in the header for section 2. Section 1 is the title page. In the upper right corner is the message, "Same as Previous." This means that the section 2 header will be the same as section 1. You do not want the title page to have a header, so you need to turn off the Same as Previous option.

If [icon] Same as Previous is on, the header in the sections before and after the section in which you are entering a header will have the same header.

3 Click [icon] Same as Previous.

You type in the header as if it were a mini-document. The header and footer text can be formatted just like any other text. In addition, you can control the placement of the header and footer text by specifying where it should appear: left-aligned, centered, or right-aligned in the header or footer space. You will enter your name followed by the page number, right-aligned.

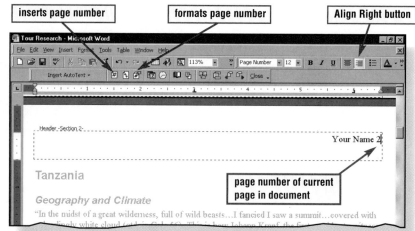

4 ■ Type **Your name**.

■ Press [Spacebar].

■ Click [#] **Insert Page Number**.

■ Click [≡] **Align Right**.

Your screen should be similar to
Figure 3-61.

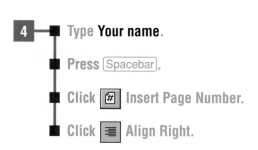

Figure 3-61

The page number 2 is displayed, because that is the current page in the
document. You do not want the title page included in the page numbering,
but instead want to begin page numbering with the first page of section 2.
To make this change,

5 ■ Click [#] **Format Page Number**.

> You can also add and format
> page numbers using
> Insert/Page Numbers.

Your screen should be similar to
Figure 3-62.

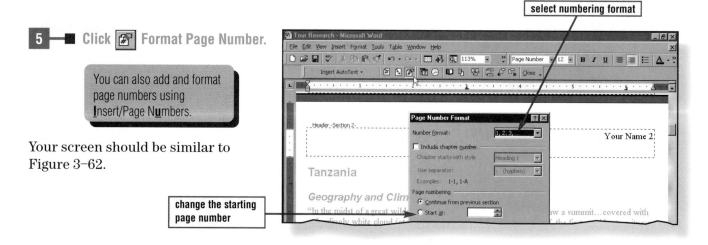

Figure 3-62

The Page Number Format dialog box is used to change the format of page
numbers, include chapter numbers, and to change the page numbering sequence. The default page numbering setting continues the numbering
from the first section. To reset the page number sequence to begin section
2 with page 1,

> The default Start At setting
> begins numbering with 1.

6 ■ Choose Start **At**.

■ Click .

The header now displays "1" as the current page number.

You want to display the date in the footer. To quickly add this information, you will use an AutoText entry.

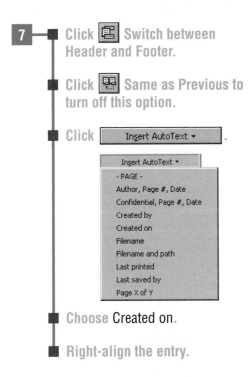

7 ■ Click 🗗 Switch between Header and Footer.

■ Click 🔳 Same as Previous to turn off this option.

■ Click Insert AutoText ▾ .

■ Choose Created on.

■ Right-align the entry.

Your screen should be similar to Figure 3–63.

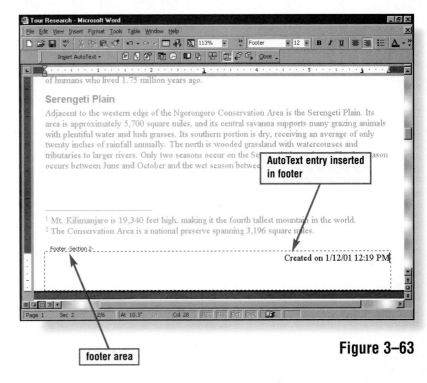

Figure 3–63

The AutoText entry is displayed followed by the date and time.

8 ■ Close the Header and Footer toolbar.

■ In section 2, scroll down to see the top of page 2 and the bottom of page 1.

Your screen should be similar to Figure 3–64.

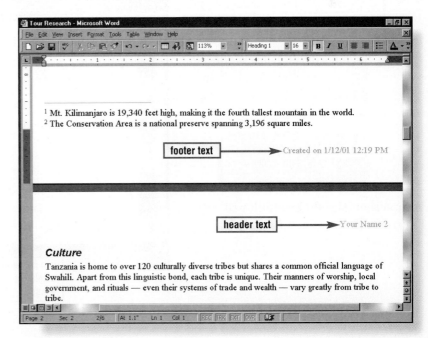

Figure 3–64

The document area is active again, and the header and footer text appears dimmed.

Showing Spelling and Grammar Errors

Before you print the report, you want to check the spelling and grammar of the entire document, including the footnotes and header. First you will turn on the display of the spelling and grammar errors again.

1 ■ Choose Tools/Options/Spelling and Grammar.

■ Select Hide spelling errors in this document.

■ Select Hide grammatical errors in this document.

■ Click OK .

■ Click ✓ Spelling and Grammar.

■ Choose Ignore All for all proper names and special terms and abbreviations. Respond appropriately to any other located errors.

Printing Selected Pages

You are now ready to print the report.

1 ■ Save the edited document as Tour Report in the Report folder.

■ Preview the report.

■ Set the Print Preview window to display two pages by clicking ▦ Multiple Pages and then selecting 1x2 pages.

The menu equivalent is View/Zoom/Many Pages.

Your screen should be similar to Figure 3–65.

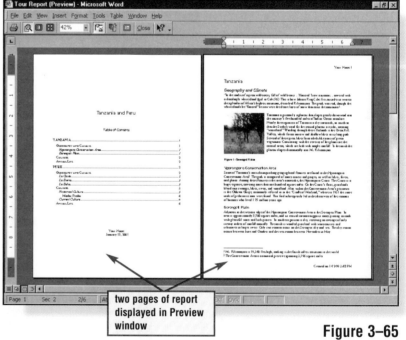

two pages of report displayed in Preview window

Figure 3–65

You would like to print only the first, second, fourth, and sixth pages of the document. To do this you use the Print dialog box to select the pages you want to print.

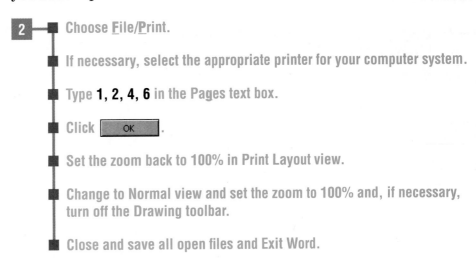

2 ▪ Choose <u>F</u>ile/<u>P</u>rint.

▪ If necessary, select the appropriate printer for your computer system.

▪ Type **1, 2, 4, 6** in the Pages text box.

▪ Click [OK] .

▪ Set the zoom back to 100% in Print Layout view.

▪ Change to Normal view and set the zoom to 100% and, if necessary, turn off the Drawing toolbar.

▪ Close and save all open files and Exit Word.

Concept Summary

Tutorial 3: Creating Reports and Tables

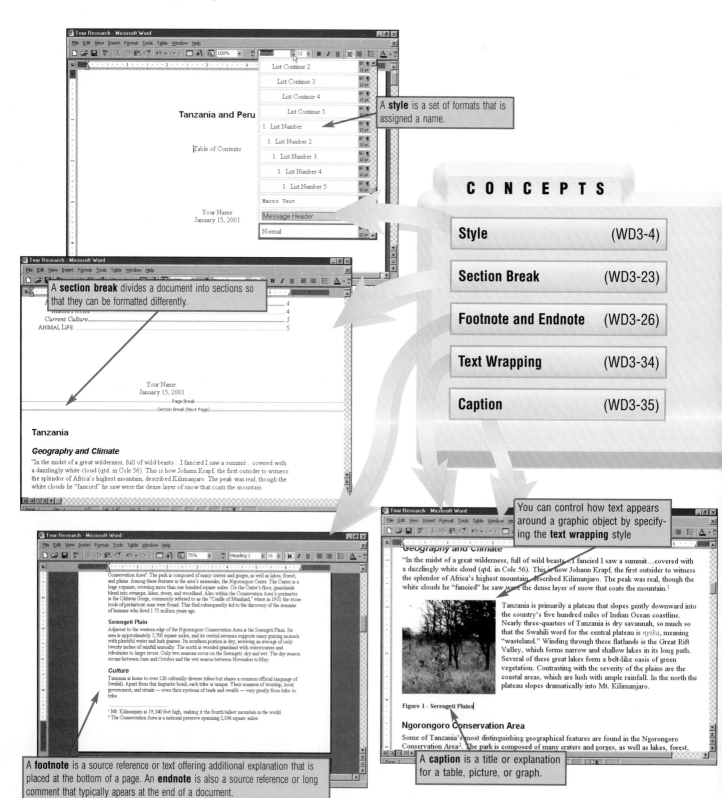

A **style** is a set of formats that is assigned a name.

A **section break** divides a document into sections so that they can be formatted differently.

You can control how text appears around a graphic object by specifying the **text wrapping** style

A **footnote** is a source reference or text offering additional explanation that is placed at the bottom of a page. An **endnote** is also a source reference or long comment that typically apears at the end of a document.

A **caption** is a title or explanation for a table, picture, or graph.

C O N C E P T S

Style	(WD3-4)
Section Break	(WD3-23)
Footnote and Endnote	(WD3-26)
Text Wrapping	(WD3-34)
Caption	(WD3-35)

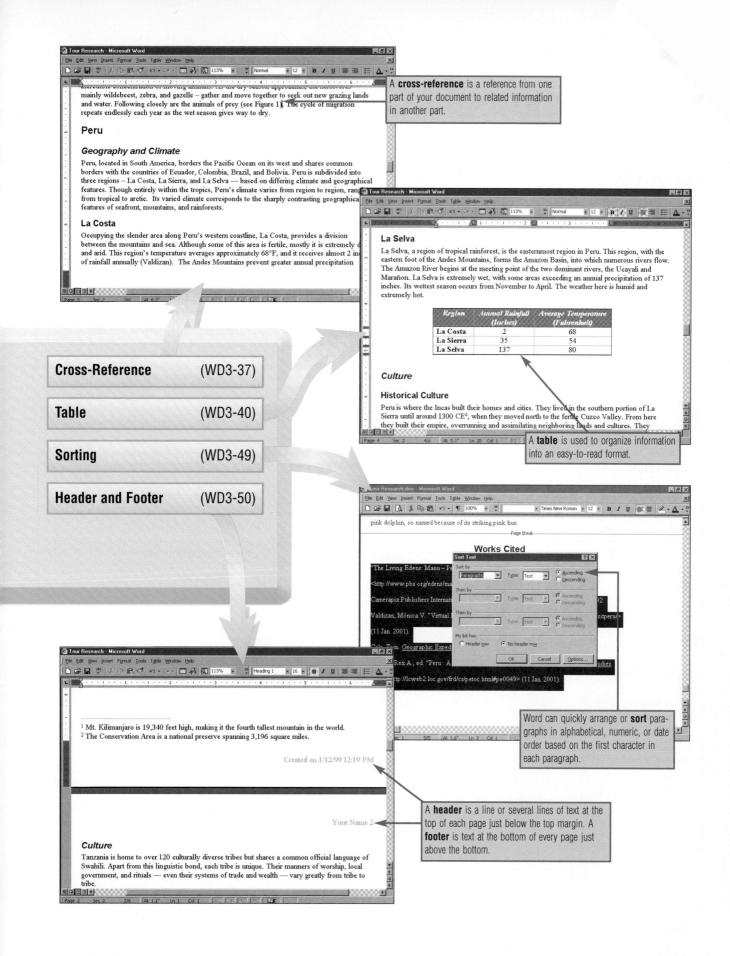

A **cross-reference** is a reference from one part of your document to related information in another part.

Peru

Geography and Climate

Peru, located in South America, borders the Pacific Ocean on its west and shares common borders with the countries of Ecuador, Colombia, Brazil, and Bolivia. Peru is subdivided into three regions – La Costa, La Sierra, and La Selva — based on differing climate and geographical features. Though entirely within the tropics, Peru's climate varies from region to region, ranging from tropical to arctic. Its varied climate corresponds to the sharply contrasting geographical features of seafront, mountains, and rainforests.

La Costa

Occupying the slender area along Peru's western coastline, La Costa, provides a division between the mountains and sea. Although some of this area is fertile, mostly it is extremely dry and arid. This region's temperature averages approximately 68°F, and it receives almost 2 inches of rainfall annually (Valdizan). The Andes Mountains prevent greater annual precipitation

La Selva

La Selva, a region of tropical rainforest, is the easternmost region in Peru. This region, with the eastern foot of the Andes Mountains, forms the Amazon Basin, into which numerous rivers flow. The Amazon River begins at the meeting point of the two dominant rivers, the Ucayali and Marañon. La Selva is extremely wet, with some areas exceeding an annual precipitation of 137 inches. Its wettest season occurs from November to April. The weather here is humid and extremely hot.

Region	Annual Rainfall (Inches)	Average Temperature (Fahrenheit)
La Costa	2	68
La Sierra	35	54
La Selva	137	80

Culture

Historical Culture

Peru is where the Incas built their homes and cities. They lived in the southern portion of La Sierra until around 1300 CE[4], when they moved north to the fertile Cuzco Valley. From here they built their empire, overrunning and assimilating neighboring lands and cultures. They

A **table** is used to organize information into an easy-to-read format.

Cross-Reference	(WD3-37)
Table	(WD3-40)
Sorting	(WD3-49)
Header and Footer	(WD3-50)

pink dolphin, so named because of its striking pink hue.

─────────Page Break─────────

Works Cited

"The Living Edens: Manu – Pe…

<http://www.pbs.org/edens/ma…

Camerapix Publishers Internati…

Valdizan, Mónica V. "Virtual …sitperu/>

(11 Jan. 2001).

Sala, Tom. Geographic Expediti…

Rex A., ed. "Peru : A…udies.

…tp://lcweb2.loc.gov/frd/cs/petoc.html#pe0049> (11 Jan. 2001).

Word can quickly arrange or **sort** paragraphs in alphabetical, numeric, or date order based on the first character in each paragraph.

[1] Mt. Kilimanjaro is 19,340 feet high, making it the fourth tallest mountain in the world.
[2] The Conservation Area is a national preserve spanning 3,196 square miles.

Created on 1/12/99 12:19 PM

Your Name 2

A **header** is a line or several lines of text at the top of each page just below the top margin. A **footer** is text at the bottom of every page just above the bottom.

Culture

Tanzania is home to over 120 culturally diverse tribes but shares a common official language of Swahili. Apart from this linguistic bond, each tribe is unique. Their manners of worship, local government, and rituals — even their systems of trade and wealth — vary greatly from tribe to tribe.

Key Terms

AutoFormat   WD3-46
caption   WD3-35
character style   WD3-4
cross-reference   WD3-37
Document Map pane   WD3-28
document pane   WD3-27
drawing layer   WD3-34
endnote   WD3-26

floating object   WD3-34
footer   WD3-50
footnote   WD3-26
header   WD3-50
heading style   WD3-4
inline object   WD3-34
note pane   WD3-27
note reference mark   WD3-26

note separator   WD3-26
note text   WD3-26
pane   WD3-27
paragraph style   WD3-4
section break   WD3-23
sort   WD3-49
style   WD3-23

Command Summary

Command	Shortcut Keys	Button	Action
File/Page Set**u**p/Layout/**V**ertical Alignment			Aligns text vertically on a page
View/**D**ocument Map		[button]	Displays/hides Document Map pane
View/**H**eader and Footer			Displays header and footer areas
View/Foot**n**otes			Hides or displays note pane
View/**Z**oom/**M**any Pages		[button]	Displays two or more pages in document window
Insert/Page Nu**m**bers			Specifies page number location
Insert/Foot**n**ote	[Alt] + [Ctrl]+F		Inserts footnote reference at insertion point
Insert/**C**aption			Inserts caption at insertion point
Insert/Cross-**r**eference			Inserts cross-reference at insertion point
Insert/In**d**ex and Tables/Table of **C**ontents		Normal	Creates a table of contents
F**o**rmat/**S**tyle			Applies selected style to paragraph or characters
F**o**rmat/Pi**c**ture/Layout		[button]	Specifies how text will wrap around picture
Tools/**O**ptions/View/Sc**r**eenTips			Turns off and on the display of ScreenTips
Tools/**O**ptions/Spelling & Grammar			Changes settings associated with the Spelling and Grammar checking feature
Table/**I**nsert Table		[button]	Inserts table at insertion point
Ta**b**le/**I**nsert/Rows **A**bove			Inserts a new row in table above selected row

Command	Shortcut Keys	Button	Action
T**a**ble/Con**v**ert/Te**x**t to Table			Converts selected text to table format
T**a**ble/Table Auto**F**ormat			Applies selected format to table
T**a**ble/**S**ort			Rearranges items in a selection into sorted order

Screen Identification

- -

In the following Word screen, letters identify important elements. Enter the correct screen element in the space provided.

a. _____   f. _____

b. _____   g. _____

c. _____   h. _____

d. _____   i. _____

e. _____   j. _____

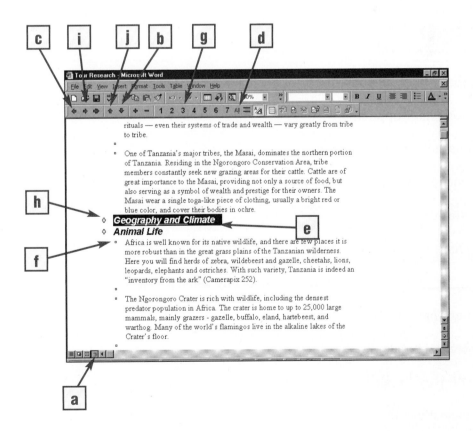

Matching

Match the lettered item on the right with the numbered item on the left.

1. note pane _____ **a.** text that appears at the bottom of each page above the bottom margin

2. table of contents _____ **b.** graphic placed at insertion point

3. footer _____ **c.** source reference displayed at the bottom of a page

4. caption _____ **d.** lower section of workspace that displays footnote text

5. footnote _____ **e.** instructs Word to end one set of format settings and begin another

6. section break _____ **f.** a title or explanation for a table, picture, or graph

7. tight wrap _____ **g.** a listing of the topics that appear in the document

8. Document Map _____ **h.** text closely follows contours around a graphic

9. inline image _____ **i.** reference from one part of the document to another part

10. cross-reference _____ **j.** displays the headings in the document

Multiple Choice

Circle the correct response to the questions below.

1. Styles can be applied to _____.

   a. characters and paragraphs

   b. documents and paragraphs

   c. words and characters

   d. characters and documents

2. A _____ is inserted automatically when a new page is created in a document.

   a. hard page break

   b. section break

   c. soft page break

   d. page division

3. Source references or text offering additional explanation that are placed at the bottom of a page are _____.

   a. endnotes

   b. footnotes

   c. reference notes

   d. page notes

4. The graphic text-wrapping style(s) that can be used in Word are _____.

   a. inline

   b. square

   c. through

   d. all the above

5. A _____ is a title or explanation for a table, picture, or graph.

   a. statement

   b. cross-reference

   c. caption

   d. footnote

6. A cross-reference is a _____ to another location.

   a. caption

   b. hyperlink

   c. footnote

   d. endnote

7. Text sorted in _____ order appears alphabetically from A to Z.

   a. ordered

   b. descending

   c. ascending

   d. rescending

8. The _____ pane displays the headings in your document.

    a. Document Map

    b. Note

    c. Heading

    d. Outline

9. A _____ object is inserted in the drawing layer and can be positioned precisely on the page.

    a. fixed

    b. floating

    c. layered

    d. pasted

10. A _____displays information in horizontal rows and vertical columns.

    a. Document Map

    b. cell reference

    c. object

    d. table

True/False

Circle the correct answer to the following questions.

1. A style is a named group of formats.	True	False
2. Outline view is the best view to use while entering the body of a document.	True	False
3. The Document Preview pane displays the headings in your document.	True	False
4. A caption can be displayed below a graphic to identify the object.	True	False
5. A cross-reference can be placed within a document to refer back to a figure or other reference in the document.	True	False
6. A hyperlink allows you to jump to another location in a document, another document, or the Web.	True	False
7. Outline view is used to apply different formats to different parts of a document.	True	False

8. A header is text that prints at the bottom of every page just above the bottom margin. True   False

9. Footnotes are source references or long comments that typically appear at the end of a document. True   False

10. How text appears surrounding a graphic object depends on the text wrapping style. True   False

Discussion Questions

1. Discuss the differences between footnotes and endnotes. When should notes be added to a document?

2. Use Help to learn more about how to position text and graphic objects on a page. Discuss how you can move and place graphic objects in a document. Discuss the different wrapping options.

3. Discuss how the Document Map can be used in a document. What must be present for the Document Map to display text?

4. Discuss the cross-reference and caption features. When would it be appropriate to use them in a document?

5. Describe the different methods you can use to create a table and explain when they should be used.

6. What is the significance of using a column and row format in tables? How are the rows and columns labeled?

Hands-On Practice Exercises

Step by Step

1. You work as a volunteer with Animal Angels, a nonprofit organization that finds homes for abandoned pets. You have been asked to make a brief presentation to a group asking for volunteers and donations. You will create an outline of the topics you want to discuss during the presentation.

   a. Open a new blank document and switch to Outline view.

   b. The topics you want to discuss are shown below. Enter these topics in Outline view pressing ⏎Enter at the end of each.

Who is an Animal Angel?

What is a Rescue Animal?

How to Become an Angel

Where Are We Located?

Adopting a Rescue Animal

What Should I Expect?

Animals for Adoption

Trevor

Misty

Adoption Fees

Events Calendar

> Student Name
> January 10, 2001
>
> **Who is an Animal Angel?**
>
> **What is a Rescue Animal?**
>
> **Adopting a Rescue Animal**
>
> *What Should I Expect?*
>
> *Animals for Adoption*
>
> Trevor
>
> Misty
>
> CJ
>
> *Adoption Fees*
>
> **How to Become an Angel**
>
> **Events Calendar**

   c. Move the topic How to Become an Angel above the Events Calendar line.

   d. Make the topics What Should I Expect?, Animals for Adoption, and Adoption Fees level 2 headings.

   e. Make the Trevor and Misty lines level 3 headings.

   f. Insert a new level 3 line, CJ, below the Misty line.

   g. Delete the "Where Are We Located?" topic and blank line.

   h. Enter your name and the date in a header.

   i. Print the outline.

   j. Save the outline as Animal Angel Outline.

2. You work for a small publishing company that specializes in travel books. Each year the company updates the regional bed and breakfast books that describe the features of B&B facilities in each region of the country. You have been asked to update the current listing of bed and breakfasts in New England.

   a. Open the file New England B&Bs.

   b. Change the order of the list (excluding the heading line) so that it is sorted by name instead of by state.

c. Use the Convert Text to Table command on the Table menu to convert the list to a table.

d. Apply a table AutoFormat of your choice to the table.

e. Center the table.

f. Add the title New England Bed And Breakfasts centered above the table. Enhance the title using the Title style. Color the title to match colors used in the table.

g. Add a header to the document that contains your name and the current date, right-aligned.

h. Print the document.

i. Save the document as New England B&Bs Revised.

☆☆

3. The Downtown Internet Cafe is planning a grand opening celebration. You have already started designing a flyer to advertise the event, but it still needs additional work.

a. Open the file Internet Cafe Flyer.

b. Change the left and right margins to 1 inch.

c. Create the following table of data below the "Users pay . . ." paragraph.

Length of Time	Rate
Hour	$8.00
Half hour	$5.00

d. Apply an AutoFormat of your choice to the table. Center the table.

e. Add bullets to the four items under "The Downtown Internet Cafe combines." Add a different style bullet before the four items under "What to do at the Cafe."

f. Insert a ClipArt graphic of your choice to the right of the first four bulleted items.

Student Name
January 10, 2001

New England Bed And Breakfasts

Name	City	State
Bay View Inn	Portland	Maine
Blue Heron Inn	Biddeford	Maine
Colonial Inn	Hartford	Connecticut
Hanging Lantern Inn	Cambridge	Massachusetts
Harbor House	Nantucket	Massachusetts
Litchfield House	Winsted	Connecticut
Mystic Mansion	Mystic	Connecticut
Quincy Cottage	Boston	Massachusetts
Windsor Farms	Windsor	Connecticut
Yankee Inn	Kennebunk	Maine

Opening Soon
Downtown Internet Cafe

... a new concept in coffeehouses

The Downtown Internet Café combines:

♦ Delicious aromas of genuine coffeehouse coffee
♦ Fun of using the Internet
♦ Tempting deserts, fresh salads, and sandwiches
♦ Fine selection of gourmet coffees for you to take home

What to do at the Café:

☐ Surf the Web on our T1 line! (That's 1.5 MB per second!)
☐ Play multi-player network games.
☐ Videoconference with people from around the world!
☐ Use our productivity software.

Users pay to access all the café's amenities using the following rate table:

Length of Time	Rate
Hour	$8.00
Half hour	$5.00

Come to our open house for free coffee and cake
March 24th from 12 to 6 pm

Created on 1/14/99 3:24 PM   Student Name

g. Insert another ClipArt graphic
of your choice to the left of the second list of bulleted items.

h. Preview the document. Make
any editing changes you feel are appropriate.

i. Enter your name and the date
in a footer.

j. Save the document as Internet Cafe Flyer Revised.

k. Print the document.

4. The Lifestyle Fitness Club produces a quarterly newsletter for its members. As the marketing and advertising director, you are responsible for developing and writing the articles for the newsletter. You have researched several topics you plan to include in the next issue and are in the process of writing up a report of your findings. The first two pages of the revised report are shown here.

Lifestyle Fitness Club

Student Name
Date

Table of Contents

HEALTH AND FITNESS

How to Be a Weekend Warrior

"The weekend warrior: You lead a sedentary life all week, sitting behind a desk, stuffing your body with junk food and poorly balanced meals... But the weekend arrives and you're all dressed up and ready to go. You eat pancakes for breakfast and pack a banana in your gear bag. You crank serves and play for hours. Come Monday, all you have to show for it are sore muscles, little energy and bad memories of too many missed overheads" (Anthony 89).

Sound familiar? Although this quote is directed at people playing tennis, it really applies to all types of athletic events. When the weekend arrives, you become an instant athlete - eating right, exercising more than usual - and by Monday morning you pay for it: you are tired, sluggish, and sore. Good nutritional habits and a regular fitness routine throughout the week will make you a true weekend warrior.

A Balanced Diet

Dietary advice for all types of athletes is the same as for the general public. That is, eat a well-balanced diet from a wide variety of foods in sufficient amounts to meet energy needs. Nutrition experts like the American Dietetic Association recommend that we eat a diet low in fat and high in complex carbohydrates.[1] Generally, nutritionists suggest that we consume no more than 30 to 35 percent of our calories as fat, at least 55 percent as carbohydrates, and the remainder as protein.

Understanding how our bodies process the foods we eat explains why this balanced diet is important. Our bodies use the food we consume by converting the chemical energy stored in food into free energy that can be used by our cells, muscles, organs and all other tissues. But since the body cannot use all the food it takes in at once, some of it is stored away for later use. Although all three nutrients, carbohydrates, protein, and fat supply energy, carbohydrates are the major source of energy. Complex carbohydrates are stored in muscles and liver as glycogen, while fat and sugar (simple carbohydrates) are stored as fat. After the body uses up all the glucose in the bloodstream, it begins breaking down the glycogen stored in the muscles before finally turning to the stored fat for energy.

Simple carbohydrates are absorbed into the bloodstream much more quickly than complex carbohydrates.[2] They provide instant but short-lived energy. Complex carbohydrates are a much more stable source of energy. They give us energy by slowly breaking down into glucose,

[1] Complex carbohydrates are foods such as pasta, rice, potatoes, and breads.
[2] Simple carbohydrates are foods such as sugar and honey.

a. Open the file Fitness Report.

b. Using the Document Map to locate the section titles, apply the following heading styles to the document.

Health and Fitness	Heading 1
How to Be a Weekend Warrior	Heading 2
Daily Aerobic Exercise	Heading 3
A Balanced Diet	Heading 3
What Fluids Are Best?	Heading 2
Equipment Update	Heading 1
Stationary Bikes	Heading 2

c. In Outline view, move the Daily Aerobic Exercise section after the Balanced Diet section.

d. Insert the following footnotes into the document.

Location	Footnote
After word "carbohydrates" in first paragraph of "A Balanced Diet"	Complex carbohydrates are foods such as pasta, rice, potatoes and bread.
After word "carbohydrates" in first sentence of "A Balanced Diet"	Simple carbohydrates are foods such as sugar and honey.

e. Create a title page for the report. Include the club's name, your name, and the date at the top of the page. Format the club name using the Title style. Center your name and the date below the title.

f. Include a heading on the title page for a table of contents. Format the heading as a Subtitle style.

g. Create a table of contents below the heading on the title page. Do not include the Title and Subtitle styles in the table of contents.

h. Center the title page vertically.

i. Number the list of tips on page 2 and bullet the guidelines on page 3.

j. Add page numbers displayed on the right in a footer. Do not include the title page in the numbering.

k. Print the document.

l. Save the file as Revised Fitness Report.

5. The advertising director of the Lifestyle Fitness Club has asked you to help with a few of the final details for the fitness report. The last 3 pages of the report are shown here.

Note: This problem requires that you have first completed Practice exercise 4 above. If you have not, you can use the Fitness Report file, however, your final output will not reflect the features added in Exercise 4.

   a. Open the file Fitness Report, or if you completed problem 4 above, open the file Revised Fitness Report.

   b. Insert the picture Bike to the left of the second and third paragraphs in the Stationary Bike section.

   c. Add the caption Recumbent Cycle under the picture. Adjust paragraph spacing as needed.

   d. Sort the three paragraphs on sugary drinks, alcoholic beverages, and caffeine drinks in the "What Fluids Are Best?" section, and make them bulleted items. Remove any unneeded blank lines.

   e. Alphabetize and format the works cited on the last page of the report.

   f. Print the document.

   g. Save the file as Fitness Final Report.

Lifestyle Fitness Club

Student Name
Date

Table of Contents

If you follow these basic nutrition and exercise principles, you will find that the cumulative effect of a health conscious diet and regular exercise will show up everywhere: at home, at work, and while being a weekend warrior.

What Fluids Are Best?

Without a doubt, plain water is best. Water is quickly absorbed into the system to replenish water lost by sweat. Here's the scoop on other fluids:

- Alcoholic beverages actually increase fluid loss by stimulating urine production.
- Caffeine drinks such as coffee have been suggested to be a performance enhancer, but their effects are still being studied. Thus far, the indications are that caffeine may be helpful in endurance events. But before using caffeine, keep in mind that it also triggers increased urine excretion, which can contribute to dehydration.
- Sugary drinks such as sodas actually decrease the speed at which the water leaves the stomach and enters the small intestines where it can be absorbed by the body.

What about additives such as glucose polymer powders and electrolytes? Most sports medicine experts agree that glucose polymers are really only a benefit to long endurance athletes. Adding electrolytes to fluids consumed during exercise is not necessary unless one exercises for more than two or three hours in hot and humid weather. Electrolytes that are lost during exercise are easily replaced during the next meal.

Because of the tension of athletic performance and the ex[...] experience, thirst may not reliably signal the need for wat[...] should weigh themselves before and after training and mo[...] training period. For each pound lost, they should drink a[...]

Therefore athletes in endurance competition would do we[...] American Dietetic Association:

- ❖ Two hours before an event, drink three cups of w[...] is best; it leaves the stomach and enters the syste[...]
- ❖ Ten to fifteen minutes before the event, drink two[...]
- ❖ Drink small amounts of water - one half to one cu[...] throughout the competition. Water taken during [...] when possible. This helps the body to keep its ter[...]
- ❖ After competition or training, continue to drink w[...] regained.

EQUIPMENT UPDATE

Stationary Bikes

You can benefit from biking without leaving your living room. Riding a stationary bike is a great way to get an aerobic workout.

 There are two kinds of stationary bikes. The standard upright has been around for years. Newer versions offer computer readouts of calories burned, miles traveled, and average speed. Fancier models calculate your heart rate while cycling, or simulate hills and valleys to vary your workout.

The new arrival is the recumbent cycle. You sit up straight as if in a regular chair only lower to the ground, with your feet out straight. Since you have to fight gravity to keep your legs upright, you actually get a better workout than in the upright version. It is better toning for your thighs, buttocks, and lower stomach.

Figure 1 Recumbent Cycle

Whichever type you choose, you will find you quickly benefit from a daily aerobic bike ride to nowhere.

6. You are a freelance writer and have written an article about the top ten scenic drives in the world. You want to enhance the document before submitting it to several travel magazines. Open the file Top 10 Scenic Drives on your data disk. The first 3 pages of the completed article are shown here.

a. Create a title page at the top of the document. Include the article title in Title style and your name and the current date centered below the title. Center the title page vertically.

b. Format the names of the top ten drives as Heading 1 styles. (Hint: use Format Painter.)

c. On the extra new page following the title page, add the heading Table of Contents formatted as Title style. Create a table of contents listing on this page. Use the Modern style and do not include the Title style headings in the listing.

d. Insert the picture Mountain from your data disk to the left of the first paragraph of the Rocky Mountain section. Size the graphic appropriately and wrap the text to the right.

e. Add the following footnote to the end of the first sentence of the third paragraph:

   This top 10 list was obtained from the Weissmann Travel Reports in the America Online Traveler's Corner.

Scenic Drives

Student Name
Date

f. Number the pages, excluding the title page.

g. Preview the document and make any adjustments necessary.

h. Save the document as Top 10 Scenic Drives Revised. Print the document.

Table of Contents

Student Nam
Date

Top 10 Scenic Drives

The high road, it seems, is the road of choice: Routes through mountainous scenery dominated the nominations you sent in for Top 10 Scenic Drives. As one person wrote about the experience of hitting the top of one Rocky Mountain pass, "you'll think you've reached heaven."

Hyperbole competed with sentiment in many of the nominations we received; multiple exclamation points (AWESOME!!!!!) lined up as thick as billboards along an interstate, and in a few cases, memories of childhood drives revealed just how long it has been since the writer hit the road ("My strongest memories are from looking out the back window of my parents' station wagon").

For those whose memories of beautiful drives needs updating, let the following list of our top 10 picks for Scenic Drives, as nominated by online users and the correspondents and editors of Weissmann Travel Reports, serve as inspiration for your summer travel plans[1]. As usual, this month's ranking is not intended to be a popularity contest; while multiple nominations were taken into consideration when compiling the list, the final results also took into account the writers' ability to convey the beauty they traversed.

1. THE ROCKY MOUNTAINS

Three Rocky roads--Rocky Mountain National Park's Trail Ridge Road, Waterton-Glacier International Peace Park's Going to the Sun Road and the Icefields Parkway, located between Jasper and Banff National Parks in Alberta, Canada, were all nominated as the most scenic drive in the world. Each is lined with spectacular scenery, and for us to try to choose the "best" among them would be like saying that air is more important to human beings than water or food: They all have their strengths, and none could eliminate the others from contention. We're left with a three-way tie. Trail Ridge Road, the highest through-highway in the U.S., begins in Estes Park, Colorado, and winds along a route that takes in terrain ranging from ponderosa pine forests to tundra. Forested canyons, hanging valleys and glacial lakes punctuate the route. The Sun Road, which runs for 50 miles/80 km from Lake McDonald to St. Mary, features stunning and inspiring vistas of alpine scenery (watch for the "Garden Wall," a landmark of the Continental Divide), while the Icefields Parkway is characterized by magnificent lakes, glacial ice fields, waterfalls and herds of animals. Honorable Mention goes to Highway 550 between Ouray and Silverton, Colorado, which offers rugged and dynamic mountain beauty with a lot less traffic than these others. Note: None of the roads open until late spring, and all are usually closed by mid-fall.

---

[1] This top 10 list was obtained from the Weissmann Travel Reports in the America Online Traveler's Corner.

On Your Own

7. The city Health Department receives a large number of calls concerning Alzheimer's disease. In response to the need for information on this topic, they are putting together a FAQ (Frequently Asked Questions) sheet with answers to the most frequently asked questions about the disease.

   a. Open the file Alzheimer on your data disk.

   b. Use the Document Map to locate the headings in the document, and apply appropriate heading levels.

   c. Number the list of ten warning signs.

   d. Use the Format Painter to add bold and underlines to the first sentence of each of the ten warning signs.

   e. Convert the scale for stages of Alzheimer on the last page to a table (Use Table/Convert text to Table). Apply an AutoFormat of your choice to the table.

   f. Display a page number at a position of your choice in the footer.

   g. Include your name and the current date in a header.

   h. Save and print the document.

8. You are a Physical Education major and have written a report on water exercises. Open the file Water on your data disk. The first page of the file is where the table of contents will appear. Pages 2 through 4 contain the body of your report. Use the features presented in this tutorial to add the following to the report:

   ■ Create a title page that displays the report title, date, and your name.

   ■ Create a table of contents on another page after the title page.

   ■ Center the title page and table of contents pages vertically.

   ■ Apply additional formats of your choice to the report.

   ■ Include page numbers.

   ■ Create a works cited page using the following reference sources.

   McEnvoy, Joseph: *Fitness Swimming: Lifetime Programs:* Princeton: Princeton Book Company Publishers, 1995.

   President's Council on Physical Fitness and Sports, *AquaDynamics: Physical Conditioning Through Water Exercise:* Washington, DC: Government Printing Office, 1981.

   ■ Save the document as Water Exercise Program. Print the report.

9. You are an Elementary Education major and are writing a report about computers and children. Open the file Computer on your data disk. You are in the final stages of finishing the report. Use the features presented in this tutorial to add the following to the report:

   ■ Apply appropriate formats to the titles and headings.

   ■ Create a title page above the body of the report. Use appropriate styles, fonts, and sizes.

- Locate and insert an appropriate ClipArt on the title page.
- Center the title page vertically.
- Add the footnote Availability of products is limited to stock on hand. after "Look for:" in the section "Software for Kids."
- Add page numbers to the report, excluding the title page.
- Create a bulleted sorted list of the five software titles at the end of the report.
- Save the document as Computer Report.
- Print the document.

☆ ☆ ☆

10. Create a brief research report (or use a paper you have written in the past) on a topic of interest to you. The paper must include the following features:

- A title page that displays the report title, your name, the current date, and a table of contents.
- The body of the paper should include at least two levels of headings and a minimum of three footnotes.
- The report layout should include page numbers on the top right corner of every page (excluding the title page). The title page should be vertically aligned.
- Include at least one picture with a caption and cross-reference.
- Include a works cited page with an alphabetical list of your reference sources.

Working Together: Word and Your Web Browser

Case Study Adventure Travel Company has a World Wide Web (WWW) site. Through it they hope to be able to promote their products and broaden the audience of customers. In addition to the obvious marketing and sales potential, they want to provide an avenue for interaction between themselves and the customer to improve their customer service. They also want the Web site to provide articles of interest to customers. The articles, topics as travel background information and descriptions, would change on a monthly basis as an added incentive for readers to return to the site.

You think the flyer you developed to promote the new tours and presentations could be used on the Web site. Word 2000 includes Web-editing features that help you create a Web page quickly and easily. While using the Web-editing features, you will be working with Word and with a Web browser application. This capability of all Office 2000 applications to work together and with other applications makes it easy to share and exchange information between applications. Several steps to create a Web page are shown below.

A background theme adds color and interest to the Web page and hyperlinks connect pages.

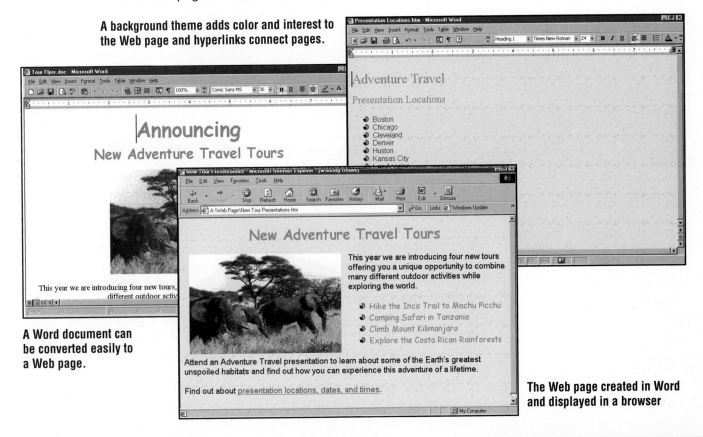

A Word document can be converted easily to a Web page.

The Web page created in Word and displayed in a browser

Note: The intent of the Working Together tutorial is to show how two applications work together and to present a basic introduction to creating Web pages. More information about Web page creation is available in the advanced Word 2000 tutorials.

Saving a Word Document as a Web Page

You want to create a Web page on the company's Web site. A **Web page** is a document that can be used on the WWW. The Web page you create will provide information about the tour presentations. Word offers three ways to create or **author** Web pages. One way is to start with a blank Web page and enter text and graphics much as you would a normal document. Another is to use the Web Page Wizard, which provides step-by-step instructions to help you quickly create a Web page. Finally, you can quickly convert an existing Word document to a Web page.

Because the Tour Flyer has already been created as a Word document and contains much of the information you want to use on the Web page, you will convert it to a Web page document.

Start Word.

Open the file Tour Flyer from your data disk.

Your screen should be similar to Figure 1.

Figure 1

Word converts a document to a Web page by adding HTML coding to the document. **HTML (Hypertext Markup Language)** is a programming language used to create Web pages. HTML commands control the display of information on a page, such as font colors and size, and how an item will be processed. HTML also allows users to click on hyperlinks and jump to other locations on the same page, other pages in the same site, or to other sites and locations on the WWW altogether. HTML commands are interpreted by the browser software you are using. A **browser** is a program that connects you to the remote computers and displays the Web pages you request.

When a file is converted to a Web page, the HTML coding is added and it is saved to a new file with a .html file extension.

2 Choose File/Save as Web Page.

The Save As dialog box on your screen should be similar to Figure 2.

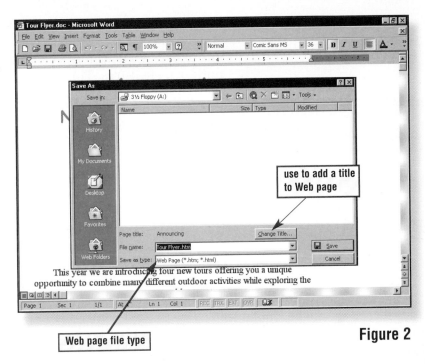

Figure 2

The file type of Web Page is automatically specified. You want to save the Web page using the file name New Tour Presentations in a new folder on your data disk. You also need to provide a title for the page. This is the text that will appear in the title bar of the Web browser when the page is displayed. You want the title to be the same as the file name.

3 If necessary, change the location to your data disk.

Create a new folder named Web Page.

Change the file name to New Tour Presentations.

Click Change Title... .

Change the title to New Tour Presentations.

Click OK .

Click Save .

Your screen should be similar to Figure 3.

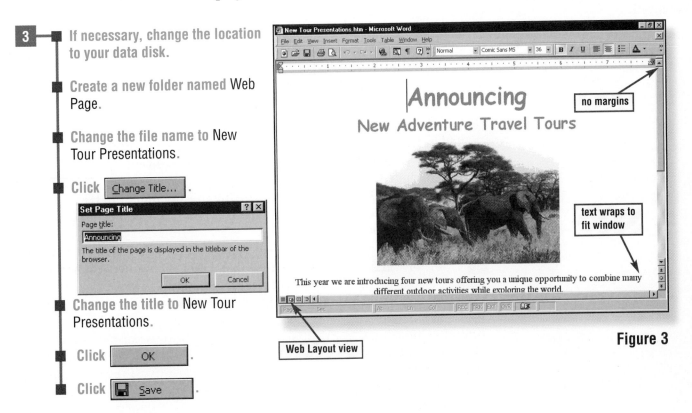

Figure 3

The flyer has been converted to an HTML document and is displayed in Web Layout view. Although the menu bar contains the same menus, Word customizes some menus, commands, and options to provide the Web page authoring features. This view displays the document as it will appear if viewed using a Web browser. This document looks very much like a normal Word document. In fact, the only visible difference is the margin settings. A Web page does not include margins. Instead, the text wraps to fit in the window space. However, the formatting and features that are supported by HTML, in this case the paragraph and character formatting such as the font style, type size and color attributes, have been converted to HTML format. To see the HTML code,

Additional Information

Some formatting features, such as emboss and shadow effects, are not supported by HTML or other Web browsers and are not available when authoring Web pages.

4 ■ Choose <u>V</u>iew/HTML Sour<u>c</u>e .

■ If necessary, maximize both windows.

Your screen should be similar to Figure 4.

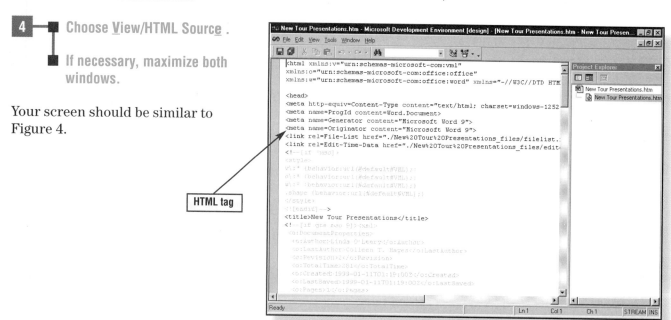

HTML tag

Figure 4

Every item on a Web page has properties associated with it that are encoded in HTML tags. **Tags**, are embedded codes that supply information about the page's structure, appearance, and contents. They tell your browser where the title, headings, paragraphs, images, and other information are to appear on the page. Converting this document to HTML format using Word was a lot easier than learning to enter the code yourself. To return to the Web page,

5 ■ Click ☒ to close the Microsoft Development Environment window.

The Web page is displayed in Web Page view again.

Making Text Changes

Next you want to change the layout of the Web page so that more information is displayed in the window when the page is viewed in the browser. You will delete any unnecessary text first and change the paragraph alignment to left-aligned.

1
- Select the entire Announcing heading line.
- Press (Delete).
- Delete the last two paragraphs in the flyer.
- Select all the text below the picture.
- Click ![left align icon] Left.
- Add bullets preceding the list of four tours.
- Scroll to the top of the document.

Your screen should be similar to Figure 5.

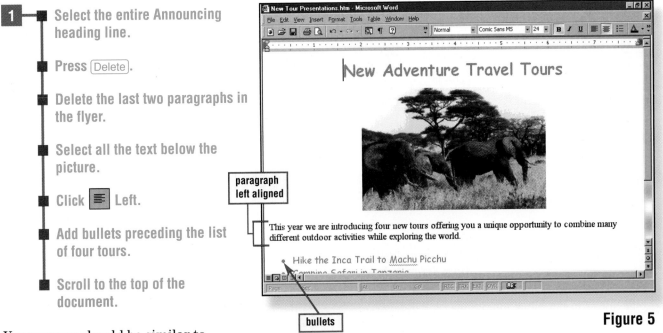

Figure 5

Changing the Picture Layout

Additional Information

Each graphic file is stored in a separate file. Word creates a link, which includes the location and file name, to the object's file in the HTML file. When graphic files are added to a page, they are copied to the same folder location as the page. They must always reside in the same location as the HTML document file in which they are used.

You still cannot view all the information in a single window. To make more space, you will move the picture to the left edge of the window and wrap the text to the right around it. Unlike a normal Word document, pictures and other graphic elements are not embedded into the Web page document. Instead they are inserted as inline images. In an HTML file an inline image is stored as a separate file that is accessed and loaded by the browser when the page is loaded. However, they can still be moved and sized as well as formatted just like embedded picture objects.

1 Select the picture and drag it to the **T** in **This** at the beginning of the first paragraph.

Click 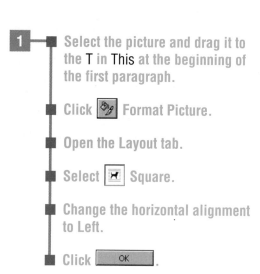 Format Picture.

Open the Layout tab.

Select Square.

Change the horizontal alignment to Left.

Click OK .

Your screen should be similar to Figure 6.

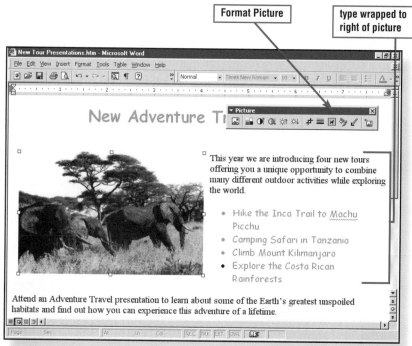

Figure 6

Now almost all the information is visible. You will remove two of the blank lines from below the heading and reduce the size of the picture slightly.

2 Move to the blank line below the heading.

Press Delete twice.

Reduce the picture size slightly as in Figure 7.

Your screen should be similar to Figure 7.

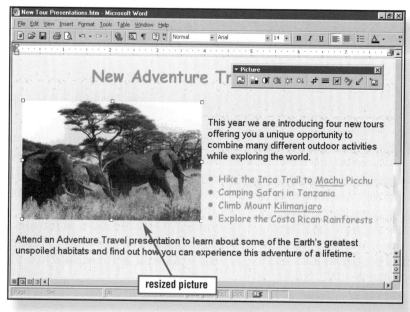

Figure 7

Applying a Theme

Because color and design are important elements of Web pages, you can add a background color and other special effects to a Web page. Many of these special effects are designed specifically for Web pages and cannot be used in printed pages. Like styles, Word includes many predesigned Web page effects, called **themes**, which you can quickly apply to a Web page.

1 ━ Choose F<u>o</u>rmat/ Th<u>e</u>me.

Your screen should be similar to Figure 8.

Figure 8

The Choose a Theme list displays the names of all the themes that are provided with Word. The preview area displays a sample of the selected theme showing the background design, bullet and horizontal line style, and character formats that will be applied to headings, normal text, and hyperlinks.

2 ━ Select several themes to preview them.

━ Select Piechart.

━ Click ▭ OK ▭.

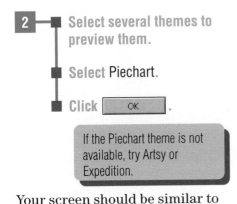

If the Piechart theme is not available, try Artsy or Expedition.

Your screen should be similar to Figure 9.

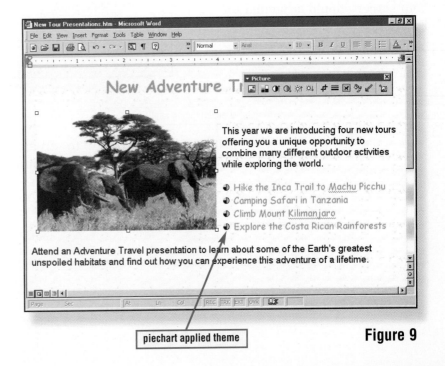

piechart applied theme

Figure 9

The formatting settings associated with the selected theme are applied to the Web page.

3 ── ■ Click 🖫 to save the changes you have made to the Web page.

Creating a Hyperlink

- -

Next you want create another Web page that will contain a list of presentation locations throughout the United States. You will then add a hyperlink to this information from the New Tour Presentations page. As you have learned, a hyperlink provides a quick way to jump to other documents, objects, or Web pages. Hyperlinks are the real power of the WWW. You can jump to sites on your own system and network as well as to sites on the Internet and WWW. The list of tour locations has already been entered for you and saved as Presentation Locations on your data disk.

1 ── ■ Open the file Presentation Locations from your data disk.

■ Save the document as a Web page to your Web Page folder with the same file name and a page title of **Locations**.

■ Apply the Piechart theme to this page.

■ Save it again.

Your screen should be similar to Figure 10.

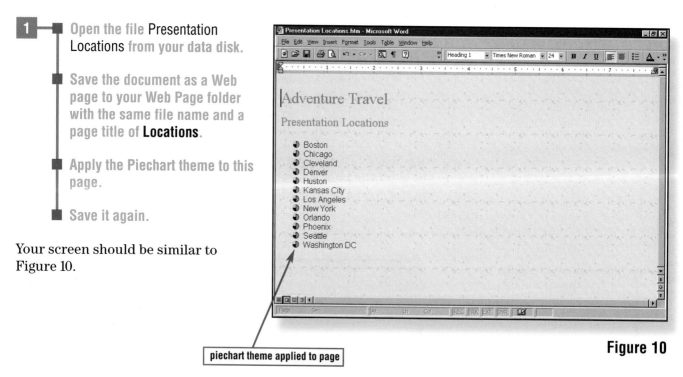

piechart theme applied to page

Figure 10

Now you are ready to create the hyperlink from the New Tour Presentation page to the Presentation Locations page.

2 ■ Switch to the New Tour Presentations window.

■ Add the text **Find out about presentation locations, dates, and times.** one line below the last paragraph.

■ Select the text presentation locations, dates, and times.

■ Click 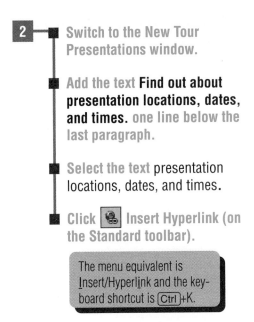 Insert Hyperlink (on the Standard toolbar).

> The menu equivalent is Insert/Hyperlink and the keyboard shortcut is [Ctrl]+K.

Your screen should be similar to Figure 11.

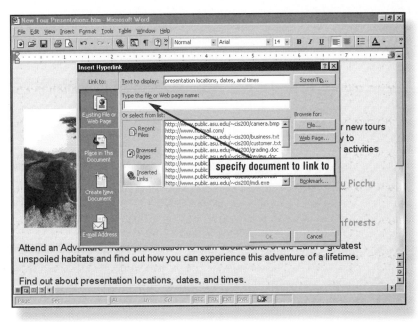

Figure 11

From the Insert Hyperlink dialog box, you need to specify the name of the document you want to link to.

3 ■ If necessary, click .

■ Click [Recent Files].

■ Select Presentation Locations from the file list.

■ Click [OK].

Your screen should be similar to Figure 12.

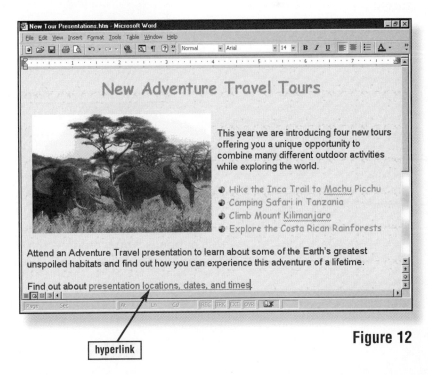

hyperlink

Figure 12

The selected text appears as a hyperlink in the design colors specified by the Piechart theme.

4 ■ Click the hyperlink.

Because the Tour Locations document is already open in a window, clicking the hyperlink simply switches to the open window and displays the page.

5 ▪ Close the Presentation Locations window.

Previewing the Page

- -

To see how your Web page will actually look when displayed by your browser, you can preview it in your default browser.

1 ▪ Choose File/Web Page Preview.

▪ If necessary, maximize the browser window.

▪ If Internet Explorer is your default browser and the Favorites list is open, click ✕ in the Favorites bar to close it.

Your screen should be similar to Figure 13.

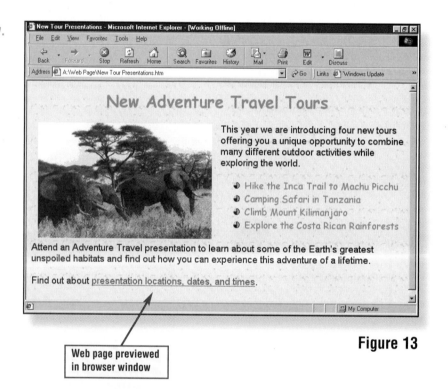

Web page previewed in browser window

Figure 13

The browser on your system is loaded offline, and the Web page you are working on is displayed in the browser window. Sometimes the browser may display a page slightly differently than it appears in Web Page view. If this happens, you would need to return Word and adjust the layout until it displays appropriately in the browser. In this case however, it looks great.

Your screen should be similar to Figure 14.

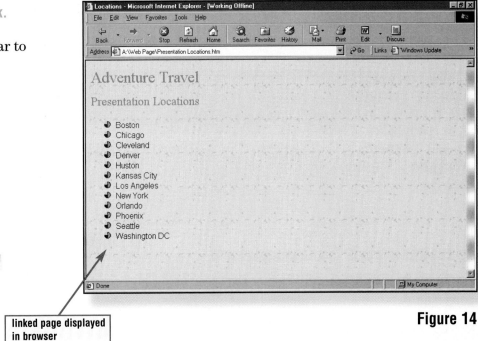

linked page displayed
in browser

Figure 14

The associated page is displayed in the browser. This page also looks fine and does not need any additional formatting.

Making a Web Page Public

Now that you have created Web pages, in order for others to see them you need to make them available on the Internet. The steps that you take to make your pages public depend on how you want to share them. There are two main avenues: on your local network or intranet for limited access by people within an organization, or on the Internet for access by anyone using the WWW. To make pages available to other people on your network, save your Web pages and related files, such as pictures, to a network location. To make your Web pages available on the WWW, you need to either install Web server software on your computer or locate an Internet service provider that allocates space for Web pages.

Key Terms

author WDW-2
browser WDW-2
HTML (Hypertext Markup Language) WDW-2
tag WDW-4
theme WDW-7
Web page WDW-2

Command Summary

Command	Shortcut Keys	Button	Action
File/Save as Web Page			Saves file as a Web page document
File/Web Page Preview			Previews Web page in browser window
View/HTML Source			Displays HTML source code
Insert/Hyperlink	Ctrl + K		Inserts hyperlink
Format/ Theme			Applies a predesigned theme to Web page

Hands-On Practice Exercises

1. Practice using Help to learn more about Web pages and making Web pages public.

  a. Search in help for information on Web page design, Web layout, Web sites, and publishing Web pages.

  b. Print the Help pages that might be appropriate for writing a report on using Word to create a Web site.

  c. Write a one-page report using the information you found.

  d. Print the report.

2. Your manager has asked you to modify the Internet Cafe flyer you created in Practice Exercise 3 of Tutorial 3.

  a. Open the file Internet Cafe Flyer Revised on your data disk.

  b. Convert the flyer to a web page and save it in a new folder on your data disk.

  c. Include an appropriate page title.

  d. Insert the picture of the Light Bulb into the flyer. Size and position appropriately.

  e. Apply an appropriate design theme to the page.

  f. Enhance the Web page by adding appropriate formats.

  g. Preview the page in your browser.

  h. Print the Web page.

  i. Resave the Web page.

3. To complete this problem, you must have completed Practice Exercise 2 in Tutorial 1. You are about to open a bed and breakfast inn in the Pocono Mountains and you would like to advertise it on the Web.

  ■ Open the file B&B Ad on your data disk. Convert the document to a Web page and save it in a separate folder.

  ■ Cut the information from Number of Rooms to Children and paste it to a new web page. Title the page Bed and Breakfast Inn Description.

  ■ Apply a design theme of your choice to the two pages. Create a link on the first page to the Bed and Breakfast Inn Description page.

  ■ Enhance the Web pages with any features you feel are appropriate. You can search the WWW for appropriate graphics if necessary.

  ■ Resave the Web pages and preview them in your browser.

  ■ Print the pages.

Glossary of Key Terms

Alignment: The positioning of paragraphs between the margins: left, right, centered, or justified.

Author: To design and create a Web page.

AutoComplete: A Word feature that suggests AutoText entries and completes them for you if chosen.

AutoCorrect: A Word feature that makes basic assumptions about the text you are typing and automatically corrects the entry.

AutoFormat: A Word feature that automatically applies paragraph and font styles to text as you type.

AutoText: Commonly used words or phrases that are recognized by the program and can be automatically completed for you.

Browser: A program that displays Web pages.

Caption: A title or explanation for a table, picture, or graph.

Cascading menu: A menu that appears with additional options under another menu.

Case sensitive: The capability to distinguish between uppercase and lowercase characters.

Character style: A combination of any character formats that affect selected text.

Clip art: A collection of graphics that is usually bundled with a software application.

Cross-reference: A reference in one part of a document to related information in another part.

Cursor: The blinking vertical bar that shows you where the next character you type will appear. Also called the insertion point.

Custom dictionary: A dictionary of terms you have entered that are not in the main dictionary of the Spelling Checker.

Default: Initial Word settings that can be changed to customize documents.

Desktop: The opening Windows screen and the place where you begin your work.

Destination: The location to which text is moved or copied.

Docked: A toolbar that is fixed to the edge of the window.

Document Map pane: When Document Map is selected, the left portion of the window that displays the headings in a document.

Document pane: When footnotes are created, the upper portion of the window that displays the document; in Online Layout View, the pane that displays the document text.

Drag and drop: A mouse procedure that moves or copies a selection to a new location.

Drawing layer: the layer above or below the text where floating objects are inserted.

Drawing object: A simple object consisting of shapes such as lines and boxes.

Edit: To change and correct existing text in a document.

Embedded object: An object inserted into a document that becomes part of the document and can be edited within the destination file using the source program.

Endnote: A reference note displayed at the end of the document.

End-of-file marker: The horizontal line that marks the end of a file.

Field: A placeholder code that instructs Word to insert information in a document.

Field code: The code containing the instructions about the type of information to insert in a document.

Field results: The results displayed in a field according to the instructions in the field code.

Floating: A toolbar that appears in a separate window.

Floating object: An object such as a picture that is inserted in the drawing layer of a Word document.

Font: A set of characters with a specific design. Also called a typeface.

Footer: A line or several lines of text at the bottom of every page just above the bottom margin.

Footnote: A reference note displayed at the bottom of the page on which the reference occurs.

Format: To enhance the appearance of a document to make it more readable or attractive.

Formatting toolbar: The toolbar, displayed to the right of the Standard Toolbar, that contains buttons representing the most frequently used text-editing and text-layout features.

Frame: The division of a window into separate areas that display and scroll independently.

Global template: The Normal document template, which contains settings that are available to all documents.

Graphic: A non-text element in a document.

Hard page break: A manually inserted page break.

Header: A line or several lines of text at the top of each page just below the top margin.

Heading style: A style that is designed to identify different levels of headings in a document.

HTML: Hypertext markup language used to create Web pages.

Hyperlink: Colored or underlined text that provides a quick way to jump to other documents, to places within a document, or to Web pages.

Icon: A small picture that represents an object on the desktop.

Inline object: An object such as a picture that is inserted into the text layer of a Word document.

Insert mode: Method of text entry in which new characters are inserted into existing text, which moves to the right to make space for the new characters; the text on the line is reformatted as necessary.

Insertion point: The blinking vertical bar that shows you where the next character you type will appear on the line. Also called the cursor.

Leader characters: Solid, dotted, or dashed lines that fill the blank space between tab stops.

Main dictionary: The dictionary of terms that comes with Word 2000.

Margin: The distance from the text to the edge of the paper.

Menu bar: A bar that displays the menu names that can be selected.

Menu: One of many methods used to tell a program what you want it to do.

Mouse: A hand-held hardware device that is attached to the computer.

Mouse pointer: An arrow-shaped symbol that appears on the screen if a mouse device is installed. It is used to interact with objects on the screen. The pointer may change shape, depending on the task being performed.

Note pane: Lower portion of the window that displays footnotes.

Note reference mark: A superscript number or character appearing in the document at the end of the material being referenced.

Note separator: The horizontal line separating footnote text from main document text.

Note text: The text in a footnote.

Object: An item that can be sized, moved, and manipulated.

Overtype mode: Method of text entry in which new text types over the existing characters.

Pane: A division of the workspace.

Formatting mark: The ¶ that is displayed wherever the [←Enter] key was pressed.

Paragraph style: A combination of any character formats and paragraph formats that affects all text in a paragraph.

Picture: An illustration such as a scanned photograph.

Points: Measure used for the height of type; 1 point equals 1/72 inch.

Ruler: The ruler located below the Formatting toolbar that shows the line length in inches.

Sans serif font: A font, such as Arial or Helvetica, that does not have a flair at the base of each letter.

ScreenTip: A box that displays a description of toolbar buttons and other application features when the mouse is held over the item.

Scroll arrows: Arrows in the scroll bar that move information in the direction of the arrows, allowing new information to be displayed in the space.

Scroll bar: A window element located on the right or bottom window border that lets you display text that is not currently visible in the window. It contains scroll arrows and a scroll box.

Scroll box: A box in the scroll bar that indicates your relative position within the area of available information. The box can be moved to a general location within the area of information by dragging it up or down the scroll bar.

Select: To highlight text.

Selection bar: The unmarked area to the left of the document area where the mouse can be used to highlight text lines.

Selection cursor: The highlight bar in a menu.

Selection rectangle: Outline around an object indicating it is a selected object.

Serif font: A font, such as Times New Roman, that has a flair at the base of each letter.

Shortcut menu: A menu that appears when you right-click an item. It displays common commands associated with the selected item.

Sizing handles: Black squares around a selected object that can be used to size and move the object.

Soft page break: A page break automatically inserted by Word.

Soft space: A space automatically entered by Word to align the text properly on a single line.

Sort: To arrange alphabetically or numerically in ascending or descending order.

Source: The location that contains the text to be moved or copied.

Source Program: The program in which an object was created.

Standard toolbar: The toolbar, displayed below the menu bar, that contains buttons for the most frequently used menu commands.

Start button: A button in the taskbar that displays a menu of commands that are used to start a program, open a document, get help, find files, and change system settings.

Status bar: A bar of information at the bottom of many windows. It displays location information and the status of different settings as they are used.

Style: A set of formats that is assigned a name.

Tag: Embedded codes in an HTML document that supply information about the page's structure, appearance, and contents.

Taskbar: A bar at the bottom of the desktop that contains the Start button, buttons representing active applications, the clock, and other indicators.

Template: A document file that includes predefined settings that can be used as a pattern to create many common types of documents.

Theme: Predesigned Web page effects that can be applied to a Web page to enhance its appearance.

Thesaurus: The file of synonyms and antonyms provided with Word.

Toolbar: A bar of buttons commonly displayed below the menu bar. The buttons are shortcuts for many of the most common menu commands.

Typeface: A set of characters with a specific design. Also called a font.

URL: The Uniform Resource Locator, or the address that indicates the location of a document on the World Wide Web.

Web page: A document that uses HTML to display in a browser.

Word wrap: A feature that automatically determines where to end a line and wrap text to the next line. The user does not press ⏎Enter at the end of a line unless it is the end of a paragraph or to insert a blank line.

Workspace: The large blank area in an application window where your work is displayed.

Command Summary

Command	Shortcut Keys	Button	Action
File/**N**ew	Ctrl + N		Opens new file
File/**O**pen	Ctrl + O		Opens selected file
File/**C**lose			Closes file
File/**S**ave	Ctrl + S		Saves file using same file name
File/Save **A**s			Saves file using a new file name
File/Save as Web Pa**g**e			Saves file as a Web page document
File/We**b** Page Preview			Displays Web page in browser window
File/Page Set**u**p			Changes layout of page including margins, paper size, and paper source
File/Page Set**u**p/**L**ayout/**V**ertical Alignment			Aligns text vertically on a page
File/Print Pre**v**iew			Displays document as it will appear when printed
File/**P**rint	Ctrl + P		Prints file using selected print settings
File/E**x**it	Alt + F4		Exits Word program
Edit/**U**ndo	Ctrl + Z		Restores last editing change
Edit/**R**edo	Ctrl + Y		Restores last Undo or repeats last command or action
Edit/Cu**t**	Ctrl + X		Cuts selected text and copies it to Clipboard
Edit/**C**opy	Ctrl + C		Copies selected text to Clipboard
Edit/**P**aste	Ctrl + V		Pastes text from Clipboard
Edit/Select A**l**l	Ctrl + A		Selects all text in document
Edit/**F**ind	Ctrl + F		Locates specified text
Edit/R**e**place	Ctrl + H		Locates and replaces specified text
View/**N**ormal			Displays document in Normal view
View/**P**rint Layout			Displays document in Print Layout view
View/**W**eb Layout			Displays document as it will appear in a browser

Command	Shortcut Keys	Button	Action
View/**T**oolbars			Displays or hides selected toolbar
View/**R**uler		🔲	Displays or hides horizontal ruler
View/**D**ocument Map			Displays or hides Document Map pane
View/**H**eader and Footer			Displays header and footer areas
View/**F**ootnotes			Hides or displays note pane
View/HTML Sourc**e**			Displays HTML source code of a Web page document
View/**Z**oom			Changes onscreen character size
View/**Z**oom/**W**hole Page			Displays entire page onscreen
View/**Z**oom/**M**any Pages		🔲	Displays two or more pages in document window
Insert/**B**reak/Page Break	Ctrl + ←Enter		Inserts hard page break
Insert/Page Nu**m**bers			Specifies page number location
Insert/Date and **T**ime			Inserts current date or time, maintained by computer system, in selected format
Insert/**A**utoText			Enters predefined text
Insert/Foot**n**ote			Inserts footnote reference at insertion point
Insert/**C**aption			Inserts caption at insertion point
Insert/Cross-**r**eference			Inserts cross-reference at insertion point
Insert/In**d**ex and Tables/Table of **C**ontents			Creates a table of contents
Insert/**H**yperlink	Ctrl + K	🔲	Inserts hyperlink
Insert/**P**icture/**F**rom File			Inserts selected picture into document
F**o**rmat/**F**ont/Fo**n**t/**F**ont		Times New Roman ▾	Changes character typeface
F**o**rmat/**F**ont/Fo**n**t/**S**ize		12 ▾	Changes font size
F**o**rmat/**F**ont/Fo**n**t/Font **C**olor		A	Changes font color
F**o**rmat/**F**ont/Fo**n**t/Font St**y**le/Italic	Ctrl + I	*I*	Makes selected text italic
F**o**rmat/**F**ont/Fo**n**t/Font St**y**le/Bold	Ctrl + B	**B**	Makes selected text bold
F**o**rmat/**F**ont/Fo**n**t/**U**nderline style/Single	Ctrl + U	U	Underlines selected text
F**o**rmat/**P**aragraph/**I**ndents and Spacing /**S**pecial/First Line			Indents first line of paragraph from left margin
F**o**rmat/**P**aragraph/**I**ndents and Spacing /Ali**g**nment/Left	Ctrl + L	≡	Aligns text to left margin

Command	Shortcut Keys	Button	Action
Format/Paragraph/Indents and Spacing /Alignment/Centered	Ctrl + E		Centers text between left and right margins
Format/Paragraph/Indents and Spacing /Alignment/Right	Ctrl + R		Aligns text to right margin
Format/Paragraph/Indents and Spacing /Alignment/Justified	Ctrl + J		Aligns text equally between left and right margins
Format/Paragraph/Indents and Spacing /Alignment/Line Spacing			Changes amount of space between lines
Format/Style		Normal	Applies selected style to paragraph or characters
Format/Picture/Layout			Specifies how text will wrap around picture
Format/Bullets and Numbering			Creates a bulleted or numbered list
Format/Tabs			Specifies types and position of tab stops
Tools/Spelling and Grammar	F7		Starts Spelling and Grammar tool
Tools/Language/Thesaurus	Shift + F7		Starts Thesaurus tool
Tools/Options/View/ScreenTips			Turns off and on the display of ScreenTips
Tools/Options/View/All		¶	Displays or hides formatting marks
Tools/Options/Edit/Overtype mode		OVR	Switches between Insert and overtype modes
Tools/Options/Spelling & Grammar			Change settings associated with the Spelling and Grammar Checking feature
Table/Insert Table			Inserts table at insertion point
Table/Insert/Row Above			Inserts a new row in table above selected row
Table/Table AutoFormat			Applies selected format to table
Table/Convert/Text to Table			Converts selected text to table format
Table/Sort			Rearranges items in a selection into sorted order
Help/Microsoft Word Help	F1		Opens the online Help program
Help/Hide/Show the Office Assistant			Hides or displays the Office Assistant feature

Index

Notes